Gentleman
Of
Fortune

An Unofficial Guide
to Army 2020

Henry B Beeching

D1425248

Martial Tutelage

Published by Martial Tutelage
This paperback edition published in 2018

ISBN 978-1-9998970-0-0

Martial Tutelage

www.martialtutelage.com

To all those who have served
are serving or will serve

Contents

Foreword

Not quite a Gentleman, almost an Officer

They won't tell you any of this at Sandhurst.

I joined the British Army because I wanted to do what hundreds of thousands of soldiers and officers before me had gone on to do. To protect their country, help protect people overseas, to seek excitement, to better myself, and to test myself.

Over the course of my career, both within the Reserves and the Regular Army, I was to discover a range of factors and aspects that despite all that I'd read and heard about, were very different to what I had expected and were to have a profound impact on me and the people whom I served with.

This book's aim is to give an insight into what life is like for serving soldiers and officers in the British Army of 2020. All of the following accounts are taken from my experiences as a young student turned TA officer and then, after graduating from the Royal Military Academy Sandhurst (RMAS) as a Regular, as an officer within the Corps of Royal Engineers.

I have written this narrative not because I believe my career path or success rate was particularly special, although it was far from normal, but because despite of all the countless books and papers that have been previously written on what life is like in the Army, none have been written about what life is like now.

This is epitomised even more so by the fact the British Army is now the smallest it has been for more than 200 years.

This book is not only written to tell my own story but also the story of those whom I served with, and I hope that in these lines you will find or recognise aspects, conversations or topics that you too have come across and will find familiar.

Some details, such as names and places, have been changed due to service and security restrictions but the message and the stories throughout are unchanged. Although I state that this is a narrative and factual story, I have kept no diary and so if it becomes apparent that my memory has played some tricks on me in regards to some detail, c'est la vie.

I realised early on that the career path I wanted to follow in the Army wasn't a well-trodden path anymore, and that I would come up against opposition. This was epitomised during a conversation I happened to have when I arrived at my first regiment with a senior officer about what I wanted to do in the next few years of my life.

'If you want to do these sorts of things, in my opinion, they're career suicide and not really conventional,' he said.

I forget what I said out loud, but I remember that what I really wanted to say was, 'If a regular career will lead me to have a career like yours, I'd prefer the career suicide, and besides, I never wanted a conventional career anyway.'

This is my story of Army 2020.

1

Overrun

The sun rises on yet another bitingly cold morning. The poor individual on sentry duty quietly knocks on the slightly open door of the ISO container that is my accommodation, my eyes blinking in the half light, wishing for just another five minutes in my sleeping bag. Wrenching myself out of it with a quiet curse, my hands automatically reaching for my shaving kit and rifle, I lurch outside and stumble across to my Land Rover and put some water on to heat atop the bonnet using my jet boil kit. I then look around at the Forward Operating Base (FOB) occupied by my troop of Royal Engineers.

As I blearily gaze over our dusty and barren compound, which is situated in the bottom of a desolate valley, guarding a key bridge, I think back to myself as to how we found ourselves here.

My brain still sluggish with sleep, struggling to tell me how long ago it was, I remember the verbal orders I received from the Commanding Officer (CO) of the Battle Group (BG):

'I need you to conduct a reconnaissance patrol out into the area north of here and evaluate the conditions of the main road and bridges along it to see if the BG can safely travel along them; then report back when you are done.'

After returning to my troop and rapidly writing up and issuing my recce orders to the section of men who were to accompany me, as we had to be out the door in less than thirty minutes, as well as readying our kit and weapons for the night's work, we set off in our vehicles into the darkness, leaving the BG harbour area far behind. The BG had not been able to provide us with any form of surveillance intelligence (ISTAR) or even additional vehicles for protection, so stretched were their resources. So we had to use our own soft skinned and thus extremely vulnerable, Land Rovers to take us from the BG's fortified location to the drop off point.

Satellite signal in the area was woeful, meaning that GPS was a 'no no', and so with a laminated map crudely spread across my knees as I sat crammed in the Land Rover's front passenger seat, radio headphones clamped uncomfortably over my ears, helmet pressing down, I led the vehicle packet out into the night.

Holding a thin pencil torch in one hand to light the map, listening for radio updates in one ear and information from my driver in the other, all the while checking the road to ensure we didn't take the wrong turn. It's always interesting when the tactical situation doesn't allow for headlights and the fiscal one doesn't allow for the issuing of night vision goggles. I laughingly recalled how in the early days of my training I was petrified of even the simplest navigation tests, how the times had changed.

4

Soon, the time had come and I signalled a halt. Headlights off, voices hushed, order of march sorted out, weapons made ready and compass bearing taken, I lead the patrol off towards our destination.

Hours later, drenched with stress induced sweat, despite the chilly night air, the recce team had successfully crept out onto the local main road at numerous points, as well as the two bridges and, thankfully, had found them intact and clear of any mines or Improvised Explosive Devices (IEDs).

A fantastic example of what a small group of highly trained and dedicated men, with me tagging along with them, could achieve in the pitch black of night. Without a whisper of sound, deep in enemy territory.

Word was duly passed back to the BG over the radios, miraculously working, that the route was all clear. Once it was acknowledged and permission was given to return to the pickup point, the patrol quickly hunkered down and took quick sips of water and bites of chocolate, and then moved quietly back to our rendezvous (RV) point. We had to get back to our pickup point, we simply couldn't afford for a local to stumble across us and pass word back to the insurgents that we were in the area.

Once back at our RV, awaiting permission to move back to the BG's main location, a new set of orders suddenly flashed down the airwaves to us:

'Return to the main bridge by the village and hold it. Wait till reinforcements from the BG come to secure the location. DO NOT move from the bridge site!'

With heavy hearts, aching shoulders and sore feet, the patrol once again disembarked from the warm safety of our vehicles and, after adhering to the vital but often more taxing military lesson, of planning a different route back to the bridge site, for only a fool retraces his steps in enemy territory, my eight men and I headed off once again.

Arriving just as the dawn's light crept over the barren hills and lit up the surrounding area, especially the small bridge site and the scrubby village that occupied the far bank, we settled into an overwatch position and awaited the reinforcements.

The insurgents were known to be in the area, they blended in perfectly with the locals, swathed in robes and headscarves, and were numerous and well-armed. Their exact locations could only be roughly estimated and the likelihood that some would be hidden within the village was very high.

Each man in my patrol knew that not only did the enemy carry weapons equal to that of our own individual SA80s assault rifles, but that they also had a substantial number of mortars and of heavily armed Technicals, 4x4s with mounted heavy weapons on the back, in their arsenal. Nerves were tense amongst my recce section, counting down the minutes until the cavalry arrived, as it was a cavalry BG that we were working with, at which point we could then return back to the BG HQ.

Five days later we were still there.

***

Looking up irritably, only as someone who has spent far too long sleeping in the field can, into my mirror as I scraped the razor across my face, I forced my mind to focus on the situation and position we had found ourselves in.

The FOB we were in, known to my troops and I as the 'FOB of Forgotten Sappers' had been initially an abandoned fort built by some unknown previous military unit, how long ago no one around here knew, or at least would tell us.

A few scattered ISO containers formed our accommodation, as well as stores area, with a thick belt of barbed wire and earth barriers helping to create our main defensive barrier. Overall, it was less than 100 square metres square, sat astride the main road and with a rough vehicle park opposite which was overlooked by our sentry positions. It was there where we had been forced, due to lack of space inside the FOB, to move most of our vehicles.

If pushed, we could just about ensure that all of our positions had interlocking arcs, despite having no medium or heavy machine guns with us, and we sincerely hoped the enemy didn't decide to engage us with their mortars or use vehicle borne IEDs.

It was a simply awful position. But we had been ordered to hold it and hold it we would. The spirit of Rorke's Drift was strong within the troop. We would stand and fight.

Luckily, after initially being told to stay in place on the bridge, my small recce team had been quickly reinforced by the remainder of my troop under the direction of my Staff Sergeant, Staff Dixon, who with foresight borne of years of experience well in advance of my own, had assessed the situation and rapidly obtained permission back at BG HQ to reinforce his isolated troop commander.

Having done the best we could upon arrival, in the finest tradition of the Royal Engineers, with no small amount of grumbling about the madness of BG HQ that had resulted with the only Engineer unit in the entire area becoming fixed and isolated on an exposed position, well away from any other friendly units, we had upgraded the FOB as best we could with available resources and awaited further direction.

We were sat in the bottom of a valley, high ground all around, astride a main road which civilian traffic used at all hours of the day, fifty metres away from a rambling village filled with armed locals, with no heavy weapons of any kind and only intermittent radio communication with our HQ. Not ideal.

Still, my Sappers (Sprs) were cheerful and performing to excellent standards. We had established a rapport with the locals and were on speaking terms with the elders, had plenty of supplies and my NCOs and I, aside from constantly checking the surrounding area for insurgents and our own defensive positions, were doing all we could to keep the lads busy.

The village opposite us had been hit two days ago by two insurgent Technicals and had been severely shot up, an insurgent punishment for the villagers for not waging jihad on us – we'd returned fire from the FOB location and driven them off without losses. The troop's accuracy and fire discipline had been very good, all thanks to the excellent Pre Deployment Training (PDT) carried out weeks ago by the NCOs.

As I put away my wash kit and turned to clean my rifle, the freezing cold of the night and the dust of the day necessitated constant weapon cleaning, a shout came from one of the FOB's sentry positions.

'Enemy! Five hundred metres! Section plus! Coming over the top of North Hill!'

The FOB erupted in activity as men boiled out of their accommodation, throwing on their Osprey body armour and webbing, rifles in hand, running to their stand to positions.

As I took my central position in the FOB, every man in the troop knowing that if they needed me, unless I was directly called away, they could find me there, I scanned the horizon with my rifle's telescopic site.

Where are they? Is this a feint? Are they enemy? Could be locals heading across the fields..., no wait! There they are! Two groups of around ten men moving over the hill with weapons! Damn, they're still out of our weapon range....

As I ordered my signaller to send a message to BG HQ, checking that there were no friendly units in the area, I quickly scanned around the FOB's perimeter to see if there were any other groups moving towards us from different directions.

To my great satisfaction, I saw none and heard the NCOs yelling to the men in their sections to watch their arcs and to call out if any other enemy came into view.

'Sir! HQ reports back no friendly units in the area!'

'Roger. They're enemy lads! Watch your arcs and remember to move your firing positions!'

As the enemy crested the hill, an uncharacteristically bad and obvious line of attack for them, they threw themselves on the ground and opened fire on us.

While their muzzle flashes lit up along the crest of the hillside in the early morning light, the section nearest to them, with a collective weapon range of 500 meters, returned fire.

Remembering that a NCO's worst nightmare is an officer meddling in his handling of his section (a former Commandant of Sandhurst famously admits to being punched in the face by a NCO during his Platoon's first fire fight for this exact reason), I kept my central position with a clear overview of the action, letting my NCOs control their sections, and carefully assessed the situation.

An officer should always be calm and composed, but commanding.

With SSgt Dixon efficiently moving around the FOB checking on the other two sections who were not currently engaged, I was in the process of requesting artillery support, as it would have been madness to move forward from our fortified location towards the enemy at that time, where my men heavily burdened with kit and weapons would have been rapidly outmanoeuvred by the light and fast moving insurgents, when suddenly fire erupted from another corner of the FOB.

I looked across the water to see that now that half hidden between the buildings in the village across the river, two enemy Technicals had arrived and were now rapidly firing into the FOB with a mixture of small and large calibre machine guns.

As the fire increased, I began to hear yells and cries from some of my soldiers – they had been hit.

Quickly, they were dragged out of the line of fire into our first aid location and assessed. The first aid drills of the soldiers that carried the injured to safety were fantastic.

With a group of insurgents on a dominant hill overlooking our entire location, and a number of heavy weapons firing directly at us from less than 150 meters, with no air support or reinforcements, it dawned on me that the situation was getting out of control and advantage was slipping to the enemy.

I needed to get the BG's Quick Reaction Force (QRF) to our location immediately to reinforce and help us win the fire fight, their heavy weapons and additional manpower would easily tip the balance in our favour.

I turned to my signaller.

'Where the FUCK are the QRF?'

'They're not available, sir! HQ says at least 30 minutes.'

'We haven't bloody got 30 minutes! Tell them we've taken casualties and need the QRF immediately!'

I looked over to SSgt Dixon who was handling the wounded and his expression was grim – we needed to make a drastic change to the situation and quick.

Turning to face the only section that was not in contact with the enemy, I yelled across for the NCO in charge to reinforce those being fired on by the vehicles. The Lance Corporal (LCpl) in command rapidly assigned his men and they charged across the exposed ground towards the beleaguered section, crashing down into any available firing position. Soon our fire equalled, and then began to outweigh, the insurgent Technicals, who'd suffered a number of causalities themselves.

Suddenly, the fighters manning the 4x4s lost their nerve and in a screech of tires and dust, drove off back into the wadis they had emerged from, my men yelling abuse at them and firing at them as they went.

Thank God.

No sooner had the insurgents crewing the 4x4s withdrawn, I turned and witnessed a new line of turbaned figures, brandishing automatic rifles, jump up out the cover from where they had been hiding less than fifty metres and fire their weapons point blank range at the exposed section position.

The men left in the positions, vacated less than a minute before by the team that had hurtled across to help fight off the 4x4s, took the full front of the fire and I saw all five remaining men crumple to the ground; their bodies still.

It was a masterful example of drawing an enemy's attention away and then attacking an exposed flank – sadly, in this case it was the enemy who had the advantage, not us.

As my soldiers dashed to and fro, firing from behind the engine blocks of parked Land Rovers and around corners of ISO containers, shell casings littering the floor, I saw even more insurgents running towards us from different directions, having displayed extraordinary field craft skill in getting so close to us without being seen – the situation became chaotic.

Order collapsed as men were shot down as they moved positions, not able to fire without drawing enemy fire from at least two other locations. My signaller was shot whilst using the radio, his body slumped against the door of the Land Rover. One of my largest Sprs ran from cover to drag him into safety but even before he had covered five yards, he suddenly dropped to the ground, shot.

Pulling men into whatever cover we could, our greatest fear was finally realised, our defence had broken....the enemy was inside the wire.

With my lungs bursting, struggling to yell out commands and wrest control back from the enemy, moving constantly throughout the FOB in order to maintain our defences, I saw that some of my men still holding out from various locations in the FOB and they poured an unbelievable rate of fire into the enemy from point blank range, who bizarrely did not seem to be falling when they got shot.

Grenades thrown from windows, magazines skimmed across the floor to those that needed them, barrels burned red hot, the chatter of automatic fire reaching a crescendo, commands yelled, bodies dragged back into cover, voices raised in urgency, we fought on.

I looked out a window of the ISO container that I was fighting from, wiping the sweat out of my eyes and saw that aside from my location, with four other Sprs and one NCO, the only other part of the FOB that was still fighting was one of the accommodation rooms, under the control of SSgt Dixon.

We needed to rally the remnants of the troop together and attempt to fight it out, hoping we could keep the enemy at bay until the QRF got to us.

'Cover us! Go! Go!'

I sprinted out towards their position, the others following on behind me. SSgt Dixon lifts his weapon and fires on automatic from his ISO doorway, the shell cases spitting out of his SA80. His remaining men following his example and a torrent of fire streams towards the various insurgent fighters scattered around the FOB, their figures bobbing and moving around in the dust and smoke.

My legs feeling like they're made of lead. Running in quicksand. Lungs heavy. Bulky webbing and helmet slowing me down. Swear I'm not moving at all. We're almost at the door.

'Boss!'

Mid sprint I spin round and see one of my LCpls lying in the dirt behind me, clutching his leg.

'I've been hit!'

The remainder of the lads with me stop and pick him up; we're yards away from safety. We haul his body up, some of them lifting their rifles on shaky arms and firing wildly towards the enemy. Despite this, enemy automatic fire explodes from all around us and my men are all hit. As they drop to the ground, in a chaos of falling, tangled bodies, all swearing and firing their rifles, I continue to drag the LCpl towards the safety of SSgt Dixon and his boys.

BAM!

I'm hit. I'm on the ground. I can't move. It's my chest. FUCK.

I crawl on the ground, exhausted, bone tired, head screaming, parched with thirst, suddenly feeling rough hands pulling on my webbing strap.... SSgt Dixon has sprinted out of cover and is dragging me into the ISO. I'm hit again. SSgt Dixon is hit. The boys behind me aren't moving, lying there in a tangled heap in the dust.

Still.

As I'm pulled off the ground, into the ISO container, dumped onto the floor with half a dozen bodies, I see figures still at the window. My soldiers, silhouetted by the swirling dust, their bodies' dark against the gloom, firing, yelling, moving, ducking, weaving, are still doggedly fighting.

Grenades bounce against the walls and explode, I see SSgt Dixon get hit again and drop. There are only five of the chaps from the entire troop still standing in the entire FOB.

I glance up from where I'm lying sprawled on the floor and shout to those of my Sprs who are still on their feet:

'Run! Get the fuck out of here! Go! Get out!'

They look down at us quickly, we gesture at them and the last five blokes charge out of the doorway. I look around at the rest of the wounded and some of them shift in a rough semblance of a firing position, waiting for the insurgents to come through the doorway, ready to cut them down.

We hear the yells and cries of my men outside, moving around FOB buildings, fighting as they go. Then suddenly, a whistle sounds, cutting across all sound. It sounds again. All firing stops.

'STOP. STOP. STOP!'

A new figure steps into the doorway, white tape wrapped around his helmet and body armour.

'That's a stop, lads. Your FOB has been overrun. The serial has ended. Where's your troop commander?'

I stand up, as does everyone else around me and we walk outside. I look around as all of my troop stand up from where they've been lying and move to the centre of the FOB.

'Righto. I'll go for the debrief. Wait here.'

As I move over to where the Directing Staff (DS) stand on the main road, clipboards and notepads in hand, the enemy fighters, a British Guards Platoon, jump into their Technicals and drive off.

The DS of the exercise we are part of, Ex WESSEX STORM, in Salisbury Plain Training Area (SPTA), give us their assessment of how well the troop held up against the enemy assault. Surprisingly, despite being overrun, we did quite well according to the DS, bearing in mind the limitations they had secretly imposed upon us.

It turns out that the enemy had been informed not to drop when their TES vests told them they had been shot but to keep on pressing us. It was a lesson to us to highlight the weaknesses in our defence but also to the BG HQ for putting their only engineer unit in such an exposed position for such a lengthy period of time without any forms of suitable protection or support. For although the entire troop were trained as infantry, many had previously served as dismounted infantry multiples overseas in Afghanistan and Iraq, we had been deployed out into the field by the BG without sufficient numbers, heavy weapons or armoured vehicles.

As the DS moved around the FOB, resetting the electronic battle simulation TES vests of my Troop, I thought back over all the actions that we had carried out during the fight, what we would improve upon and what to commend the blokes for. The old military adage, the 'shit sandwich debrief'. A good point, followed by the points to improve upon and a final good point so people don't go away totally dispirited.

We'd been part of Ex WESSEX STORM for almost four weeks, the final fifth week was just around the corner and after which we'd be returning to our regiment. The electronic TES vests which, matching with a corresponding gadget attached to the end of our rifles, which for the sake of the exercise fire blank cartridges, record exactly where an individual has fired and what injury the shot person has 'received', will soon be taken off.

The TES kit, meant to be the cutting edge battle casualty simulation technology that can be fitted to men, vehicles and even buildings, is an absolute nightmare most of the time. Randomly going off, awkward to wear, creating bizarre supposed injuries and, despite working well sometimes, is generally laughed at by all those that experienced it.

Sitting on my Land Rover, waiting to begin my debrief to the troop, whom are all laughing around me and are recalling the fun they'd had firing their rifles on full automatic for once and the simulated death poses they had all struck, I thought back on the events that had led me to this point.

I was fortunate and lucky enough to be in command of a troop of Royal Engineers.

HENRY B BEECHING

2

Beginnings

Explorations. Books. Hunting. Travels. ACF.
Languages

I was born on February 1 1989 in Hastings. I was fortunate
enough to grow up in the wilds of Southern England, our
house, an old keeper's cottage that had been expanded by
my parents, was situated in the deepest green of Sussex
countryside. It was a veritable fortress of solitude and
comfort, with not a sound from the outside world except for
the occasional traffic on the distant country lanes. On even
more treasured occasions, especially for a young English
country boy like myself, we would hear the distant roar of
Twin Rolls Royce Merlin engines as Spitfires soared and
spiralled majestically in the skies overhead, practising for
the local air shows.

The surrounding woods, streams, fields, rambling hills all
offered the most fantastic opportunities for adventures,
exploration, fishing and shooting. Kind relatives, as soon as
I was old enough to be trusted with them, they soon gifted

me with plenty of fishing rods, air rifles, catapults, snares and bows & arrows.

A keen reader from an early age, I avidly devoured any action or military history books I could get my hands on. Visits to the local library, and then my first foray to the Imperial War Museum, are implanted firmly in my memory. I'd come away each time with easily half a dozen books in tow, these being the days well before Kindles and broadband internet. Accounts of WW2 Commando raids, Imperial conflicts in distant mountainous states which bordered the Empire, Brooke in Borneo and much more, all of them fed my appetite for adventure and excitement.

Inspired by these accounts, as a boy I would often creep through the tall Sussex bracken which surrounded the house, hunting Imperial Japanese Guardsmen with a walking stick or spend a morning building a fort in the thick woodland and defy any jungle savages or pirates to try and take my fortification. In addition to setting worm baited lines in the nearby bubbling woodland streams and laying nooses in the hedgerows which were sewn with raisins, stolen from the kitchen the night before, for unsuspecting trout, pheasants and rabbits.

When I was confident enough, soon my forays into the unknown extended well past the boundaries of the wood where our cottage was situated and soon wood pigeons and squirrels, to name a few, from the surrounding parks and fields began falling to my ever increasing accuracy with the air rifle and shotgun.

As my strength and experience grew, I soon began to construct rafts in attempts to cross the vast reservoir that sat on the edges of our wood. As well as recruiting friends from school to help carry them, whose labours were rewarded with a BBQ and a few beers in the woods afterwards. Maybe it was an indication that life in the Royal Engineers would be of appeal to me in the future, but also a greater indication that significant amounts of additional learning would also be required, for every single one of my rafts sank on its virgin voyage.

A weekend was considered a rich success if I'd manage to fit in some trap laying on the Friday afternoon after school, usually with an accomplice in tow, and then a foray out in the early Saturday morning mist. Armed with a couple of guns, as well as a sack for mushrooms and blackberries, if the season was right, if all went well I'd hopefully return to the house just before lunchtime with a few trout, and a fowl or two, tucked away in my game bag.

All of these self-imposed excursions into the countryside, usually on my own, taught me not only a great respect for the wildlife and countryside that they inhabited, but also the importance of self-reliance, accuracy in shooting, discipline, planning, patience and, when I had 2 pair of hands with me, some of the fundamentals of leadership. Namely, always being cheerful when hardship arises, trying to keep my voice sounding confident, especially when I wasn't, but not overbearing, tackling the hardest task so that others would help me with it, and carefully weighing up risk versus reward.

How well I managed to keep to these over the years, even now, is not for me to say.

Videos and documentaries also formed a staple part of my diet of military exploits and adventures. My parents had accidentally stumbled upon an excellent way of keeping me entertained when the weather was too severe outside for me to go after the trout or rabbits. I was to revisit the usefulness of these recorded accounts of military success, and failure, many years later during lectures whilst I was serving at the Royal Military Academy Sandhurst (RMAS).

The family travelled a lot and I was fortune enough to see most of Europe, where I was able to pick up a working grasp of French during a stint in Luxembourg and Brussels, as well as much of the Mediterranean. This afforded plenty of opportunities to me for activities unheard of from the wilds of Sussex. Scuba diving, sailing, mountain hikes, sea fishing; the sky was the limit for the young boy from a small English rural country village.

My family did not boast much in the way of a military lineage, other than my grandfather on my mother's side, known affectionately as 'DanDan' who served in the Royal Engineers in the 50's and 60's, eventually retiring at the rank of Major to the amiable and wine-soaked region of southern France.

Over the course of a number family holidays to his house in France, and him visiting us in East Sussex, or whilst we were living in Luxembourg and Brussels, I was to learn of all the interesting places he had been and the marvels he had seen as part of his military service. From staying in luxurious flats in the Far East which rocked to and fro when the monsoons hit, to glorious old French Chateaus whilst he was employed as a military attaché to the French Army or the wondrous provisions that were allotted to his family as a result of his service.

His most famous story, told in his steady, unassuming manner, was of his time during a posting to Austria. Principally during on a weeklong exercise into the countryside and the mountains where he was instructing his troop in the fine art of explosives and demolitions, when he then accidentally blew up a local military heritage site.

With stories and wisdom like that, how could I not follow in my Grandfather's footsteps and tradition and not take up the badge and the illustrious red uniform of the famous Royal Engineers?

Thankfully it was not just tales of mishap and long since deserted outposts of the Empire that kept me enthralled in my grandfather's military life but also an aspect of his career which is none too common these days; his linguistic ability.

DanDan was fluent in French and through hook or by crook, had managed to secure a number of attaché posts with the French Army for a number of years during his career. After hearing a number of his exploits and experiences during this period of his military life, I become devoted to the idea of developing a similar level of linguistic ability and pursuing a similar path.

Visions of staying in grand chateaus, shaking hands with Gaullist looking French officers as they stepped out of cars in front of the British Embassy in some swanky part of a European city, and standing in meetings of multinational officers and acting as the translator and cultural advisor filled my imagination.

Throughout school I was not the most academic of students and suffered from a mild form of dyslexia, or just bone idealness, I never could really tell, and so I was not exactly an A star pupil. But eventually I discovered I had an avid passion for not only History, English and Physical Education, but also for French.

I was also soon introduced to the local Army Cadet Force (ACF) detachment in Bexhill and after spending my first evening there taking part in the sports evening they were holding, I became a regular member and was part of the organisation for around three years. Looking back on it now, although I never considered myself an undisciplined child, I realise that it came at a point in my life where direction and discipline from some non-family organisation was needed. There is a point in every young man's life where he craves excitement and some direction, discipline or purpose, which is often best delivered at the hands of people whom are not his parents.

During those three years with the ACF, comprised of weekends away and the occasional summer camp, where we were lucky enough to have instructors who were all ex-military, I learnt many valuable lessons.

Rifle shooting, map & compass, how to keep my kit clean in the field, marching, the rank system, Physical Training (PT), the camaraderie of the people in my unit and much more. After a while I was lucky enough to be awarded a minor command position and had my first taste of command of a small group. Needless to say that although some of the lessons I had learnt running around Sussex chasing pheasants came in handy, I also made a number of mistakes which I endeavoured, as soon as I had realised I'd made them, never to repeat. I was to have varied success in this aspect in the coming years.

Principally, getting lost in the dark whilst leading a patrol, not arriving on time for a specific event, having my rifle not as clean as it should be, writing an inaccurate set of orders, having less than perfect admin in the field, and more. All heinous and unforgiveable crimes in the military, and felt as keenly as a whiplash across my shoulders each time and as they occurred.

I believe the best lesson I ever learnt from my instructors at the Bexhill ACF detachment was to learn how to cope with a failure. To realise where you went wrong and then, without complaining or trying to shift the blame to someone else, as tempting as that may be at times. To simply crack on with the task at hand regardless of the obstacles, and get the job done. I have endeavoured to keep to these guidelines throughout my life and would strongly recommend them to anyone.

Soon, before I knew it, I was half way through my time at my local 6th form college, by this point, some of my time which had been previously spent chasing rabbits and drinking tea by the campfire had been replaced with chasing girls and drinking beer at gigs, and the decision as to whether to go to university or not loomed over me like the Sword of Damocles.

Initially I was determined not to go, I saw it as a definite waste of time, spending my time studying and getting into debt whereas I could leap straight in RMAS as a young eighteen year old officer cadet, if I passed the selection weekends that is, and be off fighting the Queen's enemies whilst my old school chums would be busy writing mind boggling essays and preparing for infuriating exams.

Thankfully a combination of wise words from my school teachers, who believed that despite of my varying grades, if I applied myself to a subject I liked I would do well, and sound advice from friends and, most importantly, my family finally resulted in me changing my decision and I looked about for a degree to apply for.

After once hearing from some long forgotten source that 'only a fool would spend three or four years of their life, expending vast sums of money in learning a skill that they neither enjoyed studying, or used afterwards', I was determined to study something I enjoyed, else I'd never be able to pass the damn thing, and that I could utilise whilst in the Army afterwards.

Language, following my grandfather's example, as well as my parents, who between them spoke French, Spanish and Russian, was at the front of my mind and I quickly assessed all my available options. French, strangely enough, was disqualified quite quickly as I was content with my current level of skill in that area, always a foolish mistake to make, and I was confident that we, the British Army, would be unlikely to be invading France again anytime soon. Although the French have still not been forgiven by us Anglo Saxons for their use of treacherous tactics during that minor martial incident in 1066.

I scanned all the European languages and found them wanting, the Americas did not appeal to me, more fool me, and anything spoken in the parts east of the Suez Canal seemed to grate on my ear. Eventually I decided to settle on two choices; Arabic or Russian.

My father had spent years working in Russia when the Wall had fallen and his stories and exploits were personally rated at times even higher than DanDan's. The incentive to study the Great Bear and its ways was very great indeed.

My other option was Arabic, a language which, if successfully learnt, would allow me to travel across the Middle East and North Africa. Now bearing in mind my absolute passion for exotic foods, especially curry, due to having grown up with countless homemade curries made by DanDan and my mother, learnt from their years in the Far East, my stomach had a significant say in matters of where I would be spending a year of my life academic study.

Thankfully in the Islamic world they heartily enjoy rice and spicy food and, what's more, I had already glutted myself with historical accounts from Lawrence of Arabia, the Long Range Desert Patrol, Gordon Pasha and many others.

These factors weighed heavily upon my decision, bearing in mind my life's love for food, books and travel, and yet the choice was still a tough one. Eventually it was my undying devotion to my stomach that settled the argument.

I chose Arabic, for as at the time I simply detested cabbage, which I knew to be a firm favourite throughout Russia, and most of the known world, although this little fact didn't enter into my adolescent equation. A cardinal sin. It was decided, I couldn't possibly study in a country where cabbage was the staple diet for countless millions.

Despite the fact that I had never spoken a word of Arabic in my life up to that point and that my father, who'd spent many delightful years in Russia, could have easily taught me the basics of Russian even before I reached university. He'd also previously spent a year contracting in Saudi Arabia and had refused to go back, even at the promise of a 50% wage increase.

Perversely, it was one of the best decisions I have ever made in my life and it has had a profound impact on me ever since.

After reaching the decision whilst sat in my 6th form common room, I leapt up and within ten excited minutes I had found two good universities that taught Arabic and required entry grades I could achieve if I really put my mind to it; as well as having military links through their UOTCs.

Many agonising months of hard study and frustration followed and I was actually on holiday in Mexico when I received my A Level grades – I had passed the entry requirements. I was going to become a student at the University of Leeds and undertake Arabic and Middle Eastern studies, which would include a year's studying in Cairo.

My hangover the next morning was simply biblical.

3

University

At the age of 19, 2008, I arrived at the University of Leeds. I simply couldn't wait to get stuck into University life, as well as my studies; a subject which I had spent the previous few months brushing up upon, in the hope that I would achieve the required A level grades and become an Arabic linguist. Or even obtain the coveted honour of being an 'Arabist'.

I was soon unpacked in the halls of Bodington and jumped feet first into all that university life could offer. I quickly made friends with those in my hall, Bragg House, as well as others, many of which are close friends to this day, and cast around for prospective societies and clubs to join.

One above all others drew my attention, the University Officers Training Corps (UOTC). It was, in simple layman's terms, a grown up version of the Army Cadets. Except for some very key differences; it was staffed by serving officers and soldiers, the work was paid and its social life just fantastic. It also trained you specifically for RMAS, for around half of the UOTC officer cadets were planning on joining the Army after graduating and it also offered you the chance to obtain a TA officer commission and attempt a couple of arduous courses. To wit - P Company, the All Arms Commando Course, and the infamous Cambrian Patrol Competition.

Back in the far-flung days between 2008 and 2011, the UOTCs around the country were very different beasts to what they are now. Each OTC had its own unique identity and had specific trades that individuals could sign up to; infantry, engineers, artillery and in some rare cases, cavalry, were the options open to an individual walking through the gates for the first time.

After passing the initial first year's training in areas such as field skills, orders, section competitions and navigation, an individual was invited to choose their arm/trade. In the finest traditions of the British military, the process was tribal to the extreme and also very competitive.

Once a person had put their name in the hat for, say the infantry wing of their particular UTOC, that was their name inscribed in the treasured accounts of that group and they were informed that they, above all else, were now part of the principal elite of that OTC and the rest were mere mongrels in comparison.

It was excellent training and preparation for what was to come in the form of the strict regimental and sub-unit pride that pervades into every corner of the British Army.

One of the biggest attractions to the UOTCs, especially the one in Leeds was the social life. It was bombastic, loud, crazy, hedonistic, heartily subscribed to, wild and just plain fantastic. With an organisation that had an attendance every

Wednesday and every other weekend of around a hundred, when LUOTC hit the streets for a night out on the town, during which each sub unit carefully recorded those who did not show up and put them to kangaroo trial on their next appearance, the exploits were brilliant.

The diversity of the membership of the Officer Cadets (OCdts) in the OTC was one of its biggest strengths. To look across the crowded barrack bar an individual would see persons who were studying medicine, science, art, politics, languages, physics and much more, as well as being from a range of different social backgrounds and parts of the country. In any conversation that was taking place, from a swaying group of intoxicated individuals on a dingy nightclub floor to a group of frozen souls stood around a flaming 44 gallon drum in the snow on a training exercise, the people would typically be as different from each other as could be imagined.

Aside from the massed social events, the actual training that took place, especially in the Engineer troop was brilliant and we got to get our hands on a wide range of engineer equipment and training serials; from bridges to boats, demolitions to inter OTC competitions. The most famous competition of all within the OTC Royal Engineer troops, although I couldn't say if it still continues to this day, was the Minley Competition.

This was held annually at Minley Manor, the home of the Royal Engineer Troop Commander training course and hosted a range of competitions. From a boat race, stretcher competition, section tasks, to name but a few, and most importantly, the bridge building competition.

Throughout the four fantastic years I was to spend at the University of Leeds, LUOTC was to win the competition, and the bridging section, twice. When the time came to leave after we graduated all the senior members of Shard's Troop left with a glint in their eye and shoulders held back with pride. I believe that it was a feat that has not been surpassed since.

It was during my first year that I first heard of a TA commission and first dipped my toe into the adult world of the British Army – it was time to see if I was ready to take a proper challenge and prove myself worthy of taking a Queen's commission.

Soon, in a speed that seemed almost too fast to witness, my application paperwork had been completed, sent off and accepted. I was dispatched to Claro Barracks in Ripon where I was to undertake four weeks of intensive infantry training which, if I passed, would then become qualified to go to RMAS and hopefully complete the last stages of becoming a TA officer in the Army.

I was confident, I was fit, I had some experience in the field, I'd read as much as I could about tactics, I was ready, I was going to pass, I just knew it.

I failed.

It was one of the hardest challenges I've had to overcome but the staff that were running the exercise, and who stated that my ability to lead and command a Platoon, as its leader, in a fire fight needed more work, were right.

I was not ready at that time. I was fit, worked well as part of section and could navigate with a map, and could do many other things well; but when it was my turn to become the Platoon commander and lead my soldiers, something still messed with my head and even though I was confident I was making the right decisions, I wasn't.

Needless to say it knocked me off my feet, and the shame of having my family and friends know that I had failed in an undertaking that I loved, was very tough, but I picked myself up, realised my errors and what I needed to do to fix them. I would go back again in the future and try again. I swore it. In fact, the final field exercise, which took place in bogs and marshes of Catterick, turned out to be one of the most physically and mentally demanding exercises I have ever taken part in. All of the students, most of who later on went on to commission into the Regulars in the future, were to suffer severe hallucinations due to fatigue throughout the exercise.

Memories of that fabled final exercise in Catterick served as excellent motivation for me in the future whenever I was on a seemingly tough exercise. All I had to do was to compare it to the hell the other OCdts and I were out through and soon enough the hardships I was currently faced with suddenly appeared to lose some of their severity.

But by now this was at the end of my first year at Leeds and further military training would have to wait as I was now off heading for my next year's study.

To the distant and exotic Middle East. To Egypt. To Cairo.

***

The sun blared down; with my shirt stuck to my back, the dusty and foul air drying my throat, wiping from perspiration from my brow, I looked out amazed into the heaving crowd of humanity whilst strange smells and the volume of strange dialects crashed against my senses.

I was in Cairo's main airport, alone, no working mobile phone, an overloaded suitcase in each hand, only a contact from the international school to find and not speaking a word of Egyptian dialect, only classical Arabic, in my head.

As I walked through the crowded arrivals hall, the air hot and humid, fighting for room in the surging crowds, I found myself surrounded by people from across the breadth and width of both North Africa and the Middle East regions.

Men in both drab and colourful robes shouted, yelled and pushed at each other in high pitched voices, conservative women wearing dark black Islamic dress that covered them from head to foot jostled shoulders with the more liberal ones who still wore semblances of Islamic headdresses but combined them with tight colourful tops, high heeled shoes and leggings.

Each and every one of them toting camera phones, bright jewellery and seemingly speaking a separate language or dialect than the person next to them.

I strolled passed the rank of waiting drivers, all holding name cards, and none held one that a name that was even close to mine. I walked past again. And again. No one was there waiting for me.

I took a much crumpled and worn printed email out of my pocket and once again read the message that the university official had sent me from the central office in Cairo prior to my departure from the UK.

'A driver from the university will be there to meet you. He will take you to your hotel, the Sun Hotel, and tell you how to find the university.'

Hours passed and the airport was starting to go quiet; I looked around and barely anyone was there. I had to do something.

Showing a type of confidence I did not feel, I proudly marched up to the information desk where various Egyptian employees and taxi drivers were lounging, holding the hotel booking sheet in front of me like it was a weapon and asked by trying to speak my best classical Arabic:

'Ain el Funduk Shams?' Where is the Sun Hotel?'

They looked at me blankly and then muttered amongst themselves, and then proceeded to throw a number of questions that I did not understand. I stood there blankly. They looked back at me, blankly.

Clearly, we had reached an impasse.

After what seemed like an age, a withered old taxi driver was thrust forward, who then took my suitcases and hurried off without a glance back. I quickly looked back at the assembled council of wise men stood in front of me, who were rapidly gestured me to follow the elderly gentleman. With as much dignity as I could muster, I turned and scurried after him.

As my bags were thrown into the back of the taxi, the stereotypical battered old heap that I was to find out is known locally as a flying coffin, I jumped in and without a moment's pause, the car juddered into action and screeched off into the dense traffic.

Where the hell am I going? Is this kidnap? Can't be, of all the nerve, I've only just bloody arrived! Let's see how this one pans out.

For thirty minutes my taxi, during which the owner and I didn't exchange a word, journeyed around the various congested and dirty roads of central Cairo and just as my nerves were starting to give and I began to make look for recognisable landmarks in case I need to describe my route to the hostage negotiators, the car slams to a halt.

I looked around. I appear to be parked up adjacent to some Middle Eastern parody of Trafalgar Square. Huge towering buildings surrounded the junction, neglected bill boards crowning them like broken teeth and everywhere I look on the surrounding pavements and roads, a great mass of moving people.

My driver urgently jabbed his finger out the window and as I leant my head out of the taxi, my nostrils assaulted with the full blast of polluted and fume rich air, I looked up and saw a decrepit but jolly looking hotel adorned with a partly flashing neon sign which proudly stated '6 Star Sun Hotel'.

I had arrived.

The next year in this strange and confusing country which locals call 'The Cradle of Civilisation' was to become my home and it would teach me more about myself, the Arab peoples and how I saw the world than I ever could have possibly imagined. Over the next twelve months, I was to learn Egyptian Arabic like a native, discover Cairo's lager soaked nightlife, almost get arrested at least twice, learn to fight, have my tolerance levels pushed further than I thought they could go, learn humility and see first-hand the cruel works of the Egyptian government and their Secret Police (Giulio Regeni was a close and dear friend).

The first week or so, I stayed in my hotel slowly venturing out into the wilds of downtown Cairo and to see some of the sights. Laughably, I lost almost a stone within the first few days as I was simply too nervous to walk into the restaurants and cafes and order food. It took the kindly hotel manager, after I was coming to the halfway point of my two week residence in his premises, dragging me down to the nearest shop and forcing me to tentatively engage in Arabic conversation with a stranger before I ate anything that wasn't the complimentary hotel food.

After walking around much of downtown Cairo, a delightful hybrid of governmental buildings and sprawling marketplaces that seemed to have leapt straight out of the pages of a Kipling novel, and charging atop a horse around the desert which surrounds the pyramids, which are littered with rubbish, large red faced tourists with Slavic accents, Arabs selling lemonade cans at five dollars a pop and some much vandalised architecture, I addressed the issue of finding my classmates and a place to live.

It seemed, after buying a local phone, that all my known associates in my class had stolen a day's march on me and already picked themselves roommates. Clearly I was in a bit of bind, as well as suffering from severe cabin fever in my hotel. When out of the blue, whilst I was in the process of walking out of the hotel with baggage in tow, no idea of where I was going to go next, my phone rang.

Pete and Matt, two classmates of mine whom I had barely even spoken to during the previous year's study, were looking for a third person to live in the three bedroom flat they had just discovered. Did I want in? Of course, I did.

What appeared like a hell of an initial risk and deciding to live with two other chaps I'd never really met, in a flat I hadn't seen, committing myself to twelve months of agreed rent, turned out to be one of the best decisions I had made the entire year.

Pete, a very left wing and linguistically gifted chap who'd spent considerable time travelling around the Americas, Matt, a dark haired half Irish half gent from Manchester who'd spent some time living in the Gulf previously and I, a young, naive and very out of his depth Englishman, were destined to become the very best of flatmates and friends.

After moving into our seventh floor and surprisingly modern flat which was perfectly situated right between the government district and its collection of seedy bars and the sprawling local markets, lessons at the international university where we were due to study at for the next twelve months, began.

A number of weeks later, a pattern of life began to emerge and our daily living during the week days could be described as thus:

6-7am: Get up, wake up the other two, brief exercise and then wait for turn in the bathroom.

7.15am: Prepare own breakfasts in the tiny kitchen, usually of flat bread and black coffee. Kill some ants.

7.30am: Gobble down breakfast whilst watching the old television set which reeled off a constant stream of heavily censored western films. Censorship was done with a heavy Islamic hand and with no thought whatsoever given to the continuity of the script, meaning that the end result would often as cause Western viewers to fall to the floor helpless with laughter. Kill more ants.

8am: Go downstairs and move through the early morning masses of labourers and clerks, across Tahrir Square to the local bus stop. Do a running jump into an overcrowded mini bus and then after a thirty-minute commute, jump out by the university.

9-12am: Have the mind overloaded with spoken and written Arabic, try not to despair, countdown till lunch. Try and ignore the sounds of the local vendors outside the windows who are trying to sell scrap iron and gas canisters from their bicycles.

12-1pm: Lunch, wander through the dusty and filthy backstreets until a suitable street kitchen is found. Eat whatever local hot scoff appeals to the stomach that day (I over ate on falafel during the first few weeks and it has taken me years to be able to even be able look the stuff it again).

1-5pm: Arabic overload once again, fight off post lunch sleepiness, keep glancing at the clock, waiting till end of lessons for the day.

5pm: Overjoyed that another day has been spent studying and especially so now that it is now over. Run outside and flag a bus, or taxi if one is feeling affluent, and repeat standard hazardous journey home.

6pm: Get back to flat, buy takeaway dinner if one is feeling doubly affluent and then, if it is Tuesday or Thursday, get changed into a gym kit and go off to the Dragon Academy for a few hours of martial arts training and classes.

8-10pm: Return from gym, get up from sofa or desk, make or warm up dinner, watch another repeat of an obscure and badly edited English film; if feeling lazy, put on one of the CDs loaned by Dad and lie on the bed and gaze at ceiling.

10pm: Flop down onto bed, ensure fan is turned on, read book or send an email home. Kill ants. Sleep.

Every morning during the week, as long as my motivation levels were strong enough, I'd be woken up by the various calls of the Muezzin. They often sounded, sadly, like distorted electronic rants due to the poor quality speakers used at the mosques, which was a great shame considering how pleasant the summons to the faithful sounds when an Imam or Mullah uses only his lungs to project his message. After rising groggily from my bed, I'd then set about starting my morning ritual.

Firstly putting on, on lowered volumes lest I incur the sleepy wrath of my two flatmates, some classical tunes such as Nessun Dorma and La Voce del Silenzio, and after prepping a deliciously tall cool glass of water, with a fresh lime squeezed into it, I would sit at my desk and happily work away at my Arabic grammar and verbs.

On the subject of limes, which our local rambling and chaotic farmers markets specialised in, we were to find, as our time in Cairo went on, that it was almost impossible to find tonic for our special weekend G&Ts. However, we soon discovered that a glass of British gin, ice and local lemonade, with a whole lime squeezed in to add that key tart taste, made for very excellent drinks indeed. They soon became known by one and all as 'Cairo G&Ts'.

The weekend, which started on the Thursday afternoon and would continue through to Sunday, was an entirely different and more interesting, if not intoxicating, affair.

Upon lessons finishing on the Thursday, Matt, Pete and I would dash off to our carefully pre-assigned and designated tasks. Two would head to a particular market across the Nile which had a shop which sold particularly good roasted chickens, accompanied with rice, lettuce and strange dipping sauces whilst the other would move to the local hooch shop. The owner after a few weeks was to become a firm friend of ours and would always furnish us with two large plastic shopping bags filled to the brim with tins of warm Egyptian Stella lager.

Suitably armed and equipped, we'd then meet back at the flat, arrange our feast on our dinner table and, usually wearing just a pair of pants and maybe a t-shirt, as it was simply red hot in the afternoon, tuck in. After feasting and gorging on a meal fit for a king, and having downed half a dozen of cans, we would retire to our rooms and relax for a bit. A few hours later, when the last Muzzein call had ended, the preparations for the much anticipated and auspicious 'flat night out' would begin.

With as much care and attention to detail and tradition as three mystic and pompous high priests carrying out a ritual of the highest importance, we'd first put on loud music, Oasis, Lady GaGa, Arctic Monkeys and The Pogues became firm favourites. We'd then shower and put our best going out attire. Typically, this would take the form of long shorts, billowy t-shirts and sandals, although socks and shoes or a shirt would indicate a special occasion was in the offing, and then head out to the first stop of our venture around Cairo's nightspots, 'Hurriya'.

'Hurriya' was a wondrous establishment, straight out of Lawrence's time. A high-ceilinged place, thick with the pall of dense cigarette smoke which the ancient swirling fans did nothing to dissipate, and littered with old hardwood tables and chairs upon which drank the rich, varied and loud community of international students and expats, Christian and not-so-strict-Muslim Arabs.

Half of the premises were reserved for the non-alcohol drinking clientele who played constant games of chess, backgammon and dominoes, it is still to my eternal chagrin that I didn't try my hand at one of these games during my time there, and the other half for the hardened drinkers. One would walk in, the proprietor would walk up, assessing you and your companions for how much you looked like you'd spend, and assign you an appropriate table. The more regular and generous customers would earn the right of being brought their own table upon arrival.

The three of us, by the end of the year, and countless spent Egyptian pounds and hangovers later, finally managed to achieve this feat and could walk in even at the busiest of times and a waiter would bring us a table and chairs even before the first round had appeared. We wouldn't have swapped it not even for a free full membership at White's in St. James's Street.

The only alcohol available in the local Cairo bars was in the form of pint bottles of Stella, which would famously give you a hangover after just one drink, and the form of bill was novel as it was simple. The waiter would come up when you were finished at the end of the evening, count the number of empty bottles on your table, and charge you accordingly.

After a few bottles, all of which were carefully recycled and washed by the staff afterwards, or maybe just recycled, the decision would be made whether to spend the whole night in 'Hurriya' or head out to more bars.

Thankfully, in order to balance out the vast amounts of lager we were drinking on the weekends, Matt and I were very fortunate to stumble across a local MMA club, 'The Dragon Academy' after our first few initial months in Cairo and this was to be our saviour against boredom and endless routine, as well as being some of the best martial arts and fitness training I've ever had the chance to attend.

It was in a small nondescript building situated in a small dark winding street but the facilities were fantastic and our instructor was one of Egypt's top fighters. Our fellow gym buddies, all friendly and smiling Egyptian locals, had been student of the 'Sensei' for years and were all masters at boxing, kickboxing and wrestling. Needless to say, Matt and I, who'd never encountered anything more severe than the wild haymakers swung in the confusion of the Rugby and Shinty pitches, were beaten black and blue for the remainder of our time there.

Since my time in Cairo, I have been fortunate enough to be taught, and at times teach, kickboxing, wrestling, boxing and, in my opinion the deadliest of all martial arts, Krav Maga. I can credit my past teachers with the honour of saying that without their careful and patient tuition, I doubt

I would have been able to deal with the stresses and tests that I would soon encounter upon entering the Army.

My biggest trial, test of patience and point of learning throughout my entire time in Egypt was not the studying, or even the exams, or even living in a country that was as different to mine as could be imagined. It was the human terrain.

Towards the end of the first three months of our time in Cairo, despite all of our reasons that had driven us to learning and witnessing as much as we could of the Middle East, we grew to dislike much of what we came to see and encounter.

The overriding and despicable attitude demonstrated by most of the men we encountered towards all women, especially western women, as sexual objects existing for the sole purpose of gratification for men. The abject and absolute poverty of so many and the dizzying riches of their elite. The general despising of all those who were not Christian, or even the right type of Muslim. The ignorance of the rest of the world and how it worked. The quick to anger but afraid to fight attitude shown by most of the men. The hatred of homosexuality and yet barely hidden desire for it, displayed every week across the Middle East on the notorious 'Man Love Thursdays' as it was the only source of affection for many men. The belief that all those in the western world were rich, godless and despotic. The way in which local religious leaders could drive their followers into a wild mob, preaching hatred from the pulpit. How the western world would be described as a place of abject sin, and yet sexual assault of both male and female, domestic abuse, police brutality, poverty and ignorance induced by blind religious devotion were common place across the Muslim nations. How religious, political and social freedoms did not exist at all, except for those who had the means and connections to afford it.

Our belief and desire to continue to learn and study the Middle East was severely dented by these discoveries during our first three months in country.

But, thankfully, upon returning, after our Christmas holidays, to Cairo, I was fortunate enough to have my mind enlightened and eyes opened as to the reasons behind the machinations of the Middle East and the people that lived there. It was to be a conversation that I have never forgotten and has surpassed all the books, lectures and lessons that I had, or have since, encountered on the subject.

It occurred during our first return visit to 'Hurriya' after coming back from the holidays, where I had just finished sipping my first glass of frothy lager and looked around the crowded bar and its assembled patrons. I noticed a gentleman on the table next to ours, he was dressed very smartly, clearly an office worker of some sort who had just finished a long day's labour and was in need of refreshment, and he was drinking a tall glass of 'Stella' lager. He was also reading the Quran.

I worked up my courage and took the biggest singular leap an Englishman can ever manage and engaged a stranger in conversation:

'Excuse me my friend, I must ask, are you a Muslim?'

'Yes, I am my friend, why do you ask?'

'How is that you can drink a beer and read the holy book?'

'Well, it is like this my friend; I work hard each day and bring home money, I love my children and my wife, I am faithful, I give to charity and I do not hate any other man for his religious choice. What matter is it to God if I have a little drink and relax whilst I am reading his teachings?'

This simple statement had me gobsmacked. I wondered what would happen if an individual was to pull out a Quran and read it in a bar anywhere in the Islamic world. I know many places, even in Britain, where one would severely run the risk of being brutally attacked for such an act.

'Are you not afraid of what people walking outside this bar would do or say if they saw you?'

'Of course, that is why I read it here, where I know I'm surrounded by friendly people. Many people outside are stupid, like they are in your country.'

Now, bearing in mind at this time that I was not exactly ready to take the accusation that the people I know of back home could be measured with the same yardstick as those whom were padding around outside the bar, I riposted:

'What do you mean?'

'What I mean is that when I speak to people I know from this area, many of whom are my friends, they hate the West. They think you are godless, that your women are whores, your lives are full of sin and beyond all forgiveness. In their eyes, they are better than you and your people, even if they cannot afford enough food for their families or vote for whom they wish.'

I looked at him silently, imploring him to go on.

'But, my friend, before you think that the people here are different or worse than anywhere else you have been, answer me this. When do your family, or people you love, see or hear of us here in the Arab world?'

'From television mainly, or videos on the internet.'

And what do they see? What does the average British person see of the Middle East?

I thought for a few seconds.

'Suicide bombings, sectarian violence, religious hatred, poverty, backwardness generally.'

'Exactly, that is my point! The typical person in the West only knows of the Middle East by the bad images they see or hear in the Press. It is the same here. The typical Arab around here, the poor labourer for instance, only sees or hears of your world by Al-Jazeera or on the MTV that shows in the cafes. He believes all your women wear bikinis, sleep with anyone who has money, that you all live in mansions and happily flout the laws of God.'

'The only difference between your stupid person over in the West, and my stupid person here, is that your stupid person has most likely had the benefit of a good education from the State and should know which information he comes across in the news to believe, and which to discard as lies. The stupid person around here, in the souks and bazaars, has not had this. They have not had this opportunity.'

'So, even though I will admit that life for a lot of people here is not good, with no real voting or good houses to live in for instance, is it not worse when you come across this ignorance in your own country? For they have had the benefit of western education, where they are taught to be moderate and are free. Whereas here some of the people you come across have never had the chance to think anything else than what they see on television or hear in the mosque.'

'Without the benefit of a free and comprehensive education, when they see or hear of something they do not like, often they take it as fact and it grows inside them like a poison, affecting all they do.'

He paused and looked at me, taking a sip of lager, before uttering one final line.

'Forgive them father, they know not what they do.'

Since that conversation and it is to my eternal shame that I do not recall the man's name, I have never come across, in my opinion, a more thorough and yet simple explanation of how different cultures view each other and how such perceptions should be viewed and judged.

His last line, which still rings in my ears to this day, impressed upon me so much that upon finishing our conversation, we departed good friends but I was not to see him again, I went home and searched it online.

It was from the Bible, Luke 23:34.

After that evening, as if by magic, a pleasant and good precedent was made for the first time. In that we were fortunate enough to begin meeting some delightful members of the local community.

Throughout the remaining three quarters of the year, we were hosted by our ever-generous hosts to a range of different events and evenings. The epitome, at least for me, was when three of us were taken to Alexandria and spent two glorious days exploring that seaside city, sampling its famous seafood and exploring some of its classical ruins.

Sadly, I was unable to repeat the feat of Captain Anson and stumble in from the desert and down a fresh pint of lager in one go. The reason being that unlike in Cairo, we were unable to find any suitable dive bars in 'Alex'.

By the kind generosity and hospitality of our Egyptian friends, we were taken out of our daily monotonous lives surrounded by blank, unsmiling, unfriendly crowds and shown the most fantastic aspects and people of Egyptian society, rich and poor. Brilliant restaurants, street side cafes and vendors, family and religious celebrations, guided tours around streets that we would have never have thought to venture down. We had been saved and soon begun to experience the famed hospitality, generosity and friendliness of the Middle East.

***

I left Cairo at the end of the year and returned to my final two years at Leeds University, confident that I could just as easily barter with an Egyptian market vendor as I could discuss politics, to a certain degree, in classical Arabic. My university friends, upon me arriving at their house in Leeds after being away for the year, had laid on a surprise welcoming back party for me and aside from being simply overwhelmed by it, for they'd even made a six foot long cloth banner and strung it over the front of their house, it was also during that evening that I first met a young lovely lady called Katie Gunn, who, years later, was to become my wife.

The next two years of me at Leeds University were to consist of a mixture of despairing at the quality of student housing, taking up kickboxing and Krav Maga, revision for exams, struggling to learn complex grammar no one in the Arab world seems to even use anymore, brushing up on my French, meeting and becoming friends with a few students from the Middle East who were studying at Leeds and most poignantly, passing P Company and becoming a TA officer.

For during the middle section of my third year of study, desperate for cash as any student, the clerk at LUOTC mentioned that was an exercise coming up, which ran between three to four weeks, was paid and involved working with the British Paratroopers. It was an exercise called Ex AIRBORNE STUDENT, would I be interested?

I couldn't fill out the paperwork fast enough.

A few weeks later, kit bags and webbing prepped as per direction from the given kit list, I found myself on a minibus with half a dozen other OTC cadets pulling into the aptly named 'Helles Barracks' in ITC (Infantry Training Centre) Catterick. With simply not a clue what we'd be doing. Maybe just a few 'look at life' training exercises, a couple presentations on the British Airborne forces and some extra PT thrown in for good measure?

When we jumped out by the main accommodation block and saw the swarm of maroon beret wearing Physical Training Instructors (PTIs) slowly make their way towards us like a pack of predatory big cats, we realised something different may be in the offing.

'Welcome to P Company, gentlemen!'

We looked around at each other, realisation dawning on a few people's faces, thankfully mine too. The next few weeks were not going to be like any of us had envisioned at all.

After throwing our kit into our communal rooms and introducing ourselves to the other wide eyed cadets, as well as one friendly chap who had already passed the All Arms Commando Course and was to become a font of wisdom over the coming exercise, we then dashed outside again for the introductory speech by the Officer Commanding Pegasus Company (OC P Coy), a fearsome Para Captain.

The deer in headlights sensation was still strong in many of us and the record does not show what exactly what was said during that talk but the gist was thus:

'Many of you will fail. All of you will be pushed to your breaking point. It is an absolute privilege for you to have the opportunity to try and pass the selection that will allow you to wear the proud maroon beret of the British Airborne forces. The British Paras are the finest soldiers in the world; everyone else is just a HAT. From this point now, until you leave, you are ours and we will constantly drive you. The reason we will do this is simple, we must make you worthy of all those men coming before you and passed P Company. All those men who fought in Arnhem, Goose Green, Iraq and Afghanistan, we will make you worthy of them.'

It left a considerable mark or impression on all of us.

Soon a member of staff, one of the huge towering PTIs, came into our room and had an informal chat about what we were to face over the next few weeks:

'Listen lads, this is tough. It's fucking tough. But it's meant to be. All you need to remember is that if you are fit and dedicated to proving yourself, you will pass. We will thrash you on the PT sessions, we will thrash you till you bleed. But, as long as you perform well on PT, we'll leave you alone. If you turn out to be weak, we'll come down on you like a ton of bricks. At the end of this course, when some of you get handed the best fucking beret in the world, you'll have succeeded in something that will last with you throughout the rest of your life.

Just remember that when you're absolutely chin strapped half way through the log race or milling competition, earning the maroon beret was one of the hardest things I ever had to do but it's of the proudest moments of my life!'

As I listened to this, I thought that if I could only pass this arduous course, I could pass anything. I could have something that not only would my family and friends be proud of, but something that I could be proud of. I envisioned myself earning the right to wear the same beret that the men who jumped on D-Day wore, proving myself; challenge accepted.

It all started the next day.

As the days passed, and the much feared 'Test Week' slowly drew closer, the tempo of the twice a day PT sessions increased, as did the drop out and injury rate. It seemed that despite the fact that almost every bone and muscle in our bodies soon ached and simply screamed for mercy, the shouts and screams of our instructors got louder and louder:

'Stand by..., go!'

'It pays to be a winner!'

'Catch him!'

'Stop being weak!'

'Chain of command? It's the chain I'll fucking beat you with until you obey my commands!'

'Start working gents, or I'll start to make it really difficult for you!'

'I'll beast you till you bleed!'

What kept us going, through all the endless route marches, sprint sessions, circuits and more, was the famed ethos of the British Airborne forces:

Utrinque Paratus. Ready for anything.

Everywhere we went in the barracks, we were surrounded by memorabilia and literature of the rich history of the British Airborne forces, as well as serving personnel who cut about in their much envied maroon beret, with wings on the arms and confident expressions on their faces.

I forget how many times I, amongst many others, looked up to the large poster on the wall near the armoury which had printed upon it the full poem of Kipling's 'IF'. Many of us, myself included, were to have memorised it before we finally departed the barracks.

During each miniature break between PT sessions, or lessons, the P Company staff would sit down amongst us, their screaming encouragements for us to run faster forgotten for a few precious minutes, and tell us their own personal accounts, or of their comrades', in Iraq and Afghanistan. We worshiped them.

Finally, the weeks had passed and before we knew it, Test Week was starting the next day. Nerves were taught, the nominal role had dropped by at least a quarter by now due to either injury, lack of fitness or lack of spine, and everyone knew full well the challenges they would now have to face in order to earn the right to wear the maroon beret.

By the grace of God, heaving lungs and shaking legs, I managed to pass all the tests during Test Week. Although I had had some close shaves.

I came close to failing the Ten Miler due to not eating enough at breakfast, only half a bacon sandwich and a spoonful of porridge due to nerves, and almost fainting on my feet at the eight-mile point. It was only by staring at the bergen in front and imagining my parents' spurring me on I managed to stay with the pack and cross the finish line.

The Milling was by far my favourite event; I saw it almost as a treat to the end of the course. Getting matched up to a bloke of my weight and height, being made to stare each other out, the instructors psyching everyone up. Stepping into the ring with all of the other students sat around on benches, with the head instructors who doubled as the judges of the fight sat to one side, and then the instructor would beckon in one's opponent.

'Sixty seconds, I just have to fight this man for sixty seconds. I'm going to kill him. I'm going to absolutely kill him. Remember, go for maximum aggression, get the first punch in, breathe in and keep bloody hitting him. Don't give him a chance. Get your footing right. Kill him.'

As the bell rang and the punches were launched, I knew that I had my man. Although 'milling' is not boxing, and students get reprimanded for trying to do so, my previous experience in the ring saw me through that fight. With each rapid jab, don't swing any wild haymakers, thrown with maximum and full force, I exhaled, kept my feet correct and used all of my concentration, driven by anger, desperation and the encouragement of the people surrounding me, to punch the man's face. After the longest sixty seconds of my life, and my opponent falling to the floor three times, the referee raised my arm in victory.

Of all the fights I have been in, despite its simplicity, brutality and likeliness to old school prize fighting, it was perhaps my most prized event.

Straight afterwards, everyone sporting broken noses, black eyes and blood-stained faces, we were marched back to our accommodation where we showered, changed and hurried outside for the final ceremony. This was where OC P Company would call out of the names of those who had passed or failed, and personally hand those who had been successful, the prized maroon beret.

This was the final example of the utter contempt, or disdain, held by the instructors of those who had failed the rigorous standards set during the entirety of P Company. It all started when the OC went through the nominal role of the students.

If an individual had failed, after answering their name, the OC would shout 'fail!' and the student would then about turn and march off behind those remaining and form ranks with the other failed individuals, facing away.

All the while listening to those who had passed get awarded their prize, their very own maroon Paratrooper beret.

Whereas if the student had been successful, and deemed worthy by the instructing staff, upon answering their name, with a sudden surge of relief and testosterone, they would hear the word:

'PASS!'

After everyone's name had been called out, the ranks substantially thinned by those who had not passed, the OC would walk up to each successful candidate, shake their hand and hand them their beret.

As the OC solemnly called out our names, my heart was in my mouth and my stomach was full of butterflies. I knew that I'd passed every event but there was still that element of fear that the staff might had seen some unknown flaw in my character or physical makeup and despite everything, would fail me. Having seen a number of very robust students get told that they had failed and then march away to stand separated from those who had been told they had succeeded, I was very nervous indeed as the roll call got closer to my name. My back was ramrod straight, hands were held rigidly by my sides, my imagination spinning.

'Beeching!'

'Sir!'

'… PASS!'

Having OC P Company award, me my maroon beret seconds later, along with the absolute surge of relief and pride, was a moment I will never forget.

Once I'd returned to Leeds, celebrating with the others who had also passed the course, I then decided to reapply to undertake the TA Officer Commissioning Course (TACC).

This time I was successful and by the end of my third year of university I had commissioned from RMAS as a Second Lieutenant in the TA.

Aside from the experience and insight of RMAS, and the lessons taught officially and unofficially by our Staff instructors, the other excellent lesson during my time on TACC was a view into the life of the TA itself and the politics between it and the Regular Army.

The TA, until it was rebranded as the Army Reserves, has always had a fractious relationship with the Regular Army and will always remain so; predominantly to the fierce sense of unit tribalism that exists throughout the British Armed Forces. In my eyes, the TA will always remain the TA, and the Army Reserves will always be a previously existing, now extinct, organisation which consisted of soldiers who had served many years in the Regular Army before returning to 'Civvie Street', but who were ready to be called upon if their country needed them for active service.

Among the various bars and messes of the British Army, when no one representing the 'other side' is present, the TA personnel are known colloquially as STABs (Stupid Territorial Army Bastard) and the Regular Army as ARABs (Arrogant Regular Army Bastards). The British military is and always has been a very tribal organisation and no amount of Whitehall interfering will ever change this.

During my TACC, the phrase that was stressed was 'One Army!' and that no difference lay between those officers and soldiers in the TA to those in the Regular Army. Except for the fact that all of us who were going to eventually go towards a Regular Commission in a couple of years generally doubted this statement, but we wisely kept our own council.

In my experience, which is a very dangerous phrase for a young officer to utter and one that usually sends SNCOs running for cover, there are many extremely dedicated and talented persons within the TA (Reserves) and some truly excellent units who have a rich history and a wealth of experience more than equal to their Regular counterparts. To name but a few; 4 Para, The Royal Marine Reserve and the Artists Rifles.

But, and there is always a but in these cases, the general experience of the Reserve soldier or officer is typically not up to the standard of their Regular counterparts, unless they served as in the Regular Army previously, and it is a significant error to believe otherwise.

It is my view that the soldiers and officers in the British Army Reserves, like all the Reserve units that have gone before them, are often not so much 'cap badge loyal' and not necessarily dedicated to their chosen unit, but rather are 'regional loyal'. What that meant was that they wish to work in their local areas, so that they don't have to travel far and suffer as a result significant inconveniences travelling to and from their barracks.

One of the many reasons so many have declined to join up and serve within the ranks in the most recent government recruitment drives is that personnel simply do not have the time or will power to travel miles out of their way to a barracks. Many even leaving the Reserves as their local barracks has been closed and they cannot travel to its replacement location; a simple fact but one clearly not realised by the bean counters in Whitehall.

If in doubt, look to the very name of the organisation before Downing Street meddling altered its once proud name, the 'Territorial Army'.

This is not a disadvantage, before I receive too many letters written in red ink and signed with an indignant 'Regards', but one of the Reserves greatest strengths is that good commanders can and always have been able to, if you study your history books that is, draw on significant pools of manpower from their region of responsibility in times of need. Classic examples of this can be seen in the lead up, and participation, in such large-scale conflicts such as, the Boer War, both World Wars and the Korean War.

Another one of the strengths of the National Servicemen, the forerunners of the Reserves today, was their diversity and wealth of experience outside of their military careers. A commander of such soldiers, as I have been fortunate to be at times, often discovers that although an individual might be only a junior rank in the group of individuals they are commanding, but that they may well be a nuclear physicist, teacher, surgeon or surveyor in civilian life, thus adding great value to their unit.

I do not subscribe to the belief that all soldiers and officers in the Reserves are rank amateurs. Having been lucky enough to work with the Reserves on many occasions, I am wary of persons who state such rhetoric, but I do believe that it is a mistake to try and replace Regular soldiers with Reserves for long periods of time and to believe that the overall skill and response level of the unit will be the same.

Due to the difficulties in attending training nights during the weeks and training weekends, predominantly because of constraints of family life, it is simply not possible to put, for instance, a Corporal from a Royal Engineer Reserve unit next to a Regular counterpart and believe that the two will be on equal terms in regards to their engineering skill, their experience and competency.

There is simply no chance that an individual, who practises a specific trade, once a week for an evening and the occasional weekend, will be at the same expertise level of someone who practises it Monday to Friday, dawn till dusk.

Amongst the various Corps of the British Army, namely those that are not in the 'Teeth Arms', the biggest concern is skill fade amongst its soldiers; especially within the Royal Engineers. As all those who have a specialist trade are often called on to serve as infantry, the strain is especially felt more so by the soldiers and officers in the Reserves.

Much funding has been spent on not only trade training for the personnel in the Reserves, let alone propaganda and recruiting campaigns, and yet unless individuals arrive from a specialist Reserve unit, very often the skill level of an individual's trade or ability as a field soldier is not as high as their Regular counterparts.

Unless, as aforementioned, they were a Regular soldier or officer before they joined the Reserves.

There is a significant argument within the British military to do away with all the different forms of Reserve units, except for specialist ones such as the UK Reserve Special Forces, and compel all personnel to undertake just one type of training, instead of trying to do everything:

'Do one thing well, not too things badly.'

This is not meant as a disparaging comment on the abilities or reputation of either the Regulars or the Reserves, but more so to ensure that continuity in training is achieved and that training can be achieved with fewer resources. Thus, freeing up resources for Regular units and mitigating any concerns about deficiencies in standards in the niche trades.

Lastly, amongst the many institutions and organisations that I have worked or lived in, the scheme for Army 2020 and replacing Regulars with Reserves en masse is generally seen as a mockery by many within the ranks, myself being one, and its deficiencies are well known.

It is my argument that replacing Regulars with Reserves on a large scale for lengthy periods of time has never worked before in the history of the British military and that there are now more reasons than ever before as to why it will not work this time. Especially due to the complexity of the equipment the Army now uses, the tempo and regularity of training which is required to keep individuals up to peak performance and lastly, the sheer amount of time soldiers and officers are now actually deployed overseas in complex and often rapidly evolving conflicts.

Hopefully the damage will be rectified before it is too late and the Regular Army will be brought back up to something resembling fighting strength. But sadly, I do not think so, mainly due to the zeal in which senior personnel in the military and government are desperately expending funds and manpower in attempts with succeeding with the theory of Army 2020. They cannot see the wood for the trees.

In order to quantify how small the British Army actually is these days, if the entire British Army was collected together, including its sick, lame and lazy, and sat in Wembley Stadium, there would be still seats left empty. But I digress.

***

2011 Leeds. There I was, standing in Carlton Barracks, proudly sporting my new maroon beret and single Second Lieutenant's pip. I felt like a million bucks.

But I was also in a quandary, for I was still in the UOTC, having declined to progress further and join the local Para unit as my studies would have not survived me actually doing real soldiering at this point, and was surrounded by UOTC cadets. Many of whom were my friends and classmates outside of work. Thus, during the day many of them were fellow students whom I drank with the local bars, whilst on certain evenings we'd all change roles and respond to the hierarchical system of the army. It was always tricky to put myself in a position of authority over someone whom I had been drinking or studying with the night before.

It is worth mentioning that part of the allure of completing P Company was the prospect of qualifying for my jumps and getting a set of wings on my shirt sleeves. But sadly, due to the high amount of P Company qualified officers and soldiers and the scarcity of RAF pilots and planes, many, myself included, were not offered the chances to prove ourselves and do our jumps.

I was to discover this was, and still is, a significant point of contention amongst those Army personnel who have passed P Company but have not had the opportunity to get their jumps due to limited RAF availability. I know of one 4 Para Private who had wait over five years before completing his last jump.

It was disappointing to realise that as a result of constant government cutbacks and subsequent minimising of military air resources such as planes and pilots, exactly just how many officers and soldiers who passed P Company with flying colours were destined to become Penguins.

Birds that cannot fly.

It is a strange feeling to be at the bottom rung of the promotion chain as a Second Lieutenant, as even though you are sporting the Queen's uniform, and that is what is saluted, it is still a tricky business finding your own way and your command presence. The entire reason being, as it has always been, is that although an individual has proved themselves at RMAS and worthy of a commission, in the Army one has to also earn the respect of those one is working with.

Especially so in the UOTC, as everyone is aware that aside from the weekly drill night and training weekend, outside of the wire you are also another penniless student who attends classes, irregularly, and is always, regularly, thirsty for the next pint.

But, I was fortunate; all of my friends and colleagues whom I worked with in the UOTC 'played the game' and through a mixture of humility and fragile confidence in my own command presence, salutes were presented and I was given modicums of responsibility. I was also helped by the fact that aside from myself, there was also a smattering of other Reserve Second Lieutenants serving within LUOTC and through by hook and by crook, we helped each other along and gradually learnt the ropes of being junior officers serving within an OTC unit.

Throughout my remaining time at LUOTC in Carlton Barracks, I deployed on a number of exercises, I even took part in a Commando familiarisation visit, where as I was the only officer, one wearing the hated maroon beret no less, I was sent in the freezing cold waters of the dip tank more times than anyone else, and I had plenty of opportunities to figure out my own command style and approach.

As well as cutting my teeth on important aspects such as giving orders, leading patrols and taking care of the administration of those under my command. All on a smaller scale than what I would face in the future, I freely admit but never the less, the lessons and experiences would put me in good stead for when I attended Regular RMAS.

Aside from my military-esc escapades, I also had to keep up with my studies, something which I have always had a tenuous relationship with, in order to graduate. The sole aim I had for my final year at university, aside from getting a degree, was ensuring that I could maintain a conversation in Arabic with as native speaker on almost any topic.

To become, or at least try to become, an 'Arabist'.

To eventually become someone whom could not only chat away with an individual from anywhere in the Arab world, but also with a medium chance of having a modicum of success in understanding what was actually being said in return. As well as having an understanding of their culture, religion and true meanings behind words and phrases.

Fortunately for me, I discovered that Leeds has a rich Middle Eastern and North African community and there were plenty of opportunities to practise my spoken Arabic and French.

My whole incentive was that as long as I could happily chat away with someone and the conversation not being too broken up whilst trying to remember certain words or phrases, I would be happy.

As a result, throughout my final year, I spent countless hours meeting and chatting with overseas students in a babble of Arabic and French, amid swaths of cups of coffee and sweets. I treasured every second.

The overwhelming courtesy that was shown to me by my acquaintances from the Arab world was simply outstanding and a finer example of spontaneous and authentic friendship I have yet to see.

From meeting at small coffee houses where instead of just meeting my Saudi Arabian friend, there would be often up to six individuals who were all close associates and family of my acquaintance, all of whom were desperate for a chance to chat and practise their spoken English.

I have found, since my time at university and in the military, people from the Arab world happen to be among some of the best linguists I have ever come across, they even manage to understand my attempts Arabic for heaven's sake, and often speak a number of additional oversees languages, as well as any number of additional Middle Eastern dialects. Whereas I believe the average Brit speaks only English, and in case of overseas travel, 'Louder English'; typically in conjunction with a heavy reliance on dramatic sign language.

I would often be invited to houses where, upon turning up, a small token of friendship in one hand, usually some assorted sweet pastries, I would be shown into the living room and over a full course of beautifully cooked food, lamb and rice being particular favourites of mine, would find myself talking about a whole host of topics.

Hours later, which flew by like minutes, upon leaving, I would often find small containers filled with food thrust into my hands by my hosts. The epitome of Arab hospitality.

No topic was off limits and, in the safety and security of a busy and crowded coffee shop, or the snug comfort of a living room with half a dozen people perched on all manner of furniture, I would find myself having frank and open discussions on subjects such as God, other religions, sex before marriage, women's rights, politics and much more.

The form and procedures were always the same. I would arrive on time, with a either a small gift for the household, one cannot overestimate the importance and stress placed on such formalities, or a pocket full of change in order to buy everyone a coffee or tug on the hookah pipe, and would then wait for the other guests, usually work colleagues or family of my host, to turn up.

Around half an hour later, over a steady stream of exchanging pleasantries, handshakes and offering of food and drink, the conversations would then begin in earnest. I would try to speak only in Arabic, the only way to learn the language properly, and they would speak in English.

I honestly believe that these experiences taught me more about Arab world and the mix of people whom inhabit it as much as, if not more, my university lectures did. One of the biggest challenges I have come across in my constant endeavour to learn foreign languages is trying to understand a conversation between two locals.

Although I will readily admit that there is still much improvement needed in regards to this struggle, the numerous hours I spent sat listening to the exchanges between my Arab friends did wonders and helped lay the foundations for me to become a translator years later in the British Army.

But before I had known what had happened, after numerous training weekends and drill nights and many boozy parties in the mess, Burns Night and the Annual Ball were amongst the highlights, tedious long hours spent studying, my head in my hands fighting the urge to throw my grammar books out the window, and endless and tedious exams, I did it.

I found myself a proud graduate from the University of Leeds with a degree in Arabic and Middle Eastern Studies.

Playtime was now over; I now had to pull my socks up for real this time and finally face my biggest test and trial. Forty four weeks at RMAS.

To try and gain a commission into the Regular Army and into the Corps of Royal Engineers.

4

Royal Military Academy Sandhurst

Juniors. Inters. Seniors

11 September, 2011, Minley Manor, the Royal Engineers Officers' Mess of Gibraltar Barracks, a few minutes down the road from RMAS.

I was sitting in my suit, my stomach doing back flips, at a table eating a buffet curry, hosted by the Royal Engineers (RE), trying not to let my hand shake too much. All the while waiting for the senior RE officer to stand up and give his speech to the sponsored RE OCdts, of which I was one of, as I'd somehow managed to convince the Royal Engineers to sponsor me through university and very kindly give me £1000 a year as a bursary, and their assembled parents.

This speech is famous amongst all whom have attended RMAS as it is aimed at the parents more than the OCdts and it is meant to put any fears or nerves to rest. But all it did, in my opinion, was to drag out the inevitable.

I didn't want to be sat in my suit eating madras curry with saffron rice, jealously watching all the various family and friends wander around, blissfully happy in their finery, as they were not the ones about to embark upon a year's training, stress and pain.

I wanted to get started. I wanted the executioner's axe to fall. I wanted to begin.

I wanted to join my intake at RMAS, which was to comprise of three Companies of OCdts, each roughly ninety persons strong; although as the years have progressed since my time at RMAS, the intakes have been whittled down severely and the flow of OCdts graduating from RMAS has slowed down to a veritable dribble.

Thankfully, the false calm of the lunch was soon over and I was in the car, filled to the brim with kit and clothing and haring around the lanes till we pulled through the main gates of Sandhurst and ended up parking up right in front of the steps of Old College.

I burst out of the car like a partridge, hurried through the crowd of new cadets, all sporting suits and worried faces, carrying their iconic ironing boards under their arms and went to find my Colour Sergeant (CSgt); the man who would become a pivotal figure in the next forty-four weeks of my life.

Walking briskly up to an infantry SNCO who standing on steps of Old College, his chest festooned with campaign medals, and holding an official looking clipboard, I halted and awaited his attention.

'Name?'

'Beeching, Colour Sergeant.'

'Beeching, Beeching..., ah yes. Ypres Company, 25 Platoon. Go find Colour Sergeant Morrison; he's your Platoon Sergeant.'

Slowly edging my way through the crowd of concerned individuals and imposing looking instructors, I eventually found my way to a central classroom where the majority of RMAS personnel were waiting. Walking through the doors, I looked around at the assembled SNCOs, all stood around the corners of the room, I tried to decipher which one of the huge, hairy and angry looking men was my new CSgt.

One in particular stood out.

A dominating figure, heavy shoulders with a prominent barrel chest, red face glaring from underneath his polished cap, his eyes swivelled and focused on me.

He walked over, moving through the crowd like an iceberg making its way through a stormy sea, pushing all to one side. Stopping right in front of me, I realised with shaking dread that this huge man's name tag identified him as 'Colour Sergeant Morrison, Yorkshire regiment'.

Looking at me, he then scanned his eyes down his clipboard:

'Name?'

'Beeching, Colour Sergeant.'

'Beeching? Yes, here you are. You're one of mine; Ypres Company, 25 Platoon.'

He rattled off the details as to where I could find my new accommodation and put my variety of belongs. I then rushed off back to the car and started overburdening myself with armfuls of heavy items.

Thirty minutes later, after a number of scurried journeys from the car to my room and frantic farewells to the family, I was standing in my new room, piled high with kit and surrounded by other OCdts who were to be my companions for the next year.

Soon, after donning on the obligatory dull green overalls marking our status as raw recruits, all ninety OCdts were marshalled into a lecture hall by various members of DS and were given an introductory speech by our new OC; Major Hawkins RE.

A stocky and very powerfully built man who not only sported the maroon beret and wings of the Airborne Engineers, but also wore the hallowed RE diver patch. Clearly, he was an exceptionally tough and capable individual.

Standing there with his arms folded, casting his eyes over us, he projected the aura of confidence, experience and one who although might have a sense of humour, would brook nothing less than absolute peak performance from the OCdts in his company. As the weeks and months were to pass by, he was to become another reason as to why I wanted to join the Royal Engineers.

After his introductory speech, under the guidance of our indomitable CSgt Morrison, 25 Platoon was soon to meet with their Platoon Commander. Captain Rouse QOGLR.

Slim and short, but with eyes that spoke of intense experience, toughness and drive, Captain Rouse left us in no doubt that he would drive us hard and expect nothing but perfection. Standards befitting a man who had not only completed both the All Arms Commando Course and P Company, but had also served with distinction in Iraq and Afghanistan numerous times, as both a soldier to start with and later on as an officer.

It goes without saying that the DS at RMAS, both SCNOs and officers, were all of the highest calibre and were the very best and brightest from their respective regiments. Everyone single one of them was not only of the highest physical and mental standards, but each individual had also served in numerous overseas conflicts.

If the military adage that 'a good leader is reflected by his unit', Ypres Company, and 25 Platoon especially, would have to reach exceptionally high standards and capabilities in order to match and keep up with those of our instructors.

During the next five weeks, we would be put through a crash course of basic military skills, marching and on the different functions and units of the British Army. The priority throughout seemed, unsurprisingly, to be on marching up and down the RMAS parade square.

Often, aside from trying to make sure trousers and shirts were ironed correctly, the hardest task for any OCdt to overcome was not falling asleep in any of the lectures we had to sit through. The hardest location to avoid giving into narcolepsy was the 'Churchill Lecture Hall', which is known by all Army past and present, as the 'largest sleeping bag in the world'.

A large ugly concrete building which can seat hundreds of OCdts at one time and allows the DS at RMAS to give any number of lectures. Convenitley, the seats are also very comfortable and often entire rows of OCdts can be seen slumped to one side, fast asleep. Much to the amusement of the OCdts still awake, as well as the eagle-eyed Platoon SNCOs and officers.

It was in one of the various lectures that took place in Churchill Hall that we were informed that aside from candidates who are undergoing UK Special Forces (UKSF) training, RMAS OCdts have the highest calorie intake in the entire British military.

Despite the extraordinary large meals that we ate three times a day, not including snacks, we all lost weight; getting up at around 5.45am, having a full day of brain busting lectures and lung bursting PT sessions, every single calorie counted and individuals were known to faint on their feet for not eating enough. It was rather amusing for the male OCdts in Junior Term to watch the female Platoon being trooped in and watched by their DS during meal times to ensure they ate enough; too many initially trying to sustain themselves with salads and the like.

Throughout the hectic days of learning the different personalities of OCdts and DS, the various skill at arms, map reading and orders lessons, as well as rigid parades and nerve wracking room inspections, our Platoon slowly began to take shape. Individuals slowly found each other's strengths and weaknesses and made collective assistance efforts so that 25 Platoon would thrive, the eternal mantra of 'the needs of the group coming before the needs of the individual' was very much so in force.

We were fortunate to have two overseas OCdts in our Platoon; Muataz from the UAE Army and Ahmed from the Sultan of Oman's Special Force. With my burgeoning background in Arabic, I slowly made friends with these two, as did the rest of the 25 Platoon, and the enjoyment of working with them quickly affirmed my desire to work with Middle Eastern militaries in the future.

For maintaining, promoting and improving relationships between the UK and its Middle Eastern allies, no finer individuals could have been found than OCdts Muataz and Ahmed.

One can only imagine the tension and nerves they must have had to overcome as part of being chosen by their country to attend RMAS. Many UK OCdts find the learning curve of RMAS to be extremely steep and intimidating, and I simply cannot imagine undertaking the challenge of passing RMAS, when English is not your first language and Britain is not your home country.

The equivalent for UK OCdts I imagine would be say attending 'St. Cyr' or the 'Führungsakademie der Bundeswehr' military institutions with only a GCSE or A level understanding of French or German, with the expectation of meeting and performing to the same standards as the host nation cadets. Very intimidating indeed.

RMAS was an excellent environment to have opportunities for British OCdts to work with officers from overseas militaries. History is abound with examples of junior officers who worked together during their time at RMAS, meeting up, sometimes on opposing sides, in future conflicts.

For example, when during the opening days of the Second Gulf War in Iraq, a unit of British Paratroopers found themselves dug in along a sandy ridge and a horde of Iraqi soldiers began advancing towards them, hands held high, with their officer out in front, shouting in English:

'Are you British Paras?!'

The British Paras looked around bizarrely at each other before one of them yelled back:

'Yes, we are. 3 Para. Why?!'

To which the young Iraqi officer replied:

'I graduated from Sandhurst a few years ago, my Colour Sergeant was from 3 Para!'

Usually there are two overseas OCdts in each Platoon at RMAS and the countries they come from highlight the range of allies and good overseas relations the UK military enjoys. It is not uncommon to find the person next to you in the lunch queue is from as far away as the USA, South Africa, Belize, Iraq or Kazakhstan.

Aside from the addition of a number of overseas OCdts in every company, each Platoon at RMAS also typically has two OCdts who have previously served as soldiers in the Army before applying to become officers. These are known as 'Ex-Rankers' and due to their previous military knowledge, experience and understanding of the system, are priceless assets to each Platoon. Showing the otherwise naive OCdts how to work smart, work the system and pick up all the little tricks learnt from years of experience which make life in uniform that little bit easier.

During the first five weeks at RMAS, where the OCdts are not allowed off the premises due to RMAS training regulations, waiting with baited breath for the first leave weekend, tension gradually builds up as more and more knowledge and lessons are heaped upon the OCdts.

Drill, always a heated topic amongst the RMAS OCdts, becomes even more intense and the room and clothing inspections become even more severe as the tests loomed closer and closer.

All of this culminates in a final parade where each Platoon formally 'passes off the Square', all the while in front of senior RMAS officers who overlook the performance with a critiquing eye and finally, the Platoon hopefully is deemed smart and professional looking enough to progress forward into the next stage of training.

The drill, marching, rifle drill, endless polishing and ironing, and much more, drove more than one OCdt to exasperation on numerous occasions.

Me included:

Why on earth are we spending so much time on this stuff? I'm not joining the bloody Guards for heaven's sake!

But looking back, one could not argue with the results, as foot drill is one of the most fundamental and effective ways of moulding a group of individuals together into a team. Each Platoon soon took absolute pride in their performance on the drill square and this unit pride was then carried onto into other vital aspects, such as fighting ability in the field or other inter RMAS Platoon competitions.

As the days and weeks passed, the focus of an individual, especially for me, became one of two things; food and sleep.

Sleep. Precious sleep. All enveloping, comforting and restorative slumber. It is the most valued commodity to anyone who has gone through military training.

It simply consumed our lives and as the intensity of instruction increased and more and more was heaped upon one's shoulders, OCdts soon craved any minute opportunity to close their eyes and rest; even if only for a few precious seconds.

If an OCdt, male or female, UK or overseas, was stationary for more than a minute, they would soon hurriedly eat whatever food that was available, often carrying their own snacks in case none could be found locally. I can honestly say that I have never eaten as much as I did whilst at RMAS.

Each morning during Junior Term, I, along with the rest of my intake, would eat a huge fried breakfast, with lashings of tea or coffee. Then, come midday, a full lunch and then to finish off the day, hours later, a simply gargantuan dinner, complete with dessert.

PT, aside from the lectures on the vast range of RMAS subject materials we all had to assimilate and memorise, formed a significant part of our lives and competition was fierce during Platoon or Company PT sessions to be amongst the strongest and the fastest by a long mile.

After each Physical Fitness Assessment (PFA), everyone's times for the run, combined with the number of press-ups and sit ups each person had managed, were published in each Platoon line. Quickly all OCdts began to realise where they stood in relation to the rest of their compatriots and who they would have to beat next time in order to progress up the hierarchy of the platoon and company.

Towards the end of my time at RMAS, I could comfortably achieve one hundred push ups and one hundred sit ups in the given time and run the mile and a half in almost eight minutes and fifteen seconds. If I could only have managed to run under the eight minute and fifteen second mark I would have become part of the famed '300 Club'.

An individual achieves this by achieving a set amount of sit ups and press ups, as well as a certain time on the run, the amounts varying with age and gender. Once they have achieved the required number or time, they are awarded a hundred points per challenge and once completing all three, their score tallies up to three hundred and they earn the right to claim membership to the 300 Club.

A club only in name but which consists of individuals who have proven themselves to be extremely fit and thus earning a significant accolade. Despite my best efforts, and having no issue with requiring the set amount of sit ups and press ups, I have never managed to run fast enough to meet the required standard run time.

At my fastest, I was only managing to complete the run in 8.23 minutes; whereas the minimum required was 8.15 minutes. Maybe one day. But God knows, I do hate sprinting with a passion.

One of my proudest moments during Junior Term was taking part in the 'Eight Mile March' competition in which all OCdts in the intake were to compete, as well as many of the DS, where each Platoon would collectively race over a four mile route, with weighted bergens, against all the other Platoons in the intake. Then, once all individuals were across the finish line, time only stopping when all the OCdts from a Platoon had completed the race, the race would begin again immediately but it was now an individual best effort.

I was very pleased to find that when I crossed the finish line at the end of the individual race, legs trembling and chest heaving, only to find that I had come 16th out of my entire intake of roughly two hundred and fifty OCdts. It was at that point that I realised that although I was not the fittest by any stretch of the imagination, I was capable of performing to high physical standards and this slowly started to build up my confidence and standing within 25 Platoon.

On the subject of physical acumen, each Wednesday afternoon the Platoons would parade outside of our accommodation in Old College and been marched down to gym, at which point OCdts would chose a sport to take up for the afternoon and for the next few hours would be blissfully free from officers and SNCOs in their company.

Quick to ensure that I did something to mitigate the overwhelming stress I found myself, some self-inflicted and some as a result of the RMAS programme, on the first 'sports afternoon' I put myself towards selection for the

Boxing team. There were a number of other clubs available, some more martial than others, from polo to judo, cross country running to beagling, but boxing was what I needed.

In order to separate the wheat from the chaff, the boxing coaches, some of which were serving RMAS PTIs, whilst others were experienced OCdts who were in Senior Term and thus had the time spare to give instruction, instructed us to shadow box in the main courtyard.

This way, instructors were able to ascertain who had experience and who were either bluffing or just very hopeful. Thankfully, as the instructors walked around telling individuals, who were all busily huffing and puffing, throwing rapid punches at the air and dancing around, whether they had been selected or not, I was amongst those who were chosen.

During the whole of the Junior Term at RMAS, I was then part of the Boxing team and aside from the twice a day training sessions, I was also able to indulge in the right known as a 'boxer's breakfast' and after training finished at 6am each morning, I, along with my other boxing hopefuls, was allowed to eat a truly mammoth and delicious breakfast to replace the calories lost as a result of the early morning training session. Principally a big plate heaped with fried eggs, toast, beans, sausages, bacon, tomatoes washed down with countless glasses of tea, coffee, orange juice and the odd bowlful of cereal and porridge.

Left alone in our delightful isolation, earned by proving ourselves apart from the other mortals as boxers, we would glean any additional precious minutes of rest we could whilst we ate. Savouring the temporary moments where we could relax before returning to our rooms to shower, change and then proceed to join our Platoons in the daily RMAS training routine.

In my opinion the numerous cafes around the UK which have competitions to see who can eat a particularly large meal in a certain time would struggle to find an OCdt in Junior Term who was part of the boxing team that could not only eat the meal, but within time and most likely, then ask for more. Not too dissimilar to when my friends and I, whilst studying at Leeds University, when after a heavy night's drinking, would visit the celebrated local greasy spoon café 'Popina's' and try to complete its mammoth 'breakfast challenge'. Except that very few students ever completed the Popina's challenge, whereas almost every RMAS OCdt would have finished their gigantic meals in double quick time and then asked for additional helpings.

The pride of being part of the boxing team and again, being 'a band apart' was fantastic and was an excellent opportunity to show to the Platoon DS, who held an individual's prospective career in their hands, an OCdt's levels of tenacity, discipline, courage and last but not least controlled aggression.

I also found it a very useful way to not only help alleviate stress and frustration but also to develop my boxing skills, the phrase 'you are only as good as your last fight' was always on my mind. The instructors being of a very high quality and they had a number of innovative ways to improve the performance of their fighters.

One of my proudest moments was being put into the ring to take part in the 'last man standing spar'; this would commence by two individuals sparring, well, boxing in reality, and as soon as an individual couldn't continue anymore and bowed out, the victor was kept in and new fighter was brought in.

The aim being to see how tough the individuals were, if they remembered their training when the punches started being thrown and what mistakes they made when they became fatigued.

Whilst I was waiting in the wings with the other boxers, watching the two in the ring hammer each other, I could feel the nerves building as all other training soon ceased and the ring became the centre of attention. When it was my turn to step in, head guard slipping over my eyes and gloves wet with sweat, I felt all the eyes of the assembled staff and OCdts were on me.

My opponent, I forget his name, looked mean, menacing and worst of all, capable. Before I could catch my breath or try to remember the plan I had formulated before I stepped into the ring, the coach stepped forward, rapidly confirmed the rules and then stepped back with a final order to start.

A flurry of exchanged blows, fists smashing noses and bashing rib cages, we then quickly drew apart. I was hurting, but when I saw my opponent was hurting too, sucking in deep breaths of air, I started to become more and more confident.

He wasn't moving forward and after the initial baptism of fire he seemed slightly nervous; as was I, but I tried not to show it. I moved forwards.

Less than one minute later, my opponent was led out of the ring by a PTI and a fresh contender was put in his place. I still stood, victorious, my face bruised but breathing steady, arms feeling strong.

Moments later, my second opponent lay on the floor. I had broken his will to fight, as well as his ability to do so in a quick flurry of blows; aiming jabs at his head but then as he drew his arms up to guard his face, quickly ducking down and hammering his chest. I had finished my second fight and was ready for a third. Pride slowly surging through my limbs like a fire, I was still ready to carry on. Then a third boxer was brought forward.

I began to grow nervous as the build-up was repeated, fully aware I was not as fresh as he was and he could any second floor me like I had done to my two previous opponents. I looked at him over my gloves.

'Box!'

He was more wary than the previous two, cleverer, moving back and forth dancing lightly on his feet, throwing quick and powerful jabs at me, trying to get me into a corner.

As we traded blows, trying to trick the other into giving a significant opening, I found myself in a corner and knew I had seconds before I was completely stuck and would be at the mercy of his stronger body shots. As he threw a hook to my head, I ducked underneath and moved to my right; his left side was now exposed to me. I hit the side of his face with a strong right, and then hammered his side with short rapid hooks.

It was one of the sweetest combinations I think I have ever pulled off in the ring.

After hitting his flank, his defence crumbled and a few moments later the PTIs called a halt to the proceedings and we were both taken from ring.

Three sparring partners beaten in a row, not too shabby, I thought to myself.

Karma, being the severe and balanced mistress that she is, ensured that these victories did not go to my head, for the next day during training I came up against a much more experienced boxer who simply took my defences apart and beat me black and blue.

You only get better at training against someone who is better than you.

Aside from what makes up an OCdt's time at RMAS, such as the various exercises, tests, assignments, mishaps and successes, one activity that secretly featured heavily at times was the aspect of sex.

Almost a taboo subject and never really spoken about, it was no surprise to any of the OCdts that, bearing in mind the high level of stress all of us existed in, as well as the sheer level of physical fitness the OCdts reached whilst living in close proximity to each other, many male and female OCdts did seek companionship at times.

The easiest comparison that can be made to an outside reader to the environment that existed at times behind closed doors at RMAS at times is that during a recent Winter Olympics, the Olympic Village officially ran out of condoms as the various international competitors proved more 'enthusiastic' than suppliers had initially predicted.

The various relationships that formed, however brief, were generally known about by the OCdts and RMAS history is abound with various stories in which individuals have been discovered in compromising and hilarious situations. Such as the infamous female OCdt who reputably fell out of a first floor window due to a combination of poor balancing and over enthusiastic amorous exertions with her partner. Since that incident, all windows in the OCdts' accommodation rooms were all altered so that the lower window pane cannot be opened, only the higher one.

Relationships, or liaisons, principally took place in Inters and Seniors when individuals had slightly more time, and energy, to spare. For in Juniors it was all we could do to simply keep our eyes open at times and all of our thoughts were devoted solely to figuring out when we'd next be able to get some sleep.

Perhaps the most infamous of liaisons that took place during my time at RMAS, in which a friend of mine was involved, was when the Medical Centre took delivery of a new audio testing booth. Whilst staying in the centre as patients, perhaps they were less poorly than the experts thought, two OCdts took it upon themselves to utilise the listening booth, the size of a telephone box, for a use not at all stated in the instruction manual.

During Junior Term, as the amount of map reading, infantry skills and command instruction increased, the exercises and tests set by the RMAS staff rapidly increased in tempo, intensity and importance.

But as a result, as the weeks went by, our identities as individual OCdts and Platoons were gradually emerging and taking shape.

Unit pride was now fierce and even though the different companies in our intake competed fiercely for primacy, the Platoons themselves also constantly measured themselves against each other. The three different companies that comprised our intake also soon took on their own identities:

Ypres Company – 'Easy Company'. The OCdts and instructors in my company took pride in this name as we believed our performance and dedication whilst deployed in the field was in line with the ethos of one of the most famous infantry companies to have ever existed, 'Easy Company, 101 Airborne'. Every other OCdt and instructor in RMAS referred to us by this given pseudonym apparently due to our apparent more 'lax' attitude toward drill and parades.

Months later, towards the end of our time at RMAS, when Somme Company were still often paraded en masse before and after meals on the main parade square, OCdts from Easy Company would often open their bedroom windows which overlooked the square and politely ask the OCdts on parade to keep the noise down. The reason being that they were intruding upon Easy Company's post meal nap.

The jury is still out as to which theory behind our given nickname was correct.

Gaza Company – 'Knuckle Draggers'. Gaza Company soon became known for generally having a significant portion of the fittest, strongest and largest OCdts in our intake, as such, we likened them to heavy bruisers that should only be brought out of their cages if the need for brute force arose.

It was surprising how much the OCdts and instructors in Gaza Company took great delight when they learnt of their assigned 'nom de guerre'.

Somme Company – 'Rather be at the Somme than in Somme'. The poor OCdts in this company were simply pushed harder by their instructors, both in the field and in the barracks, than the other two companies combined. Mainly due to the fact that they had the only female Platoon in the intake and their DS clearly wanted to show that no exceptions, in regards to standards, were to be made.

It was a source of great morale to the OCdts in Ypres and Gaza companies that if at any time the current situation was unpleasant, say during a particularly difficult field exercise, it was common knowledge that the OCdts in Somme Company were bound be having it even worse than they were. Towards the end of our time at RMAS, the instructors had even started using the promise of sending an OCdt to Somme Company for a short stint as a threat.

The common joke being that an OCdt in Ypres or Gaza would rather volunteer to fight in a hellish, suicidal and soul-destroying conflict like the Somme in 1916, rather than go and be part of the regime that the unfortunate OCdts in Somme Company lived under during their time at RMAS.

By the time it had come to finish Junior Term, the SNCOs and officers who made up our instructors had successfully galvanised us into competitive, fit and keen OCdts. Some had failed to make the cut and had been removed from the Academy, those of has who progressed felt a surge of satisfaction for having made it past the first stage.

Intermediate Term. The fabled stage of an OCdt's instruction where he or she is treated with a modicum of maturity by their instructors, except in Somme Company, of course, and a little leeway is given. Additional focus was now also paid to our academic education and significant time was given over to attending small but intense lessons given by experienced civilian lecturers who specialised in different aspects of military history and theory.

Due to the amount of time spent in study, as well as the slowly increasing periods where OCdts were left to their own devices in their accommodation, although not those unfortunate souls in Somme Company, the atmosphere was a tad more relaxed and some of the tension of the daily routine dissipated.

Exercises were still intense but equal focus, at least for a time, was put onto OCdts' academic performance and thankfully the subject material often proved interesting and current. The instructors who took the classes had mostly been teaching at RMAS for years, some even had prior military service, and had a significant wealth of knowledge, as well as experience in getting OCdts to engage in points they otherwise would not have thought of.

Hilarity often ensued in these classes as OCdts were encouraged to relax into the academic setting and as such, many promptly fell asleep whilst at their desks. The instructors would usually let them snooze for a few precious moments and then would cheerfully wake them up and charge them a pound for the accidental nap.

The overseas OCdts within our intake, especially those from MENA countries, were grouped together in their own classes and the discussions that took place in these lessons were sometimes of the most fiercely debated at RMAS as different cultural and regional perceptions clashed. Much to the amusement of their patient and understanding lecturers.

Opinions on issues such as current events and previous conflicts, how prisoners should be treated, adherence to rules of engagement, treatment of civilians and suspected insurgents, the military being in theory a non-political organisation and much more. Topics such as these were always guaranteed to result in raised voices, waving arms, accusations and expletives and it would go on and on.

And it would mean plenty hilarity for the UK OCdts listening in the adjacent classrooms.

Aside from learning about military engagements, both conventional and non-conventional, past and present, as well as perceptions on current events, such as The Arab Spring, considerable focus was also made on teaching OCdts the importance of media and how to engage with its various forms.

Napoleon's phrase on the media does sum up, in my opinion, its constant relevance to all military leaders and operations:

'I fear one thousands bayonets less than I fear three hostile newspapers'.

This was done by being shown previous examples of where the media has been both a boon, and a hindrance, to military commanders and how it has affected situations.

Ranging from how it has highlighted errors and crimes committed by military personnel, such as Camp Breadbasket and the prisoner abuse which took place there, how refusing to engage with the media has resulted in it accidentally giving away vital information, occurring in the Falklands conflict where leaked media photographs gave away the size of the British Naval forces, to how correct use of the media has helped achieve a military objective, such as the secret messages via BBC radio broadcasts during World War Two to SOE operatives around the globe.

Winston Churchill's, 'We will fight them on the beaches' speech was spread throughout the world through a correct and effective use of the media, both British and international, and is infamous for inspiring the British nation to fight on, and emerge victorious, against overwhelming odds.

Winston Churchill's grasp of the power of the media, as well as his ability to not only contribute to it, but also to sway opinions, was clear even at an early age:

'Of all the talents bestowed upon men, none is so precious as the gift of oratory. He who enjoys it wields a power mightier than that of a great king'.

Military, and political, leaders around the world would do well to remember these lessons and ensure that their subordinates, as well as themselves, appreciate the full power and impact of the media, especially in today's society. Bearing in mind the rapid advances, and the subsequent increase in both power and effect, of social media and news agencies.

For as history shows, more so now than ever, it is often not the individual who wins the fight that appears victorious on the international stage, but the individual who prints the best picture, or writes the best article, first.

To a self-confessed book worm such as myself, the Department of War Studies in Faraday Hall was absolute heaven and I thoroughly enjoyed the class discussions and written assignments, which culminated in an essay competition known as the 'Commandant's War Study Paper', that took place in them. As well as the visits to the RMAS library.

The library itself was an absolute treasure trove of accounts of previous conflicts and the soldiers and officers, as well as civilians, who were involved in them. Many were the books which stated different theories and opinions on how previous wars were conducted and the subsequent lessons that need to be learnt. If only the RMAS timetable had allowed, I would have spent all of my spare time sitting in that fine old library.

Aside from burying into books, writing essays on military studies on conflicts such as the 'Dhofar War' or 'Grozny' and revelling in the minute freedoms we were allowed by our instructors, I was also fortunate to be able to become involved in the infamous 'Sandhurst Cup'.

The 'Sandhurst Cup' is a competition that runs at the prestigious American officer academy West Point where teams comprising of OCdts from around the world undergo a series of challenges in a competition that requires extremely high levels of fitness, team work, intelligence and robustness.

The rivalry between RMAS and West Point is fierce in the extreme, no less so because it is usually that OCdt teams from these two institutions that frequently win the competition, but also due to the particular fact that there is no rivalry like that which exists between allies.

Selection for the RMAS team was very tough but the honour of representing the Academy drove many, including me, to try and pass the selection.

On one auspicious Wednesday sports afternoon, those who wished to undergo training and selection for the team were detailed to make their way to the rugby pitches, wearing full green kit; combats, boots, webbing and helmet. None of us knew really what to expect, apart from the fact that it was bound to be a real sound thrashing.

After countless partner carries, sprints, press ups, squats, more sprints, burpees, stress positions, crawling and more, many of us were struggling to breathe as the team training staff put us through our paces. We also did not know how long the 'selection phase' would go on for and so many of us were in a quandary, trying our hardest to impress the RMAS training staff but not wanting to expend all of our energy in case we ran out of puff too soon.

Suddenly the head instructor, a Royal Tank Regiment (RTR) Captain, halted us in whatever heinous exercise we were carrying out, all breathing in deep gulps of air as fast as we could and made us stand up:

'Gents, I want you to jog across the fields until I say stop. Females, I want you to start jogging after the blokes when they're 100m metres away!'

Duly we all plodded off, glad for the brief respite, our clothes and bodies filthy from the mud and rain, trying to catch our breath and give our muscles a chance to recover. When we were around three hundred metres from where we had started, the RTR Capt yelled after us:

'Female OCdts, I want you to about turn and sprint back to me. Gents, sprint back too; anyone crossing the touch line after a female won't be in the team!'

Well, it goes without saying that after around an hour of constant, intensive and draining physical exercise, none of us were ready to do a three hundred metre sprint, over muddy and wet ground.

As we hurled ourselves despairingly towards the staff, slowly passing some of the slower female OCdts, my body screamed in fatigue and pain but thankfully my desire to be part of the team kept me going just that little bit more. Although I was not the first male OCdt to cross the finish line, I certainly beat all of the female OCdts, who had had at least a hundred metre initial head start on us.

All that kept myself and many other OCdts from collapsing onto the soggy floor after crossing the finish line was the thought of the instructors taking this as a sign of weakness. Once everyone was in, the instructors duly took away all of the OCdts who had not done well in the final foot race. I had passed the initial phase.

Throughout the following days and weeks, akin to boxing training in Junior Term, with each term lasting roughly fourteen weeks, there were more early morning PT sessions and even additional ones in the afternoon. No one was given any slack and the intensity of the training programme soon rivalled, and then surpassed, the toughness of our normal PT lessons with our Platoons.

As with all small units that train and live together, camaraderie within the RMAS team hopefuls soon grew and despite the fact that we all knew only a third of us would be selected in the end, team spirit and the willingness to help each other was very strong indeed.

Morning runs in full webbing and patrol packs, intensive gym circuit sessions, races over the obstacle course, swimming lessons but whilst fully clothed, as well as lectures on topics such as weapons systems like the General Purpose Machine Gun (GPMG), soon filled all of our spare time. And although we all became as lean and as fit as racing hounds, we all still looked with dread towards the final assessment day.

Due to the fact that our days were busy enough with lectures, writing essay, prepping for and carrying out field exercises, Platoon PT lessons and much more without the added addition of the RMAS Team training sessions, the days flew by and after a of weeks, the assessment day had arrived.

All of the team hopefuls were given an allotted time to be at the race start point, what the race consisted of we simply had no idea, and duly I turned up on time, wearing full green kit with my helmet tucked under my arm and my heart thumping around my chest.

There were two other OCdts there waiting for me, clearly my competition for the race and no sooner had we started chatting to try and alleviate our nerves, a member of the team DS walked out of the woods and led us to our start point.

Walking along a thin earthen track which wound its way through the trees, we soon came to a line of chalk on the ground and duly prepped ourselves; after only a few seconds, helmets already slipping over our eyes and squashing our ears, the DS looked at his watch and then looked up:

'Go!'

Throughout the entire race the three of us were neck and neck and ran ourselves ragged, trying to gain a lead over the other two as we tackled a series of obstacles, bearing in mind that due to our training we were all exceptionally fit, this was no mean feat.

As we sprinted, the instructors screaming and yelling encouragement in our ears, egging us on, I slowly gained on the lead OCdt and drew level with him; the finish line was still nowhere in sight.

After what seemed like miles of running we saw a small hill to our right with the RTR Capt stood atop it, arms folded:

'Pull these tires to the top gents! Be first!'

We turned and hurriedly dragged the waiting tyres up the hill, already slippery and smooth from the feet and tires of the OCdts who had run before us; it seemed that we were making no progress what so ever against the hill and that the challenge seemed impossible.

The other OCdt and I were level with each other, almost half way up the hill when I made a mistake and decided to change my grip the rope.

Big mistake.

In order to do so, I had to halt my progress for a second and adjust my hands on the rope; not only did this then allow the lead OCdt a chance to pull ahead of me, it almost meant the OCdt behind me drew level and then overtook me. The technique I decided to use also turned out to be worse than my initial one and my pace slowed down, yards from the finish line.

I ended up coming third.

Very disappointing indeed. Out of all the OCdts that ran the final race, lasting for roughly ten minutes of gust busting effort, typically only the first out of each three passed and the slower two were rejected.

No RMAS Cup or trip to the US and competing on behalf of the Academy for me.

It was a bitter blow.

Despite the conciliations of my comrades within 25 Platoon, days later I still felt disappointed in myself that I had failed in something I had worked so hard for; especially as I had come up short in a test of physical strength and stamina, something which I had always previously fared so well in.

It took our Platoon's PTI, Staff Davies, taking me aside at the start of a circuit session in the gym a few days later and speaking to me about the RMAS cup selection to raise my morale and address at the issue.

After informing him that I had failed at the last hurdle due to not being stronger enough, especially in the shoulders and arms, he quickly drew up a personal PT programme that, if I followed it, would improve my strength, as well as speed.

Soon, during spare time in the evenings, I could be found either in the gym putting myself through a gruelling regime of pull-ups, dips, press-ups and burpees or out on the running track, improving constantly my sprints.

Addressing areas where I had previously been weaker and slowly seeing improvement in my subsequent performance helped combat the initial depression I had gone through due to failing a physical test and boosted my confidence in myself. This would stand me in good stead in the near future.

After a week or so of this, my morale now considerably higher and my muscles aching from the new exercises I was putting them through, word came through on the RMAS rumour network that opportunities had arisen for some OCdts to go abroad and visit other countries and their militaries; one of those countries being Oman.

Thankfully, due to my friendship with Ahmed and Muataz, as well as the other MENA OCdts in our intake, when I went to my Platoon commander and expressed a desire to be part of the team that was going to Oman, he accepted the proposal and said he would support my application.

Within a week I found out the answer; three other OCdts and I were going to be sent to Oman, all expenses paid, as part of a 'RMAS liaison team'.

My morale went from a watery average to sky high.

Finally I was going to go back to the Middle East but this time with the military and I would get to explore a country and culture I had read so much about. Ahmed and Muataz even provided valuable little insights before our visit to the Gulf nation that proved extremely useful upon arrival, such as the costs for common things such as taxi trips, places to visit, cultural norms, or gifts in the bazaars.

A country with strong links to its past whilst developing its infrastructure and population, Oman in my view is perhaps the perfect combination of an ancient Arab culture and modernisation. With a population absolutely devoted to their Sultan and an appetite for work, the small population of Oman is perhaps one of the happiest nations on earth that I have ever come across.

Aside from touring around the countries numerous military establishments, many of which were excellent, and seeing various cultural sites such as the markets and towns, we also had the chance to visit areas of Oman which were infamous during its conflict with the Communist backed rebels during the 1960's; such as 'Mirbat' or 'Jebel Achkdar'.

Sadly, occasions such as touring the desert in a 4x4, partying the night away in Salah and Muscat, touring Omani military units, hobnobbing with Generals and drinking pink gins at sunset at the Ambassador's Residence eventually had to end and we eventually returned to RMAS, ready to get back to the real world.

During my time in Inters I was fortunate enough to have the Platoon Commander role during the initial phases of both a field fortification exercise, as well as an urban one.

Ex FIRST ENCOUNTER: An exercise that focuses on teaching the OCdts the importance of dug in positions and fighting from cover. During this phase, every single company in the intake deployed to the field and, each Platoon Commander in the company liaising with each other to ensure cooperation, digging in Platoon trench systems that soon evolved into company strength positions of interlocking arcs and firing points.

This exercise is famous due to the fact that, at least up until recently, all of the digging is done with spades and picks, no heavy plant equipment whatsoever. Hands quickly blisters and sleep deprivation kicks in as the hours turn into days, no rest or sleep being allowed until every trench in each Platoon position is completed to the correct dimensions and standards.

I was fortunate during this phase as I had sufficient time to prepare my set of orders and delivered them before 25 Platoon deployed into the field. But not one to make a rod for one's own back, despite the history books sometimes proving otherwise, I was eager to make the best of the advantages allowed to me and ensured that every single of the orders process had been thoroughly covered.

I could not afford to leave anything open to criticism due to the fact that I had been able to write them in the warmth and comfort of my room and had a number of hours in which to compile them.

During an OCdt's delivery of orders, be they section level or higher, written and presented in a wet field at 3am or in the warmth of a classroom, every single detail is analysed, by both the other OCdts and the Platoon DS. From how well the OCdt delivering the orders covered the necessary headings in their Tactical Aid Memoire (TAM); how confident they sounded and came across or how effective the plan they had created actually appeared to minor malapropisms and any nervous ticks.

It is a nerve wracking process to have delivered one's orders and then stand there, papers in hand and listen to all the faults, as well, if one has merited it, the good points, that have just been made. The final gut lurching moment on which everything, especially the new OCdt Platoon Commander's final grade, hinges is when the DS ask the other OCdts in the Platoon one final question:

'Alright, raise your hands if you feel confident in the plan and your new Platoon Commander'.

Thankfully, mine went well and 25 Platoon performed admirably during my time as their OCdt Platoon Commander, not only being the first Platoon to complete all of our trenches during the exercise, but also then going over and assisting the other Platoons in Easy Company. I was elated at how well the Platoon had worked, not because it might have reflected more strongly on the report made on my time in command, but just to see what could be done by a group of determined and hardworking individuals.

Ex BROADSWORD: Out of the different exercises that took place during Inters, and RMAS in general, this was the one that stood out most in my memory and for many reasons. Some hilarious, others insightful, but all memorable. A truly fantastic exercise which was as amusing as it was hard work and, at times, extremely physically painful and demanding.

The exercise focuses on operating within an urban environment, the whole exercise complex consisting of old accommodation buildings, streets, shops, and a large FOB on the edge of the town. Added in is the additional challenge of commanding a group of one's peers, who's suggestions on they feel might solve a problem, or fire fight, may only worsen or complicate the overall situation for the beleaguered Platoon Commander. The reason being that the Platoon might, if the commander is not quick on their toes, turn into a democracy and not an autocracy.

During the exercise phase, which lasted a few weeks, the different companies of our intake rotated between serving as International Security Assistance Force (ISAF) personnel operating within a rural area and then in the small urban FOB, as well as in turn taking on the role of a belligerent and complex civilian population.

As each company took its turn at operating out of the nearby FOB, which was built along the same lines as those initially built in Northern Ireland during the Troubles, another company put on civilian clothes, as well as learning in detail their prescribed identities, and carried out the role of a small population consisting of a number of conflicting societies, religions and social groups.

During the phase in which Easy Company was deployed as ISAF troops in the town and carried out a range of reassurance patrols, strike and seize operations and numerous crowd control scenarios in which countless rocks, stones and Molotov cocktails were thrown at us. We learnt exactly how difficult it is to live and operate effectively amongst civilians whose loyalty and attitude towards you can turn on a sixpence.

The insurgents that lived and hid amongst the population, many of whom favoured and protected the insurgents, proved very difficult indeed to catch. Unless an individual has actually tried to actually chase down and capture a lightly armed, plain clothed, terrorist, it is almost impossible to realise how difficult, especially from the commander's point of view, it is to do this.

Purely and simply, a small, mobile and effective terrorist command cell operating amongst a population which protects them, through loyalty or fear, as well as blending in perfectly with the local civilians, is a very potent force.

Chairman Mao summed up the ease in which effective insurgents can operate and how bloody hard it can be to catch them:

'The guerrilla must move amongst the people as a fish swims in the sea.'

The sheer intensity and violence of when a population riots also cannot be underestimated or understated. Standing in the shield wall, shoulder to shoulder with your comrades, wearing full body armour, elbow and knee pads, helmet and visor, body length shield, gloves, baton and all clothes tucked in to protect skin from the flames, it is a fearful amount of clothing and equipment to try and operate in.

Especially as the population, who are perhaps standing no more than twenty feet away from you, are yelling and screaming for all their worth, throwing all manner of missiles directly at your face, the smoke from flaming tires and Molotov cocktails drifting across the scene, lungs parched and body aching from the repeated charges coming from the rioters.

During the particularly heated fights, where diplomacy and riot dogs had failed to subdue the rioters, we would find ourselves repeatedly knocked onto our backs as a solid wall of humanity charged at us; our batons slashing against legs, flanks and arms but seemingly doing no damage.

In order to maintain order and to stop the shield wall from breaking up under the onslaught, this is where effective control by the section commanders and previous team training come to the fore. I have seen individuals knocked back at least ten feet by charging rioters, only to pick themselves up off the floor for the umpteenth time and move swiftly back into the line, ready to face the next charge; yelling fiercely in anger and pride, refusing to be beat.

When not getting battered by protestors and run ragged by countless scenarios which the insurgents put on to test us, such as staged executions of locals and IED strikes, we also took our turn at becoming civilians and making life hell for the OCdts playing ISAF in the village.

As soon as OCdts, and instructors, don civilian clothing during Ex BROADSWORD, all reason seems to go out the window and everyone becomes determined to have as much fun as possible; as well as being as bloody awkward as they can for the operating OCdts.

Amongst many of the traditions for the company playing the civilian population, the 'Town Tramp' is perhaps the finest.

At the start of the civilian deployment, each individual is assigned a character and a tribe; whilst the most well-spoken, affluent and cultured individual in the company is ordered to be drunk for the week. Allowed to only wear one set of hand-me-down clothes, not allowed to wash or consume anything except alcohol, the individual quickly becomes a dribbling wreck and causes havoc and merriment in equal measure throughout the rest of the exercise.

Other OCdts are also given free rein to chase the 'Town Tramp' whenever they feel like it, often causing ISAF OCdts to peer over their parapets in confusion as half the village charges past, howling like banshees, after an individual draped in a shabby overcoat, cider bottles taped to his hands and running for all his worth. The 'Town Tramp' is also not permitted to sleep inside any of the buildings and often finds refuge in an abandoned railway car or even a derlict helicopter.

Previous 'Town Tramps' have been sons of Lords, MPs, millionaires, city bankers and even overseas OCdts. Sometimes, if the instructors are feeling kind, the 'Town Tramp' is allowed a friend to keep him company, the two soon becoming double trouble for all concerned.

During the times in which ISAF is operating amongst the civilian population, the 'Town Tramp' is worth his weight in gold as common sense no longer factors in his logic and he becomes an absolute nightmare for the troops and a class act for watching civilians.

Walking up to patrols and chatting absolute gibberish to the poor soul in command, pick pocketing webbing pouches, getting into unlocked Land Rovers and refusing to come out, all the while beeping the horn and blowing raspberries at the exasperated ISAF OCdts outside the vehicle, and causing mayhem.

When the 'Town Tramp' is rolled out, it is genuinely one of the most looked forward to events of the exercise and actually gives ISAF OCdts great experience in dealing with an apparent mad man whilst operating in an urban area.

Aside from the local alcoholic and social degenerate, the civilian population also consists of a number of other realistic characters military personnel are likely to encounter in urban operations. All acted out by OCdts dressed in civilians clothes with as much dash, flash and panache as if they were treading the boards in a Broadway Show.

Right wing religious leaders and fanatics form a significant part of the overall exercise and OCdts quickly learn how difficult local figureheads, especially religious ones, can be. With the population divided between Christian and Muslim communities, sectarian violence soon occurs and the ISAF forces have to decide on how to best mitigate it.

'Easy Company' was fortunate enough to have within its ranks both the son of an English vicar and an overseas OCdt who was the son of an Islamic Mullah.

Much amusement arose when these two individuals, both chosen as the local religious hot heads by the DS, harangued each other from the safety of their own religious buildings, directly across the road from each other, with powerful renditions of both the 'The Lord's Prayer' and 'The Call to Prayer'.

Like any large community, prostitutes also made up some of the local population and although no 'services' were actually rendered, OCdts soon fully immersed themselves in their roles. Donning horrendous makeup, tight miniskirts and flirting outrageously with patrolling ISAF units.

'Want to battle into my urban area?'

'I've been a very bad girl, sir. You may need to lock me up, although it'd cost you a few quid....'

Due to only one company having female OCdts, and a small number at that, the prostitutes were very often male OCdts in drag; they were usually the very worst behaved and most vocal in advertising their services to the local patrolling ISAF troops.

Lord knows what the overseas OCdts, especially the ones from MENA nations, must have thought when seeing at least four or five tall, hairy, muscled male British OCdts sauntering past in high heels, lipstick, wigs and swaying hips, giving out ribald comments to all whom they saw.

The Long Bar was the social hub, pub, shop and centre of village; a building sited less than two hundred metres from the ISAF FOB. It was the focal point for the entire population. Perhaps to help OCdts who were playing civilians get into the roles quicker or perhaps to lend Dutch courage to those about to charge into a shield wall, beer was available on sale for the civilian population.

All OCdts and DS who were playing local civilians thoroughly enjoyed the Long Bar and its alcoholic drinks, as well as snacks and hot drinks, and many an evening the music would be played on into the night and the entire company would stand in the warmth of the taproom, drinking lager and playing darts.

Sadly The Long Bar no longer provides alcohol, for not long after I graduated from RMAS a visiting US senior officer, one perhaps unused to the occasional silliness and long standing drinking culture that exists within the British Army, voiced negatives opinions on seeing OCdts drinking whilst on exercise and it was soon stopped.

There is a common belief amongst many British officers and soldiers that the senior British officer who subserviently, and cowardly, sided with the US delegate and stopped the tradition of beer at The Long Bar should have had their rank stripped from them due. Mainly due to a lack of back bone, team spirit, selfless commitment for such blatant brown nosing.

I ask you, what self-respecting rioter would charge into a shield wall without a bit of liquid courage?

Soon the exercise came to a conclusion and we returned en masse to RMAS, albeit covered in deep bruises for where batons, missiles and charging bodies had struck us. We were now approaching the final stages of our time as OCdts, Senior Term (Seniors) and soon, as the last of the final fourteen weeks of the term drifted by, we would become officers in the British Army. We only had a few more tests and exercises to overcome.

The time quickly came for the interviews with the units that OCdts wished to join. It was here that an OCdt's performance, both as an academic student and as an officer in the field, would be intensely analysed by a board of senior regimental officers. During this time is when the unit that an individual desires to join, in my case the Corps of Royal Engineers, goes through every success and failure of an OCdt's time so far at RMAS, every recommendation and comment noted down by their Platoon DS. At the interview's conclusion, the board then decides whether they want to accept or not the OCdt applicant into their particular military fold.

During this ten-minute interview is where your prospective unit 'has a look at you'.

I was particularly nervous as I walked into the interview room for although I was confident in my track record of fitness, as well as my academic studies and performance in the field, I also had some black marks on my record. Principally getting my team lost on Ex LONG REACH, as well as having had to retake the 'Orders Process exam', having failed that particular test as a result of overconfidence and generally needlessly complicating things. A curse that I've always struggled to shake.

Many OCdts have been 'back termed', meaning that they made to redo their training with a new RMAS intake, for failing such exams, and the subsequent retests. Needless to say that I was feeling the strain when it came to the retests was putting it lightly.

I can still remember the absolute gut churning fear and panic that was filling my stomach when I re-sat the Orders and Navigation exams. Thankfully, through hard work, and no small amount of support from my Platoon, including Muataz and Ahmed, I passed the Orders re-sit texts with flying colours. It was laughable to think, afterwards, that before the initial Order test I'd sat for days teaching Muataz and Ahmed the do's and don'ts of the Orders Process, mostly in Arabic, but yet had, in the excitement of it all, managed to muck it up myself.

In regards to the retest navigation exam, this time it was held at night and although everyone else was taking part, I knew I had to do well on it to prove my capabilities to my instructors, and anyone who has operated across country at night knows how difficult this can be. But, with a combination of remembering my past errors, such as aiming for the far away markers first, not the closer ones, fool, and being able to run for long distances without getting winded, I thankfully passed the test with flying colours. When I staggered across the finish line, after having run for roughly two hours straight in the pitch black of night, the congratulatory grins I saw from my Platoon members who were there remain with me still.

During my formal regimental interview, in which there were six senior RE officers present, one of which was the Corps Colonel, but only three spoke to me; the other three sat to one side and made silent notes in their notebooks. Not surprisingly I was asked about the mistakes that I had made during my time so far at RMAS. In response I replied that I knew that there was no excuse for the mistakes that I'd made, especially as they were such simple ones to avoid in the first place and that I'd accomplished far harder tests in the past but had somehow managed to mess these ones up. But that I was determined to learn from my past errors, and I hoped that my subsequent performance at RMAS after the failed tests had shown that I'd learnt from my past errors and hadn't made them since.

During their time at RMAS, an OCdt is rightly informed by their DS that the ultimate skill and knowledge any OCdt must have is a thorough understanding of infantry tactics, and the know how to carry them out when required. For throughout history, it is widely acknowledged by all nations and militaries, that the hardest and most important parts of a military are their infantry units.

For as General Montgomery once said:

'Without the infantry you can do nothing, absolutely nothing at all.'

As a result of the focus in RMAS which is put on infantry skills and the zeal in which all units should attempt to do their best to defeat the enemy wherever they are found, as well as having being taught by some truly fantastic RE officers, I had had set my heart on the Royal Engineers and wanted to do my utmost to prove myself tough enough to serve with some of its famous units. Namely 23 Engineer Parachute Regiment and the Royal Engineer divers.

For no small reason is the interview an OCdt has with the board of senior officers from the cap badge they wish to join called the most important interview of your career.

Before I'd gone into the interview, on which my future military career path would depend, I'd brushed up on as much as I could on interview techniques, how to deal with difficult questions and suchlike, even going as far to ask family members for pointers and what sort of commonly made mistakes I should take care to avoid.

Walk in confidently but not arrogantly, look everyone in the eye but with a charming smile, a brief but firm handshake, sit down easily but don't fidget, maintain the right posture in the chair, be sure of yourself but polite and deferential to the interviewers and don't try any crap cliché one liners.

Not long after all the OCdts in my intake had had their interviews, it turned out that one particularly odious OCdt had committed quite the foul during his own interview for a particularly renowned and capable fighting regiment. Principally by coming across as an utter pompous tit:

'So, we like for our junior officers to be cultured and well-read if possible, so with that in mind, could I ask what book you last read?'

There was a pause whilst the OCdt dramatically collected his thoughts before replying to the board of officers.

'A book of my own poetry'.

Needless to say, he didn't succeed in that particular interview and it was a stark warning to any other OCdts who thought that an outrageous accent and a deliberately quirky hobby was all that was needed in order to secure a posting to the esteemed Household Division.

Thankfully my interview went well and not long after, I was informed via letter that I had been accepted into the Corps of Royal Engineers. It was a momentous occasion.

I believed that it was me being honest about my strengths, as well as my weaknesses, which carried considerable weight when it came to the board making their decision on whether to accept me into the Royal Engineers or not. The relief, and joy, when I opened my letter and saw that the Royal Engineers had accepted me was almost palpable.

When individuals were not engaging in RMAS activities, over the weekend that is, OCdts, myself included, continued the time honoured tradition of spending most of our time away from RMAS within a mile of Piccadilly Circus or the King's Road area.

The tailors of Jermyn Street, as well as those in the surrounding area, such as 'Cordings', truly my favourite gentleman's outfitters, a place which I am proud to admit I have never been in sober, continue to do well over the weekends as many OCdts visit each establishment, wallets getting progressively lighter and shopping bags getting heavier.

Aside from purchasing truly outrageously coloured trousers and clashing tweed jackets, RMAS OCdts also contribute heavily to the livelihood of many of the club and bar owners existing within central London. It is no surprise that the first thing many OCdts wished to do, upon leaving RMAS for another much anticipated 48 hours off, was to venture to London and find solace in alcoholic oblivion.

Those Platoons blessed with particularly wealthy overseas OCdts often collectively spent hundreds, if not thousands, of pounds on Platoon night outs, often resulting in great hordes of inebriated OCdts, always identifiable by their choice of outrageously coloured trousers, stumbling happily from one nightclub to the next.

Those who did not saunter into Town, or any densely populated park of the UK, usually took the fastest route to either their partner's or family's place of residence and spent the following days eating as much food as possible and sleeping as often as their social planning would allow. It was often amusing to hear OCdts, upon returning to RMAS from a visit home or to their girlfriend, say that upon sitting down to a family meal or particularly fancy meal in an expensive restaurant, they often found themselves not only being the first one to finish their meal, but also the first to ask for seconds or the pudding menu. Much to the incredulous and amazed looks of their relatives, partners and any other persons who may have been sat in the vicinity of their table.

Many was the Sunday afternoon, if not evening, when a steady stream of OCdts could be seen slowly making their way in a steady stream from the train station to the camp gates; bleary eyed and with a full belly but grinning, hoping the memories of the past two days or so would see them through to their upcoming leave weekend.

The instructors at RMAS typically often dread 'Seniors' as due to the OCdts realising that their time at RMAS is drawing to a close, combined with a fact that most will have secured a posting in their desired regiment or battalion, the élan of some of the OCdts wanes significantly.

Or, in the words of a huge black American OCdt on loan from the United States Military Academy (West Point) to RMAS, who warned me during one lunch break about the dangers of becoming lax in 'Seniors':

'Motherfuckers just start to mentally check out.'

Heavy was the punishment that was dished out by the RMAS DS whenever an OCdt was found to have not being plying themselves as diligently as they used to back in Juniors and Inters, and many is the OCdt who has, within a few days of commissioning from RMAS, being 'back termed' by their DS as a punishment for their lax attitude; a stark warning and example to all.

'Pour encourager les autres.'

What was also interesting about the later stages of our time at RMAS was that it was also the time when the first serious government cuts were being made to the British Army, with thousands of officers and soldiers being forced to leave for good the military forces.

Done in truly cunningly political fashion, many had been given the option whether to take redundancy and bizarrely many who volunteered for it were then refused and other personnel were cut instead. The reason behind this subterfuge was that some government officials had realised that it would not be financially viable to give redundancy to military personnel who had volunteered for it, as they had already shown a willingness to leave the Army.

Instead, the government sacked officers and soldiers who had not volunteered for redundancy. This meant that many of the individuals who had applied for redundancy in the first place, but did not get it, threw their hands up in disgust and signed off anyway.

That meant that the government was able to get rid of more military personnel at a cheaper overall price; for after getting denied redundancy, and seeing others getting it, hundreds officers and soldiers left the Army outraged and annoyed without the substantial government payoff they had been hoping for.

Two birds with one stone.

The peculiar aspect of the cuts was that it was not just the lower third of the cohort that got fired, but also the middle and top percentiles. Allegedly this was so that the officials in charge of the process would not appear biased.

Meaning that even the instructors at RMAS, ones who were integral to the successful training of the Army's future officers, the very best and brightest of their various units, were also getting sacked, whilst they were still working at RMAS. It left a strange impression on everyone and was a sign of the strange and nonsensical goings on that we were soon to encounter in the Regular Army.

This was combined with the fact that we were frequently informed that we would be the first RMAS intake in years who would not be deploying straight into a conflict, as Afghanistan and Iraq were, laughingly, referred to by all politicians and senior officers as supposedly settling down, which made for some very strange thinking and unknowns for us all.

My focus soon switched to trying to get myself on a place in the Royal Engineer Dive School and starting the process which would hopefully qualify me as a diver; this meant competing with the other RE OCdts in my intake, who were also applying for places on the RE arduous courses.

The arduous courses, such as the Dive School, or P Company or the All Arms Commando Course, were heavily oversubscribed and OCdts competed fiercely against each other in hopes of getting allotted a place after RMAS. After which they would then go onto their RE officer training, already 'badged' with an arduous course to their credit, as well, potentially, the substantial dive pay added to their monthly pay cheque.

Thankfully my performance at RMAS was merited high enough by the RE examiners and I was awarded one of the two places available for officers on the next RE Dive course. Thus during my remaining time at RMAS, I became dedicated to making myself as physically fit as possible.

For although I was confident in my abilities, I was fully aware that in order to pass the course, I would have to demonstrate physical fitness and my experience during the Sandhurst Cup selection had proven that no matter how confident an individual may be, there would always be or come someone better.

There is always a bigger fish.

Additionally, as anyone who has had the pleasure of gracing the halls of RMAS will happily admit, there are many peculiarities that exist during an OCdts time at the Academy which do well to introduce them to the oddities they will face during their spell within the regular Army.

For instance, everyone who has ever borne a weapon during their time within the military, especially the British Army, lives in fear of having a 'Negligent Discharge' (ND); which means accidentally firing one's weapon when not permitted to do so. Factors which influence an OCdt, officer or soldier within the Army, committing such an offence usually are tiredness, poor weapon handling drills or a combination of the two.

When an ND occurs, punishment is severe and even more so for an officer, who is expected to know better; typically involving restriction of pay, legal consequences, additional duties and a severe reprimand from the chain of command. It is a severe 'no no'.

Towards the end of my time at RMAS, if an individual accidentally fired their weapon, usually because they were tired and had forgotten that the safety catch was off, the OCdt concerned would immediately carry out the following drill in order to try and avoid punishment.

The OCdt would be walking along on patrol, or lying in a sentry position, and would carelessly pull the trigger, resulting in a resounding 'bang!' and everyone, including the DS would freeze.

If the OCdt was clever, they would immediately shout 'Contact!', and what this meant was that they had seen the enemy and therefore were legally engaging them, and then throw themselves into a firing position and begin firing deliberate shots towards the imagined enemy position.

If the OCdt's popularity level and general standing was high within their Platoon, the rest of the OCdts would leap to their defence and immediately echo the cry of 'contact!' and fire their weapons into the surrounding bushes; thus convincing the DS that some enemy had indeed been seen.

Thus vindicating the carless OCdt.

However, if the OCdt's overall rating within their Platoon was not to an acceptable standard, upon hearing the shot and the following cry of 'contact!', the remainder of the Platoon would stand around listlessly, innocently commenting loudly to each other that they had not seen or heard no enemy whatsoever.

Mob justice at its finest.

The importance of rumours, aka the 'Rumour Mill', within RMAS also cannot be understated. Despite the fact that every member of each Platoon read the daily 'standing orders', which detailed what was to happen each day and when to happen, greater value was usually put on 'what somebody had heard!'.

During the later stages of RMAS, the power of rumours and how quickly they seemed to spread from corridor to corridor, from Platoon to Platoon, had reached such dizzying heights that one of the OCdts in 25 Platoon decided to take action.

By carefully placing himself within hearing distance of some nearby officers and SNCOs one day, the individual starting talking to his accomplice in loud whispers how the order had come down that all OCdts that were going to the grenade range had now been ordered by HQ to take their ceremonial bayonets with them.

At this, the OCdt then walked away and informed the rest of 25 Platoon of this information plant; thus, we waited in our rooms, seeing if the rumour would take shape.

Gleefully, not fifteen minutes later, an OCdt from another Platoon rushed into our corridor and breathlessly informed us that Easy Company was now ordered to take their ceremonial bayonets with them to the grenade range; at the order of the DS.

The faces and subsequent loud and incredulous comments and expletives from the DS at the grenade range when ninety OCdts proudly disembarked from their buses, faces, webbing and bodies camouflaged, ready to engage in the exciting martial ritual of throwing grenades, with shiny white and gold ceremonial bayonets bouncing off their hips, became something of legend amongst Easy Company.

Looking back, I would say that my experiences at RMAS taught me a number of vital lessons essential to any leader, junior or senior.

Firstly, be fit; for God's sake be fit.

No matter how physically fit and capable an individual may think to be, RMAS and their future career as an officer will push them beyond their limits, and there is always someone fitter. If an individual is not fit enough to run faster than their platoon or section or not able to deliver effective and convincing QBOs as they're too busy trying to catch their breath, they have failed as a leader.

The remarkable thing at RMAS was that due to the way in which the PT lessons are organised, simply everyone is pushed to their limit and finishes the end of the lesson feeling completely exhausted; be they the slowest member of the Platoon or a former SAS Trooper.

Meaning that if an individual turns up at RMAS unfit, they are at a disadvantage pretty much for the rest of their time at the Academy as although they will indeed get progressively fitter, so will the fitter members of their Platoon. Thus, the gap between the slowest and the fastest is almost insurmountable and it is very difficult for an OCdt to advance up the physical pecking order, unless their competitors either injured themselves or deliberately slack off their training.

Generally, most people will prefer one form of exercise over another, and will harbour an abhorrence of one or two in particular. It has always been burpees and sprints with me. But the key thing is that in order to improve, an individual must practise what they don't like. If someone hates press-ups, pull ups or running with a bergen, it is imperative that they, as a leader, practise them as often as they can. There is something very special about having done hours of work on an exercise that you hate and then, at the end of a PT session, realising that you ran faster or further than everyone else. Be fit!

Secondly, do not judge anyone on their appearance, especially in regards to their physical and mental arduousness. I have seen OCdts whom look like they should belong on the front cover of health and fitness magazines fall flat on their faces, gasping for breath, whilst heavier or slimmer individuals race past them, not struggling at all.

Whilst I have also witnessed individuals whom have always demonstrated a fine understanding of military tactics and logic, as well as always appearing cool and composed, usually with a witty quip thrown in for good measure, both in the classroom and in the field, but when it comes for them to deliver their orders, to step up, they falter, hesitate and make fools of themselves. Whereas often OCdts who have had no prior military experience before RMAS, couldn't march correctly or initially even know how to use a compass, quickly grasp the key military concepts and progress towards the top of their peer group.

On that note, coping with failure and continually aiming for success is extremely important and essential to a successful career, military or civilian. I do not believe anyone who has passed out of RMAS has not at some point during their weeks there, failed or struggled severely with a test or trial. One of the most important lessons I learnt courtesy of my instructors and Platoon at RMAS was to admit when I was wrong, or when I had failed, and then move on and do better.

Not letting the past failure haunt me, but using it instead as an incentive to learn from my errors and do better next time.

There were also a number of lessons that were taught, or brought home, to me whilst I was training within RMAS, all being simple and timeless, and were to become the difference between me simply surviving in the field and successfully operating in the field.

Such as having an excellent pair of boots; early on I personally had a pair of Altbergs, the best boots in the business, tailor made and throughout the years I wore them, they were worth every penny and it became clear how easy life would become when I was wearing a good pair of boots.

Look after your feet and they'll look after you.

Additionally, ensure that numerous pairs of good socks are bought and before embarking on a march, try them out. Nothing, simply nothing, cripples a soldier faster than wearing ill-chosen socks. Their feet quickly become torn to shreds and the soldier or officer concerned, becomes useless and a burden on everyone else around them. Inexcusable, unprofessional, and very embarrassing indeed.

On the subject of appropriate foot admin, talcum powder is also worth its weight in gold. For when one is completely wet, filthy and exhausted in the field, there are very few sensations better than changing into a fresh pair of socks and dusting your feet, and the inside of your boots, liberally with talcum powder. It also comes in very handy when creating a good model pit whilst in the field.

For model building, the map which shows the operation which is about to take place, in the field, be it in a muddy hole dug in the Catterick soil, or a sprawling masterpiece on the floor of a derelict farmhouse, it is imperative to ensure that the individuals tasked with building it have a number of coloured cords, bottles of talcum powder, small but clear markers which can be drawn on to show units or points, and a good amount of white tape, with them.

A good model is vital to a commander putting across to his team what is going to happen, or what is meant to happen, in the following operation. A picture speaks a thousand words, and thus makes the model essential during the summary phase of the orders. Where the commander really sells the operation, making their team really understand why they're doing it and that'll it definitely succeed.

In regards to how packing kit, principally webbing and bergens, I always found it good practise to put the same items in the same pouches and segments time and time again, so that even in the pitch of night, as head torches always break or get lost, I could unerringly reach into my bergen or webbing and know where to find, for instance, a new pair of socks, set of batteries or spare head torch.

As comfort, especially in the field, is simply everything to servicemen and a good one will do everything they can to ensure they have as many comforts as possible in order to ensure their life is as easy, or as pleasant, as possible. Often this stems from simply having spent time customising and adjusting one's webbing and bergen. From taping down loose straps, buying or making pads for the inside of the webbing belt, thus being more comfortable around the waist and on the hips, to obtaining different clips or pouches so that items can be got at quicker, with minimum fuss.

A handy thermos (brew flask) is simply a vital battle winning asset to anyone, regardless of their rank, and should be obtained and tested as quickly as possible. For when the rain is coming down in sheets, the wind is blowing a gale and the temperature is dropping rapidly, being able to reach into a webbing or bergen pouch and pull out a flask of hot tea or coffee, is simply wondrous, and also fantastic for raising morale, as well as body temperature.

On the subject of items, especially as a commander, NCO or officer, I always found it extremely useful to have a good waterproof notepad, usually in its own miniature command pouch, attached to my webbing for each access, and a number of pencils, sharpeners and good waterproof brightly coloured markers. I can't remember the amount of times

I've seen individuals have their orders, written on normal paper, disintegrate in the rain or find themselves unable to write on a map as the non-permanent ink keeps rubbing off.

Additionally, always have a small container of wipes so that TAMs or maps, for instance, can be cleared of any out of date, or incorrect information and can thus be updated correctly.

Each TAM should also be marked up as per the commander's style or taste, with tabs showing where important sections, or chapters, are; such as QBOs, Ground Briefs, Recce Orders. This massively cuts down on time when orders and direction suddenly need to be given. Especially as there is nothing sillier than seeing a fresh faced commander struggling to find the correct Orders page in their unmarked TAM in the middle of a fire fight, dropping paperwork and scattering notes everywhere, whilst their subordinates all sit around expectantly as valuable seconds tick by.

Waterproof everything. Not only each pair of socks and pants, shirts and trousers, to name but a few, in one's bergen, but also the webbing pouches. For although it may seem silly to waterproof a water bottle pouch, or the mess tin pouch, it is also extremely unsettling and unpleasant to find that after a day of running around and crawling in the mud, that your rations and water bottle to be covered in muck.

As well as socks, the right choice of underwear is also very important and not commonly mentioned. Each person prefers different styles, as it were, and it is essential to find out what works for you, for the word chafing strikes fear into the hearts of all military personnel. Be it baggy boxers, tight cycling style shorts, thongs, or even nothing at all, find out which you prefer before embarking upon any strenuous, or lengthy, stretches of exercise. Lastly, in case of disaster striking, always have a small pot of Vaseline hidden close by somewhere in your kit…, just in case.

Lastly, help everyone in your Platoon, even the ones you don't like, as you never know when you'll suddenly have to rely on the good graces of those around you. Also a commander should never lose their temper, as tempting as it may be at times to fly off the handle, as a commander not in charge of their emotions quickly loses not only the respect of their subordinates and superiors, but also the control of the overall situation or battle.

Before our time at RMAS drew to a close, there was a case that stood out in my memory as one of the finest incidences I was fortunate enough to be part of, which was the placement of a number of American West Point and Danish OCdts into our intake.

As part of generating better understanding and cooperation between our militaries, these individuals arrived at RMAS roughly half way through 'Seniors'and trained with us, including going on exercise with us, for a number of weeks.

The American OCdts were the top of their own intake, having won their placement within RMAS by taking part in a number of arduous competitions at West Point beforehand and aside from being immensely friendly, professional and excellent ambassadors for their nation, they were also immensely physically fit.

So high were their physical standards that soon, with a few Americans in each Platoon in our intake, they were all soon competing with the fittest RMAS OCdts during our PT lessons. Such was the sudden and unexpected competition amongst the first during the various foot races, be it hill sprints or partner carries, that our DS soon became frantic after seeing vast numbers of the British OCdts coming in behind the Americans.

Finally, with liberal use of good old fashioned British military cunning and studying the enemy, the OCdts within RMAS stumbled across a way to beat our Colonial Cousins. The principal weakness of the West Point OCdts was that most of them were under the age of 21 and thus had not begun drinking.

Thus, upon coming up with a suitable battle plan, the OCdts of Easy Company jovially dragged all of the Americans down the nearest bar one night and treated them to a full night of alcoholic soaked British hospitality.

The next morning our efforts bore fruit as the British OCdts, who were all hardened drinkers and well used to doing morning PT whilst still under the influence, were standing ready, albeit swaying slightly, whilst the 'Across the Pond Contingent' was clearly, to use a common military phrase, 'in the hurt locker'.

As soon as our PTI sprinted off, the Platoon following on behind like a pack of hounds, individuals soon began to fall to the side, bent double and heaving loudly, all of them cursing feebly in trans-Atlantic accents. It was a credit to the OCdts of West Point, and their instructors back in the States, that despite this heinous tactic played upon them by the smiling and devious British the night before, all of them stuck with the Platoon throughout that brutal PT session.

The epitome of the success in which the American OCdts cemented their reputations within their various British Platoons was on 4 July, the anniversary of the American War of Independence. Upon waking up in their various rooms at RMAS, they each found a small poster on the front of the door stating:

'To our traitorous American cousins, although we decided to leave the running of your juvenile country to yourselves after you proved too bothersome and ungrateful back in 1775, please know that a few years later we came back and burnt the White House on 24 August 1814.

Due to the destruction and flames visited upon it by our glorious and courageous Red Coats, it had to be painted white in order to cover up the damage; which is why it is now called the White House.

'Happy Independence Day to you all, from your British comrades.'

To complete the message, below the text on the poster, there was also a print of the White House on fire with Red Coats marching away from it.

I believe that almost all of the American OCdts took the posters back with them to the States as souvenirs.

The Danish OCdts proved an entirely different kettle of fish as all of them, as a pre-requisite to joining their officer academy, had served many years as private soldiers prior to applying to become officers. Many of them had already experienced and served multiple tours in Afghanistan.

With fine Nordic beards on display, a constant irritation to the DS at RMAS, abundant military experience, fluent in usually at least three languages each and polite to a fault, they were quickly taken on as Platoon mascots by those fortunate enough to have some Danish personnel working with them. Our Platoon's assigned Dane was quickly referred to by one and all, including our instructors, as 'Thor'.

Needless to say that they did not fall for the trick Easy Company played on the Americans, for although they, too, allowed themselves to visit the bar that night, in true Viking fashion they simply drank the British OCdts beer for beer and emerged the next morning none the worse for wear.

At last, aside from a few more exercises that took place in the wild and rainy depths of the Welsh and Scottish countryside, in truly heinous weather, Easy Company's time at RMAS was finally ending.

Looking back, I would have realised that I view, and I believe I am not alone in this view, that the British Army is perhaps the worst travel agent in the world. Meaning that where ever I have been sent by the Army, be it the very darkest depths of the Scottish Highlands to parts of the glorious Home Counties, I never want to visit those parts of the country ever again. So stark are the memories of being on exercise there and the variety of punishing and arduous conditions that prevailed there.

Although one day I will return to the Black Mountains of Wales, take a luxurious B&B nestled in a quiet village for a weekend and upon waking up each morning surrounded by thick and gloriously soft bed linen and pillows, I will tuck into a full English breakfast whilst still in bed, look out of the window at the Welsh countryside and yell from the comfort and safety of the cushions:

'Not this time! This time I'm in Wales but not I'm tabbing or running anywhere! Take that, you bastards.'

For after completing the final RMAS exercise in the Galloway forest, during which my left leg became infected and I spent a number of glorious days recuperating in hospital, the focus in our intake switched to drill, boot polishing and practising for our final parade at RMAS.

Quickly the remaining weeks flew by and after much marching up and down the square in our thick and heavy blue uniforms, the sun glaring in our eyes as we stood rigidly on parade in front of the assembled crowds, our commissioning parade and its massed pageantry went by in perfect style.

And yes, a fly did actually land on my face and crawl around, before blissfully flying off after waiting an agonising few minutes.

The Queen was rumoured to be viewing our parade but, in the end, an esteemed American General took on the duty instead. Thankfully there was no fainting by any of the assembled swaying ranks of sweating OCdts who were standing there in the glaring August sun, their massed bayonets shimmering proudly.

After a truly mammoth party, and labouredly packing up my belongings into my car, once again I drove out of the gates of the Royal Military Academy Sandhurst a commissioned Second Lieutenant.

But this time, I was part of the Corps of Royal Engineers.

5

Corps of Royal Engineers

RE Diver. Royal Engineers Troop Commander Course

September, Portsmouth, Horsea Island, HMS EXCELLENT, Diving Training Unit.

My nerves were in pieces. I was in the car on my way to start RE diver training, some of the most brutal training that takes places within the Corps of Royal Engineers. If I could see my way through the next five days of selection, I would be able to secure myself onto the full course that immediately followed and then, I would be able to serve with RE diving teams and wear the hallowed badge of a Royal Engineer diver.

The training regime which I was about to face is famous throughout the Corps of Royal Engineers and qualified divers commonly joke with nervous applicants by whispering names of the various tests they were to encounter:

'The Camp Familiarisation.'

'The Mud Session.'

'Usually we were up for about 18 hours a day, not including the set up for the next day's training....'

'Being underwater was the best part, as that was the one place I could get away from the instructors.'

Having spoken with a number of RE divers beforehand, whilst at RMAS and during visits to prospective RE regiments, I knew that what I was about to face was going to be my hardest test yet, physically and mentally.

Ever since 1838, the Royal Engineers have had their own divers, often working in partnership with the divers from the Royal Navy and their history is a testament to the capability and dedication of those individuals who have worn the badges of RE divers.

Royal Engineer divers occupy a secretive but lethal part of British Army history, seldom known about except by those who have worked alongside them, a dedicated, highly skilled selected band of individuals.

From enabling early immense construction projects of the Victorian era such as military dockyards and tunnels, to swimming ashore in the dead of night amongst the freezing Atlantic rollers to scout out the shores of Normandy in preparation for D Day, to clearing Iraqi harbours of time delayed mines courtesy of the Saddam regime, the divers of the Royal Engineers have a rich and proud history which I desperately wanted to be a part of.

Working as part of small teams, utilising highly specialised equipment in the most arduous conditions, relying only on the determination, strength, intelligence and fortitude of myself and the other divers, I wanted all of it; to be a part of it.

Driving through the gates into the small, reclusive looking compound which held both the Royal Engineer and Royal Navy diver training facilities, I quickly removed my bags from the car and went in the main building.

As I pushed the doors open and slowly walked in, the corridors quiet with not another soul in sight, I looked around at the various memorabilia and photographs that were scattered along the walls. Faded grainy black and white pictures showing grinning men smoking pipes in antiquated diving suits aboard WW2 destroyers and prints of 21st century dive teams operating in Iraq and Afghanistan all sat stride dusty shelves and various souvenirs from the watery deep which lay scattered along the floor.

I soon came across a member of the permanent dive training team and I was directed towards my accommodation room. A dingy chamber lit by a few solitary bulbs, grey bunk beds with ageing mattresses lay in the corners, peeling and faded walls and various sad looking chairs lay scattered around. Clearly life here was not going to be five stars.

Whilst dumping my bags on the nearest bunk that looked the least decrepit, the other course students began to wander in. Aside from two other junior RE officers, the majority of the individuals on the selection were from the Royal Engineer Commando and Parachute regiments. All of them were, by their chosen unit, extremely fit and capable men. Tough and reliable individuals who had already proven themselves on previous arduous courses and operational deployments.

After five minutes of shaking hands and making nervous jokes, trying to take our minds off what was coming, an instructor walked in and led us to a room where the head dive officer introduced himself, and the course, to the rest of us.

Despite cheerfully covering the tests and challenges we would have to overcome in the following five days in order to qualify for the following five week course and expressing his confidence in us that we would pass, as long as we didn't give up, our nerves were still tense afterwards, with all our thoughts on what was to come the next morning.

We filled out of the room, chatting with a humour that none of us felt, and after a brief dinner out in the nearby town, no alcohol, we crept into our beds and waited for tomorrow to start.

First off, in the misty early hours of the morning, after shaving and brushing our teeth, we kitted ourselves out into our PT kit and went into the small gym that was in a room adjacent to ours. In order to qualify for the five day selection course, candidates first had to prove that they could carry out the required number of dips, pull ups, sit ups and press-ups, as well as a final mile and a half run. This was where we had to prove to the instructors that we could accomplish these minimal physical tests easily, that our basic levels of fitness and determination were high and that we would be able to face the real challenges that were rapidly approaching.

The reason behind the fantastically high levels of fitness and mental capability all Royal Engineer divers must achieve are simple. In order to be able to comfortably operate underwater engineering equipment, often bulky and extremely heavy, in waters that are typically freezing, clouded and constantly push the diver to and fro with its currents, a diver must be extremely strong so as to accomplish the task at hand. Also the fitter an individual is, the less oxygen they use with each breath and thus are able to stay underwater for longer.

Mental coolness, fortitude and resilience are of equal importance as due to the dangers posed to RE divers whilst underwater. From the equipment they are using, the environment they are operating in, to overseeing a number of divers at the same time whilst running a dive site, RE divers must be able to deal with any stressful situations quickly and effectively.

Freezing cold rain and driving winds swept off the coastline and rattled against the windows as we took in turns to tackle the initial challenges. What was surprising was that despite how competitive spaces are on the various dive courses, a few individuals failed on these simple tests; one completing the PFA run in over eleven minutes. I believe it was the slowest time anyone had ever run the mile and a half on the dive course.

Thankfully I passed all the tests but what worried me was that instead of being at the front, or at least near it, like I had been at RMAS, I found myself, for the very first time ever, in the middle of the pack on the run. Many of the other students were faster than me. It was very disconcerting indeed.

Once we had all crossed the finish line on the run, lungs wheezing and bodies bent double, we ran to breakfast, as no students were allowed to walk anywhere outside, and quickly took on some much needed calories. Even more surprising it was the poor quality of the food at the cookhouse (Galley).

After spending a year at RMAS eating truly excellent food in order to replace energy lost due to the constant PT regime, I was surprised to find that a training establishment like the Diving Training Unit which had a much harder PT regime than RMAS, only issued such small portions of inferior quality food to its students.

God bless government spending cuts and handing over once excellent military run dining facilities to cut price civilian companies. If I ever win the lottery, I'm going to donate a significant sum to that cookhouse, so that future students and divers can get the quality and quantity of food they need.

After a hurried disappointing breakfast, we quickly jogged back to the main building and waited for the dread 'Camp Familiarisation' to begin.

This would be where we would be run ragged around the entire camp, including the facilities that were dotted around the lake, being pushed to our limits. Competing in mammoth sprints, squats, press-ups, burpees, partner carries and much more.

It was only the first day and not even 9pm, but we knew that if we failed any of the approaching tests, we would be 'binned' from the course.

Nerves were tense as we stood in the freezing cold rain in our shorts and t-shirts, waiting like greyhounds for the whistle to go, having no idea how long we were about to thrashed, just knowing that we would have to give it our physical all, right from the start and not stop until the PTIs said so.

'Stand by....go!'

We hurtled off, sprinting around the various buildings that formed the Diving Training Unit, before we quickly dropped into a series of partner workouts were one individual would sprint around a certain circuit whilst the other would complete an agonising set of abdominal exercises.

Every two students had a diver instructor bawling in their ears, watching their every move, commenting on how slow they were or how the other students were catching them up. 100% scrutiny at all times.

Then, once the instructors were content and our stomachs and legs were on fire, we sprinted off again, covering another few hundred metres at top speed before we dropped to the floor again, conducting partner carries, duck walks, bear crawls and more. We then set off again.

The worst thing about it all wasn't the burning sensation in my limbs, or the pain in my lungs, but the sensation of having to push myself to my very limits, almost immediately, in order to keep up with the front runners in our group.

That, above all else, was the hardest challenge to overcome; the feeling of not being first was the most severe drain on my confidence and on my determination to keep trying going. Having never come across such a sensation before, where all my previous competitors had been aspiring officers and thus expected to be fit, I found it very difficult to deal with. As an officer, one should always be at the front of their group of soldiers. The phrase is 'follow me', not 'wait for me'. I cracked on.

The 'Camp Familiarisation' went on and on. The weather changed from freezing cold coastal weather to sudden fierce sunshine; which quickly warmed us up but then as time went on and our bodies became even more fatigued, the fierce early morning heat began to affect us all. Eventually, after pushing myself further physically than I had ever done so before, as the training regime at RMAS and on P Company did not even come close, we were halted by the staff and told to make our way back to accommodation as a group and have lunch.

Aside from the sensation of utter and complete exhaustion, the realisation that I had passed another one of the tests of the selection course filled me with an immense pride. This helped, along with trying not to show the others how fatigued I was, to keep me on my feet and head up, ready for the next tasks.

Lunch went by quickly, another disappointingly small meal, many, including myself, at this stage were eating food in our accommodation room that we had brought with us, and this time we jogged off to the diver training facilities by the lake.

This was where the instructors, who although they drove us like demons and would suffer no weakness, were actually rather pleasant and keen for us to pass, would introduce us to the equipment we would dive with. The excitement of getting to grips with the specialist diving gear and actually getting into the water was strong within the group and we turned up to the facility a group of eager, but very nervous and very tired students.

Within minutes, we were hurriedly throwing on our dive suits, having been a set time limit to accomplish this, with punishment for anyone being late, and were jumping into the freezing cold waters of the lake. The cold salt water stinging our eyes, the suits making our movement awkward, we began a series of swimming races using only our fins and countless 'in and outs', exercises where divers would fully pull themselves out of the water and then jump back in.

The physical tests just kept coming, with no let up and everyone being measured against the others. It was peculiar to realise during these challenges that a diver within the

Corps of Royal Engineers (or within the Royal Logistic Corps, as 17 Port & Maritime Regiment also sends candidates to diver training) did not actually have to know how to swim in order to qualify.

Years later, I met a fully qualified RE diver, an extremely tough and capable man, who could not physically swim unaided, often having to use a float while paddling in the local swimming pool. One only has to be able to float on the surface and be able to move underwater.

Hours later, once again changed back into normal working clothes, we were all sat in one of the equipment hangers, which was collectively known as 'The Cage', with all of the various staff of the Dive Training Unit. We went through formal lessons such as knots and kit maintenance whilst the instructors gave us informal chats on what we were going to face in the coming days, and how to deal with it.

The relaxed but professional attitude of the instructors, some of the most physically fit individuals I have ever come across, struck me as very profound. It did much to calm our nerves to know that aside from thrashing us on PT challenges, the staff had all been in our shoes as students previously and at times, could be (very rarely) considered as 'friendly forces'.

We went to bed very late that night, having stayed for many hours around The Cage, gleaning valuable nuggets of information from the staff, and after collapsing utterly exhausted onto our beds; we realised that we still had four days of selection training to go before the actual course would begin.

Thankfully we were so tired that all of us fell asleep almost immediately, so that this did not have much of an impact on us.

Thus the first day ended.

**

The next morning, muscles tearing in protest as we swung ourselves out of our creaking beds, pain wracking our bodies due to the exertions carried out the day prior, we sluggishly prepared for the day's challenges.

Once again, after a hurried wash up and change into PT gear, we found ourselves stood outside in the shivering grey mist of the morning, waiting to set off again in pursuit of the PTIs.

Today, instead of running around the Diving Training Unit buildings, we would be heading off to the local castle, a few miles away and after doing God knows what, return an hour or so later for the next challenge to overcome.

The PTIs immerged from the main building, smiling and wishing us good morning (to which we replied with false cheerfulness) and then one of them uttered the dreaded phrase:

Stand by …, go!'

Within seconds, racing after the sprinting PTI who was rapidly disappearing off into the distance, we realised that today was to be completely different from what we had faced yesterday; simply, the pace of running was easily as twice as fast.

What was worse was that we could see where we were running to, the castle off in the distance, and we knew that not only would we be thrashed before we got there, we would have an unknown amount of challenges to overcome at the castle itself and then, we'd have to run all the way back to the Diving Training Unit afterwards.

Knowing that you are running flat out, simply as fast as you can, trying to keep up with the group and merely minutes into a run that will probably run on for at least an hour or two, is simply demoralising in the extreme.

Along the route which we were running, right on the beach walkway, there were bins and street lights every hundred metres or so and at every one of these points, we were halted and, in pairs once again, had to compete in a series of mini 'pain stations'.

This would vary from continuous partner carries, burpees, seemingly endless knees to chests or any other amount of heinous body workouts the instructors could think of. All of which were competitive and every student, be they at the front trying to keep pace with the lead PTI or struggling at the back, had the same crippling thought running through their minds:

'How long can I keep this up?'

Eyes starting to blur with sweat, vision starting to turn hazy, the pain in the lungs all-consuming and every breath a torture, limbs as heavy as lead, skin flushed with exertion, we eventually stumbled into the car park of the castle; where the instructors mercifully gave us two minutes to drink some water and rest.

After what seemed like mere seconds, we were split from our partners into two groups, one of which would sprint around the castle (a good three hundred metres at least), whilst the others would carry out more abdominal exercises; such as flipper kicks and squat thrusts until their partner finished their run. Upon which, when each runner crossed the finish line, they would immediately swap places with their partner and the exercises would begin again. This went on forever.

Each time the runners set off, already exhausted before they had arrived at the castle, they would race around the gravel track that surrounded the castle, endeavouring to be the first back so that they and their partner had the most amount of time to rest before the final runners came in.

My body temperature at this point was sky high and I soon felt like I was boiling from the inside; my limbs and muscles were working so hard that let aside from not being able to cool myself down, I was even starting to struggle to see properly.

As I sprinted round, trying to come in first each time but gradually, over time, ending up towards the back of the pack, my lungs felt completely incapable of taking in enough air and my legs screamed in absolute agony as I forced them to run.

All the while my mind was telling me to give up, that I wasn't going to be able to finish the next sprint, that I was embarrassing myself by not coming first, that I was letting my partner down and that soldiers were outrunning me, that I wasn't setting an example.

The mantra being 'follow me' not 'wait for me'; an officer who slows their soldiers down is not worthy of being an officer. Somehow I kept going.

Thankfully, I found myself able to catch my breath slightly as I took my turn on the abdominal exercises whilst my diving partner kept sprinting round. Sadly though, he was immensely fast and my breaks never seemed to be long enough.

After God knows how long, my head dizzy and body simply red hot, my lungs feeling like they're made out of wet tissue paper and every single muscle hurting worse than they ever had before in my life, the session came to a finish.

Whilst we stood around hurriedly drinking in volumes of water, our brains telling us to drink slower but our bodies overriding such wisdom in the demand for hydration, the staff stood round us and informed us of the next stage. We were to race from the castle back to the Diving Training Unit; best effort, every man against the other.

'Go!'

Off we lumbered, more so stumbling than running, somehow forcing our bodies to keep going despite the aches and searing pains.

All that kept me going at this stage was seeing the back of the individual who was in front of me and becoming determined to catch him up; knowing that although I wasn't going to be first, I was damn well not going to be last.

After seemingly running on forever, my legs not appearing to be able to cover any distance at all, the finish line getting no closer and the paranoia of those behind me overtaking me becoming overwhelming, I rounded the last corner and saw the last three hundred metres to the finish. I dragged my legs forward, forced my head up, fought back the panic of not being able to breathe properly, kept my arms moving, the encouragements of the DS loud in my ears.

Now with less than two hundred metres of a straight tarmac road to go, stumbling across a small bridge, struggling to coordinate my limbs, body feeling like its cooking from the inside, floating on an absolute sea of pain, I ran on; not wanting to quit, determined to show that I wouldn't give up, no matter what.

One hundred metres or less to go, I could hear the encouraging yells of those who had already finished, I felt the encouragement given by my dive partner, Rob, who was running next to me, and I kept going.

The resounding sound of my feet slapping onto the road became a drum beat, the dizziness in my head becoming an all-consuming roar, my legs and arms completely out of sync with each other, somehow still moving forward, pain and desperation wracking my body and mind, my skin and organs feeling as if they were on fire, determined not to give up, I kept going.

Then everything went black. I'm face down on the concrete. I can't move. Arms dragging me along the floor, urgently trying to pick me up. My legs are collapsing under me, I have no strength.

I can't help. I'm thrown into the front seat of a Land Rover, where did that come from? Why can't I breathe properly?

Eyesight flashing in and out of consciousness. Images pass before my eyes, I can make no sense of them, I'm lying slumped over a dashboard. The Land Rover's tyres screeching as it hurtles along a road.

The driver shaking me, glancing at me and then the road, rapidly speaking to me, shaking me harder. I can't move. My tongue won't respond. Can't talk. Limbs feel limp.

Hands forcing my head up and pouring water over my face and past my lips. What's going on Staff? I'm sorry Staff. What's happening?

My body feels like it's made of rubber, I can't stand up or talk, breathing isn't working. Images of panicked faces in front of mine, asking me questions, I stare at them dumbly, eyes out of focus.

My clothes are torn roughly from me, a cup of tea forced into my hands and I'm made to drink.

How did I end up in the showers? The instructors are standing all around me; their faces flush with concern, asking me questions, trying to keep me awake as I lie on the shower room floor, freezing water washing over me. I continually pass in and out of consciousness.

Why won't they let me sleep? I'm so tired. I just want to succumb back into the darkness again.

Something different now. New faces. Fresh voices. Different voices. Is this a hospital? How did I get here? What's happening?

Cool hands gently lay me down on a bed. Soft hands feel my brow and take my pulse. Voices raised in urgency, questions asked and answered rapidly. But muted, as if from far away. Damp cloths laid over me. Deliciously cool.

Fading into darkness once again.

***

'Hello? Is this Henry Beeching's mother? Yes? Ah good, this is his OC from the Dive School; well, the first thing is that he's okay but he is in hospital....'

This was the introduction my mother had over the phone from the Diver Training Unit OC who informed her that I had collapsed whilst on a run. My body had actually cooked itself from the inside, organs severely overheating and coming within seconds of causing irreversible damage; almost dying.

My body had been pushing itself so hard that it had been unable to generate enough sweat to keep itself cool. Eventually, my body 'pulled the plug' and I passed out mid stride. It was my body's reaction, it effectively going on strike and refusing to work for me anymore in order to stop any more damage being done to it, before it was too late.

The medical treatment I had received from when I first blacked out, slamming down onto the tarmac road face first, unconscious before I even hit the floor, had been first class. The DS, immediately recognising what had happened, had tried to keep me awake and cool me down, making me drink and putting me into freezing cold showers in order to force my body's temperature to drop. I had been rushed to the local hospital which fortunately had the only facility in that part of the country for dealing with such incidents.

Aside from continually passing out, and temporarily coming to over a period of a couple of hours, the only time I came fully conscious before the doctors had managed to bring my internal temperature down, was when I laying in the operating theatre and my ears picked up, through the fog of delirium, the following conversation between two nurses:

'Oh Christ! What's his temperature? Has anyone taken his temperature?'

'No, not yet! Someone get some water, cool him down! What's his blood pressure?'

'We need his temperature, get the thermometer, get the rectal thermometer!'

Upon hearing this fearsome statement, I lurched upright from the operating table like a startled zombie and my body pulled itself together with one herculean last effort so that I could utter my opinion on this proposed medical treatment:

'Not the rectal thermometer! Oral only!'

Upon feeling a nurse gently pry apart my dry and parched lips, her hand cool on my brow and open and close my jaw, holding the thermometer in place, I gratefully passed out again. Panic over.

The only thing that could have made that day worse would have been to have a thermometer jammed up my backside as well.

After a number of hours, when my body returned to normal, I was informed that I couldn't return to the Diver Training Unit. That the doctors were unsure as to the heat damage that had been done my organs; not knowing whether I had just missed causing irreversible damage or whether it was already too late. All that I could do now was wait a few days in hospital (in the end I was in hospital for roughly a week) and then, as long as I didn't deteriorate, I would then be sent home for a few days and then be transferred onto the next Royal Engineers Troop Commanders Course (RETCC).

Then as the weeks and months go by, I'd be gradually allowed to slowly start physical exercise but I'd have to have regular checks with the doctors to ensure that I didn't accidentally trigger another collapse.

Weeks and months without exercise? No thanks. I knew that after coming off the Dive course, the last thing I needed was forced sedateness. I'd take things slowly at first, of course, but I knew that in order to be able to start boost my confidence again, the first step would be proving to myself that I wasn't physically weak.

Lying invalid for a number of days (although thankfully some of the dive team instructors managed to come up and visit me), after having collapsed on an arduous course, was almost more than I could bear.

For me, the war was over. The following days were purely intolerable; lying there confined to my hospital bed, thoughts and questions constantly running around in my head, trying to balance out whether I should feel angry or disappointed in myself.

Thankfully, after what seemed an age, the time had come for me to depart and I gratefully picked my bags (which had been dropped off during one of the visits from the DS) and made my way to the train station; onto the next stage of my career, to begin to learn how to become an officers in the Corps of Royal Engineers, to the RETCC.

Initially the various medical services that exist within the British military wanted, and quite rightly, to put me on a prolonged period of restricted exercise and series of body monitoring programmes; thus ensuring that I didn't have a relapse and accidentally trigger another heat injury.

But at that time I simply couldn't imagine anything worse than an enforced stretch of time where I wasn't allowed to do any exercise what so ever; what I needed (especially in regards to my mental confidence) was to get back out there and start training again.

I needed to prove to myself that I wasn't weak, that I was still strong.

Thankfully, as time went by, I managed to convince a string of Army doctors and nurses that I really didn't need to go for check-ups at special medical rehabilitation units, but instead could be trusted to do my own recovery programme; it was a risk, I admit, but it was one I'm glad that I took for I was never to suffer any form of heat illness or side effects again.

For a long while after, weeks and months, I struggled to come to term with what had happened. The disappointment, loss of focus and direction, the pain of seeing individuals who wore the diver patches on their uniforms; it was all too much to bear at times.

But thankfully, I was saved from this spiralling circle of self-loathing by a chance conversation, months later, with my old dive partner Rob over coffee in an RE Mess one day:

'I was running right next to you and then you just went down. At full speed. You didn't give up, you just kept going well past the point where your body could keep up. Stone cold before you even hit the ground. There is nothing to be ashamed of about that'

After all the previous conversations I'd had with individuals, both civilian and military, about my failure on the course, I realised what I needed was to have had a brief and frank opinion given to me by a qualified RE diver.

Knowing that they had faced the same challenges as me (and had gone on to do much more arduous ones), and thus I knew that they would give me an honest opinion as to what had happened that day and any direction they gave, I would take to heart and listen to attentively.

That brief exchange of words, from one of my peers, pierced the gloom of my depression and gave me an incentive, instead of a defeat, in which to move forwards with once again. It is an ethos that has never left me and has put me in good stead ever since.

Cheers Rob.

After a short stay at home, I then arrived at Brompton Barracks, the home of 1 Royal School of Military Engineering Regiment (1 RSME Regt). I quickly moved into my room and met my new course mates, many of which I had been at RMAS with. The following number of weeks at Chatham were incredibly tough, as coming from a non-engineering background, it took me a while to get to grips with the equations that made up life as an RE officer.

What I found amusing during my stay at Brompton Barracks was that aside from the insanely dull lectures given on health and safety, amongst other things, I could find no books written by previous RE officers on what life was going to be like undergoing Young Officer (YO) training on the RETCC.

Despite the fact that the RETCC was the longest 'officer to trade' course taught in the entire British Army lasting roughly six months, from start to finish.

Weeks later, after having spent far too long sat in dull lecture halls in Brompton Barracks on even more dull, but sadly important, lessons on riveting subjects which covered the fundamental knowledge of engineer constructions, we thankfully headed off to another barracks to take on the remainder of the six month long RETCC.

3 Royal School of Military Engineering Regiment (3 RSME Regt), Gibraltar Barracks, Surrey. This was where we would learn how to conduct engineer recces (and the subsequent reports), how to identify and destroy different bridges, handle explosives, build a variety of crossing points, fortifications and other such paraphernalia.

In addition to getting the chance to chat to serving RE soldiers and officers about what we could expect to come across when we were finally assigned to our future regiments.

The barracks was situated amongst the rolling fields, winding lanes and scattered woodblocks of southern England. This location was perfect for carrying out engineer training for officers, NCOs and the Sprs in the Corps of Royal Engineers.

Its sprawling layout was encompassed by a single barbwire fence and within its perimeters were numerous scattered buildings, small and large, that made up the regiment; offices, headquarters, classrooms, sports pitches, fitness facilities and trade training areas.

Laughingly, despite the number of months that were to follow and the endless lectures, exercises, countless forms and sketches, briefings and orders, easily 95% of what I was do for most of my time whilst employed in my future regiment, I was to learn upon first arriving within my troop.

I was seldom to touch upon what I had been taught on the RETCC, except for the rare opportunities where I was fortunate enough to get the chance to deploy out into the field on exercise and do conventional military field engineering.

Such as aspects which were to consume my life, and the life of my fellow officers, whilst commanding soldiers, such as 'Soldiers' annual reports', 'Midyear reports', 'JPA objectives and preferences', 'Penalty statements', '5 liners', 'Admin instructions', 'Joining instructions', 'Adventurous training', 'JSATFAs', 'ECI Checks' and so on, were not covered at all during my time at RMAS. And less than 24 hours was spent on them whilst I was studying on the RETCC.

Also, conversely, having been taught for roughly an entire year on how to prepare, write and deliver different sets of infantry section and platoon orders, such as Recce orders, QBOs and Deliberate Attack orders, for a while on the RETCC we were not taught how to produce engineer 'Construction orders'.

Consequently, meaning that although all of us could happily command a group of soldiers carrying out an infantry role, we simply had no idea how to command or order them whilst trying to complete an engineering task.

This meant that when it came for a RE 2 Lieutenant studying on the RETCC to stand up and deliver their set of orders for, say a construction of a bridge, a water point or demolition, often they had no idea how they were meant to write or deliver them.

We usually learnt how to correctly create and deliver a set of engineer orders after the nominated and unfortunate Lieutenant had had their orders ripped apart by the DS. The DS would then list off all the errors that had been made, and then detail off what the 'DS Solution' looked like.

And all the while we'd be quietly whispering to each other about the indignity of not having been taught such valuable pieces of information beforehand.

After raising this point a number of times and yet, for a long while, still learning what was required only after some Lieutenant had bravely stepped up in front of the instructors and withstood the withering criticism, the lists of missed points and of omitted information and of incorrect formatting, we finally gave up and just cracked on.

C'est la guerre.

On a slightly separate note, the dining facilities of Gibraltar Barracks deserve particular note, especially one famous cafe that every single officer and soldier within the Royal Engineers recalls fondly; namely, the 'Jackson Club' (Jacko's).

Jacko's has always been, and always will be, a refuge for trainees of all ranks who are undergoing instruction at Gibraltar barracks. A medium sized unassuming building that offers a range of cold and hot snacks and drinks, as well as seating, television and pool to weary trainees who are usually exhausted after a morning's PT thrashing or who have stayed up all the previous night to get a piece of assigned paperwork completed in time.

Most famous of all is the 'Cheesy Beans' meal option at Jacko's, a greasy and piping hot (as well as utterly delicious) combination of soggy toast, cheap beans and low quality melted cheese; a meal that sticks to one's ribs and fortifies one for the challenges ahead.

It is common belief that no one in the Corps of Royal Engineers can claim to be fully part of the RE family till they have had some 'scoff and a brew' at Jacko's; the 'Cheesy Beans' option continuing to be the most preferred option by all ranks.

During the next four to five months we were billeted in within Minley Manor, a place of myth and legend. A beautiful large sprawling manor house which was cluttered with numerous turrets, crenulations and winding passages, situated in quiet isolation across the road from the main barracks location (foot access was only by a tiny bridge).

Placed in the middle of idyllic rambling green lawns and quiet gravel lanes, follies, ha-has, mini orchards and half hidden forgotten cottages, it was a perfect place for RE officers to recuperate after a long day's study or work.

Inside, amongst its various carpeted floors and wooden panelled rooms, decorated with numerous hunting prints and portraits from which long since deceased Brigadiers and Generals glared down at us, of which officers would wander through armed with cups of tea and coffee, was the celebrated Minley Manor Bar.

A medium sized room, from which there were chandeliers, richly decorated shelves stacked with old tombs, glass fronted cabinets and most importantly a fully stocked bar running from wall to wall, it was a perfect Officers' Mess.

In order to gain the best insight as to what our home for those long months looked like, one only has to watch an episode of Jeeves & Wooster, for it was the Minley Manor Bar where they filmed all the scenes that took place in the 'Drones Club'.

There was even a photo of Bertram Wooster (aka Hugh Laurie) in one of the old photo albums that lay dotted around between various scattered tea cups and toast racks on the tables, standing in full three piece suit with a happy aristocratic smile upon his face.

Posing in the same bar where over the years countless RE officers, young and old, had played riotous drinking games that were truly in line with the ethos of boisterous alcohol fuelled fun that was the lifeblood of those members of that notorious gentleman's society in P G Wodehouse's novels.

Sadly, we were to be one of the very last officer cohorts to pass through, and at times pass out, its hallowed halls and vaulted rooms as due to increasing demands from Whitehall and offices within the MoD, Minley Manor was put up for sale.

Jokingly details also soon emerged through the rumour mill that despite the Manor being a large property and sitting in the middle of truly inspiring grounds and gardens, what was available to prospective buyers was 'slightly' less attractive than one would initially imagine.

Principally that as the Manor was a 'listed building', no real changes could be made to the interior or exterior (bearing in mind it had been an Officers' Mess for years and areas were indeed slightly worn to say the least) and despite being surrounded by sprawling lawns and forests, only an acre or two would come with the sale of the Manor.

The reason being that the surrounding area was actually in fact almost completely comprised of vitally important military training areas and was used frequently by the RETCC and the Spr recruits over the road, and was essential to conducting overall engineer training.

Thus a potential buyer investigating the potential purchase of the Manor would swiftly be informed that they could make almost no changes what so ever to the decor of the buildings and that their real estate would be minimal in the extreme.

Surrounded by fields and woods that were filled at all hours of the day, and night, by soldiers and officers of the Royal Engineers; running around, firing rifles and setting off explosive charges.

One can imagine scene of a relaxed country pile in which a wealthy individual has retired to after a long week spent in London (or the Gulf), and is taking the rural airs whilst touring their quiet grounds with a cup of tea in one hand whilst the soft music of birds drifting across the early morning mists.

When all of a sudden, two hundred metres away, 3 Section suddenly bursts from a tree line in full war rig, attacking a lone enemy trench, the sounds of harsh cries, automatic fire and grenades filling the air.

Quite spoiling the spouted image of a relaxed country pile in which garden parties and winter balls can be held in refined isolation by meandering crowds of talkative wealthy civilians.

Any takers?

***

Aside from revelling in the delights of 'tea and toast' most mornings in the Mess and when the weather permitted, reading the papers out on the veranda after meals, one of the biggest advantages of Minley Manor was the opportunity for us to talk with serving officers, junior and senior ones, over meal times or over drinks in the bar.

During our various attempts to glean whatever nuggets of useful information we could about what life was like in the regiments of the Royal Engineers, we were also shocked to find out how many soldiers and officers had 'signed off'. Meaning that although the personnel were still serving within the Army, they had decided to terminate their contract and had less than one year remaining within the army, during which most of their time was consumed with preparing for the return to civilian life. It was a sign of things to come.

It was very surprising to find out that so many of the officers and soldiers, and not just within 3 RSME Regiment, who were typically in the top percentile of their peer groups and had been specially chosen to teach recruits, were so exasperated and annoyed by how the army was now being run and thus had decided to quit. The most common of grievances were often summed up in the phrase of:

'Not enough blokes, not enough money, not enough resources, not enough time, RHQs' priorities are all fucked and the workload just keeps increasing.'

In general, the personnel of the British Army and the wider military don't actually disagree with the political handling of the army and its personnel, as the British Army must always answer to the political will of the UK, as often members of the electorate are commonly led to believe. Instead they strongly resent the policies the army is mandated, or forced, to follow at times and the subsequent supposed inability by their chains of command to highlight the errors in such policies to their political masters.

The British Army of 2020, being continually faced with ever increasing cut backs and suicidal saving measures mandated by Whitehall, the MoD and its career handlers up in APC Glasgow HQ, now regularly faces a number of problems which are becoming known as '2020isms'.

One such excellent '2020ism' we stumbled across whilst studying in Gibraltar Barracks was that the head instructor of all the RE armoured vehicles, their formations and uses, had never ever been inside an armoured vehicle in his entire career.

He was an officer who had served most of his career, up until the doctrine of Army 2020 decided otherwise, within the Royal Engineer Parachute Regiment and in various RE Dive teams. The ludicrous nature of his appointment, mandated by senior Army personnel at APC Glasgow, was lost on no one and made for some interesting times during his lectures to us.

Across the road, amongst the numerous troops of young Sprs frenziedly learning under the watchful eyes of their JNCOs, most of whom were Para, Commando, PTI or Dive trained, we buried our heads into the various forms, sketches and briefings that made up our YO education.

During the various tests which filled our six month course, intense focus was put onto assessing the YOs on how well they delivered orders, gave presentations and carried out back briefs. Every single aspect of an officer, and how they carried out their assessed piece of work, would be severely scrutinised and the smallest fault or area where improvement would be needed was highlighted.

This caught us by surprise at times as the RE officers and SNCO instructors carried out a level of scrutiny far in excess than anything we had come across during our time at RMAS; hammering us on details as exact and minute as our tone of voice, particular stance, placing of briefing aids or even just our choice of notebook:

'It doesn't look professional, Mr Beeching!'

The reason for the level of importance being laid on such attention to detail was that depending on how confident and clear a YO came across to their audience, how their presentation was laid out, utilised and much more, depended on how well their intended audience would receive the given information, process it and then act upon it.

This is especially applicable to all RE young officers and SNCOs as due to the nature of their job within the Corps, aside from briefing and delivering confidence to their Sprs, they regularly also have to do it in front of much senior military figures.

The senior officers being briefed are often not Royal Engineers and thus the RE personnel most do as much as they can to convince their audience of the validity of the information given.

As well as reinforcing the belief that the Royal Engineer delivering the brief fully understands what they are talking about. At the same time asserting themselves, and the information they are providing, so that it comes across as credible and thus should be trusted by individuals who significantly outrank them and have been in the military for far longer.

My thanks go to the RETCC instructors for eventually managing to put the message through my thick skull of the importance the lessons they taught. Such as the importance of rehearsals, fully understanding the subject material and preparing for difficult questions, examining previous mistakes, turning up early and setting up effectively and finally, for learning to look and sound confident. As well as the subsequent consequences of what would occur if these precautions were not observed.

It may sound silly but aside from learning the tricks which would enable me to correctly present my trade knowledge, command presence and overall conduct to an audience, be it a group of tired soldiers in a woodblock at 3am or two senior officers who are sat across opposite me in a briefing room, we all soon learnt the importance of 'looking professional'.

As frivolous and superficial as it may sound, looking professional ('Swept up', 'Ally') in the military is extremely important. First impressions count a lot in the army and a lot can be done to initially convince a group of soldiers that they should be inclined to follow, if not at least to listen to, an officer if the individual concerned looks smart and professional.

This can apply to how an individual wears their webbing, how they've shaped their beret or how they've sorted out the straps on their bergen or day sack, shaped the hood on their combat jacket or any other number of ways in which military personnel continually alter their issued equipment and clothing to look impressive and capable to others.

It should go without saying that this approach must then also be backed up by the leader, soldier or officer, also then proving themselves to be a capable, intelligent and an effective commander and thus able to lead their group; so that the assigned task or mission gets completed.

Any doubt an individual may have on this argument only has to look at a group of military personnel, from any country or region, when they come across other armed forces. They immediately assess, almost simultaneously, how 'warlike' or 'professional' the other group looks and make their judgement on them accordingly; often without having exchanged a single word between themselves beforehand.

I know of an officer who despite having served on a number of overseas tours, having won the Sword of Honour at RMAS, and being a qualified Army diver, is still known through the Army for having once delivered a set of orders to his troop whilst accidentally wearing two different boots on his feet.

Another small trick we all soon learnt, bearing in mind we were all newly commissioned 2nd Lieutenants training in a barracks littered with soldiers, young and old, and were keen to maintain our thin venire of authority, was a method known as 'The Officer Run'.

This bizarre and rather comical run consisted of when an individual for whatever reason, say having left some work in their room or was late for class, needed to get from one point to another, rapidly. Thus, as an officer should never be seen to be running, thus indicating they were 'flapping', by others, especially soldiers, and as such the officer would then adopt the following technique.

Hurry out of their building and upon seeing no one around, sprint at full speed until the next corner and, having slowed to a nonchalant walk, peer around the bend and see if anyone was around. If there were people walking nearby, the officer then slowly saunters past them and then upon moving out of sight, speeds up to full sprint again. This process is repeated until said officer, or NCO (it must be said), then reaches their destination.

The heavy reliance the British Army and wider military has on civilian contractors and instructors was also made aware to us during our time on the RETCC. From cooks, drivers, quartermasters, managers and instructors, significant tasks and responsibilities which in previous years used to be the domain of the military forces and management, are now assigned to civilian companies.

Some of these contractors are excellent and are a credit to their companies, often having served in the military for a number of years beforehand and do much to enhance the area or barracks in which they work.

Sadly, in my experience, this is often a rarity as the military will have unwittingly, for the most part, signed itself to a ludicrously expensive, lengthy and binding contract which typically puts the military at a significant disadvantage and causes no end of headaches to the serving military staff.

These contracts are often created and signed by senior military figures with money saving measures in mind but more often than not, the military unit involved ends up worse off than before, ending up paying much more than it previously did for a typically sub-standard service.

Typically procedures which are often simple enough, such as procurement of items even as minor as light bulbs, take far longer than humanely imaginable and end up costing far more than what they would do than if it'd been permissible for military personnel to buy them directly instead.

Again, our initial introduction whilst on the RETCC to the perverse relationship the British military has within civilian contractors was to put us in good stead when we went on to join our various units in the UK and abroad.

One lesson that has also remained seared upon my memory, since my time at RMAS and then during RETCC, was the needless way in which commanders will often keep their subordinates back from going on leave for seemingly no particular reason, especially on a Friday afternoon. Except for perhaps giving them an inane and heavily clichéd one-way chat or a 'weekend safety brief'.

I have always hated this and since the start of my time as an officer within the army, I have always become determined never to keep my soldiers back from going on leave needlessly, having remembered how much I myself despised officers for doing it do me in previous years.

Conversely, I also learnt to use this as a form of reprimand on occasion for individuals within my command who had done something to warrant a punishment. Knowing full well that since the dawn of time, if you want to inconvenience a serving soldier or officer and drive them hopping mad, all you have to do is restrict their leave somehow; be it only delaying them just for a few agonising minutes.

Overall though, I struggled throughout my time within Gibraltar Barracks; but not with understanding what was being taught, as that came easily as our instructors were exceptional. But when it came to a test, such as a briefing or set of orders, my brain for some reason, seemed to continually leave out vital aspects. This drove my instructors, and me, stir crazy.

It was as if mistakes and lessons were constantly being laid before me but my brain constantly refused to learn from any them.

As a result, a few days before the end of the six month course, I was transferred onto the next RETCC and was made to do the whole thing again.

God how that smarted.

But, as having to take the whole course again was perhaps one of the biggest obstacles I had had to overcome, I became determined to let nothing get in way of proving myself as an officer.

Failure was not an option. As such, I remembered all my previously made mistakes, rigorously went through my notes, studied and thankfully, months later, succeeded in passing the RETCC the second time round.

The time had finally come for me to step out of the training world and join the field army. To start my life as a troop commander in the British Army, to become a 'Troopy', and to prove myself worthy of leading soldiers in the field.

I would say that out of all the lessons I learnt from repeating the RETCC, from humility to determination in the face of adversity, as self-imposed as it was external, the skill of preparing and rehearsing for a delivery of orders or presentation was perhaps the most significant and vital aspect to my successful completion of the course.

In short, when assigned a set of orders to deliver, I would do all I could to write down what I was going to say and then practise it time and time again. I would go over what I'd written, check for repetitions or silly errors, I'd then go away and do something else for a while and then return to it, to check it again.

I cannot overestimate the importance of, once you've spent a long time looking at it and checking it, going away, if only for a few minutes, and doing something else. Upon returning to your work, minutes or hours later, you'll be surprised how your brain is able to pick out errors you'd previously missed.

Additionally, I found that as a result of having gone over my speech, or pitch, so many times, I would often come to know most of it by heart seldom refering to my notes, thus reinforcing to my audience my credibility on the subject and overall competence.

Once I'd rehearsed my delivery, and content, as many times as I could until I felt comfortable with it, I'd then do a full run through in front of some of my peers. Having a fellow YO, who I trusted to give an honest opinion, as well as having a good level of expertise themselves, evaluate my work was useful indeed.

From how I spoke, to phrases that I overused, or shuffling my papers when I was nervous or not maintaining eye contact the right way throughout, the flaws in my delivery of a presentation were sometimes best brought out by a work colleague.

Thus, once all of this had been done, I would always find myself as best prepared as possible to walk into the room and present my work. More importantly, I would be full of confidence because of the knowledge I had seen and addressed any unforeseen flaws what I was about to present and would, all going well, stand the best chance of succeeding.

Forewarned is forearmed.

6

Life in Regiment

The Troop. Within Regiment. Outside of Regiment

It almost goes without saying that I found regimental life in the Army of 2020 completely different to anything I had imagined. Over the next two years I was, at times, to both love and loathe my time as a troop commander within an Engineer Regiment. I was to have my dedication to serve within the British Army pushed to its very limits and would come close, on more than one occasion, to leaving. I would also to grow to love the troop of Royal Engineers that I was given to command, cherish the pleasure of leading them both in barracks and whilst in the field, and surprise myself in how far I was willing to go in order to protect and advance them.

Despite my varied experiences, good and bad, as a troop commander in Army 2020, I am still glad to say that being placed in a position where I could command and lead groups of British soldiers was simply the greatest honour I have ever been awarded.

In short, having the chance to serve with officers and soldiers of the British Army is something that I will never forget. I have never been through so much stress or confusion in my entire life, but I have also never laughed as much as I did when I was with them.

From arriving through the gates of 21 Engineer Regiment, based in my old stomping grounds in Ripon, I knew that despite almost two years of training, not counting my time within the TA, I would still face a very steep learning curve indeed. But this did not serve to intimidate me but instead I used it as a catalyst, I couldn't wait to meet my soldiers and actually start life within the Royal Engineers.

After first walking into the Officers' Mess, a small building tucked away on top of a small rise at the back of the barracks, hidden by a screen of trees, I quickly learned the name of the troop of Sprs who would come to dominate my life the next two years.

Support Troop, 7 Headquarters and Support Squadron, 21 Engineer Regiment.

I couldn't wait to get my feet under the table and to start to get to know them.

Having studied at Leeds for four years and spent much of that time gambolling around the countryside in various forms of military training, I'd specifically asked to be sent to 21 Engineer Regiment as I knew the barracks was almost unique. By which that usually a regiment lives in a good barracks but in a simply awful area or in a terrible barracks but is surrounded by nice countryside; Ripon had, in my view, a rather perfect combination of the two.

Meaning that aside from working in a barracks that looked rather charming, except for the awful and inexcusable state of the Sprs' accommodation blocks due to the severe restrictions placed on obtaining funds from the regiment by RHQ in order to fix them up, the surrounding area was simply stunning and a pleasure to train and live in.

The area for miles around consisted of rolling dales, green fields and hills, interspersed with meandering streams and dense woodblocks.

An abundance of wildlife, typically in the form of vast herds of deer or clutches of bemused pheasants, made morning PT runs almost pleasant at times.

Strangely enough, the weather in North Yorkshire always fascinated me, be it during my walks between my office and the Mess, or whilst out on the local training area. As the sheer mix of violently hybrid colours and constantly changing moods of the sky often kept me spell bound.

Be it during the peak of summer or the depths of winter, I always found complete delight in viewing the sights that the countryside and skies of North Yorkshire offered me.

'Good morning Troopy, welcome to 21. The blokes will be glad to finally have a Troopy.'

'Oh really? Why's that?'

'Well, they haven't had a troop commander for roughly two years.'

This was the introduction given to me by one of my Sgts, Sgt Brown, as I was being shown round the various offices and hangers that my troop, and its various vehicles and stores, were situated. So not only would I have to learn my job rather sharply, but also I'd have to work to prove to the troop that despite having functioned without an officer for two years, as a result of a diminishing amount of available

YOs in the Corps, I was needed and my position had credibility.

Certainly not something that had been covered in my prior leadership training.

From when I first decided that I would try and join the British Army, I avidly starting reading as much as I could about the 'common errors' junior commanders, especially officers, make when first meeting their troops. From demeaning their more experienced, but junior in rank, NCOs through feeble attempts in order to try to reinforce their validity as the overall leader, or running their soldiers into the ground in mammoth PT sessions in order to establish their dominance, the errors of eager but misguided junior commanders are legion and well documented.

Classically, not long after arriving within 21, I was sat having lunch in the Officers' Mess one day and overheard a conversation about a new Troopy in another regiment who upon his arrival, almost immediately, had made a catastrophic error in attempting to establish himself. The troop had been first paraded outside his office by the troop SSgt and after minutely examining all of them, in meticulous detail, the Troopy had then turned around then in full view of everyone, inspected his SSgt!

Needless to say this not only made him look like a mini Hitler, as well as embarrassing all who were present, as well as infuriating his SSgt, the ultimate senior and professional man in the troop, but that also this Troopy, unsurprisingly, did not go on to have a good time during his first few months in command.

Again, it was an example of how bad leadership can have an instant and powerfully negative effect on the individual concerned, but also how quick the story spread throughout the Corps and everyone came to know of his particular folly.

As such, I became fixated with the idea of trying to remember all the previous mistakes, some deliberate and others accidental, leaders had made when first working with their commands and not make them myself. Such as those who are too informal with their soldiers, who try to be their 'mate' but then end up having no respect from them as an authoritarian. Soldiers want a leader, not a friend and they will look down upon, and rightly so, any leader who is so weak in command that they try to assert themselves by being their 'buddy'. A true leader, male or female, young or old, will garner support and loyalty from their subordinates by being strict but fair, understanding, brave, loyal to their team, willing to lead by example and lastly, intelligent. Any other short attempts will result in failure and a weak team.

My approach when first starting to work within my troop was to get to know my NCOs and to slowly learn the way in which things were run within the troop through talking with them. As well as learning as much as I could about the soldiers I was commanding and the individual nuances that made them separate from each other.

This started where upon being shown my office, a large but dingy upstairs room shared with my two troop Sgts, as I was not to get a SSgt until my last six months in post, I was handed the Troop Commander's Notebook and immediately got to reading the notes and reports on my men.

Before sitting down and reading it, I'd had private chat in my office with Sgt Brown and Sgt Churcher, an ex-bodybuilder from Cumbria, who I was to discover over the following months was an absolute fountain of knowledge and superb voice of reason, and put it across to them quite bluntly that although I was fully aware I was the new troop commander and that ultimately the responsibilities would now lie with me, I would also be heavily relying on them to steer me in the right direction and rein me in if needed.

The Troop Commander's Notebook is an essential document, or collection of documents, and records every single report, course certificate, desire, success and failure, personal details and facts about each soldier in the troop. It is the sole responsibility of the Troopy, in working with their NCOs, to keep this valuable record up to date and current. It is the record in which a commander can refer to when examining an individual under their command and is an excellent tool for not only keeping track of what a soldier has done, or wants to do in the future, but it also helps ensure that a soldier's career progresses correctly.

It is worth its weight in gold and when a troop commander has a large number of soldiers to command and keep track of, I had fifty, it is the one way of ensuring that all the information on a soldier is recorded and stored in a handy location.

Upon going through the vast sheathes of paperwork which described in detail the personality, and career details of each one of my Sprs, I stumbled across some excellent phrases written by previous individuals on some of the personalities in my troop:

'Like an unguided rocket.'

'Constantly vibrating.'

Fantastically, these were phrases that were all devoted to describing just one man, LCpl Hollings (aka 'Speedy'). No sooner than I had read his file, Speedy then came into my office to introduce himself and I got my opportunity to assess him for myself.

A young LCpl who had previously served a number of years in 23 Parachute Engineer Regiment, both in the UK and whilst on tour in Afghanistan, who was also a qualified PTI and had taken apparent delight in searching for Taliban IEDs whilst on his last deployment. He was a very interesting character to say the least.

His very nickname came from the fact that when he was going through his basic training, his instructors were so struck by his seemingly boundless energy that they became convinced that narcotic supplements were involved somehow. Thankfully a completely false belief, but one that was also extremely funny none the less. Speedy turned out to be one of the most energised and enthusiastic individuals I was to come across whilst serving in 21. Standing before my desk, airborne wings proudly worn on his shirt sleeves, with a cheerful and eager face, sizing me up as much as I was him, I knew I would like working with him.

There were many other soldiers within Support Troop who would become key figures during my progression as a troop commander, and even in the darkest pits of paperwork induced despair, would somehow manage to keep me sane; Ady, Sunny, Stevie, Mikey, Dale, Tomo, Ledge, Hayto, Raks, Riggers, Boot, Ampong, and more.

Through the following two years and numerous trials and tribulations my troop and I went through, as well as no small number of successes I am glad to say, I was to learn how essential my NCOs, especially my JNCOs, were to the troop and to me.

The young soldiers who'd proved themselves time and time again that they could not only handle the responsibility of being a JNCO, but who often, due to the scarce manpower of Army 2020, took on positions and jobs that were typically assigned to individuals of much more senior ranks.

Sadly, I was to find out during my time as troop commander that due to the constant and every increasing workload, very little rest, and lack of understanding from senior officers, too often preoccupied with their own tasks to realise how hard working my NCOs were, many of them were in the process of leaving the army.

Typically, one would imagine that the very worst, most lazy and inept soldiers are the ones who 'sign off' and quit the military but another 2020ism is that although that may have been the truth in years gone by, now troop commanders are discovering that it is, in fact, their best soldiers who are now quitting.

By the end of my time at 21, almost ten of my Sprs had signed off, all of them high calibre and very intelligent individuals indeed; all of them, to a man, annoyed and frustrated at the way the military was being run and how they, and they families and career, were being handled by RHQ and higher chains of command. Tired of being overworked, underpaid and undervalued, weary of often performing at the top of their peer group but not being promoted due to restrictions arising from their trade, sick of being away from their families for lengthy periods of time on needless exercises or getting severely reprimanded for the smallest mistakes and having their achievements ignored; the JNCOs of the British Army, especially the Royal Engineers, in my view, are leaving in droves.

In writing his final words before being consumed by the elements of the Antarctic in 1912, the intrepid and dauntless explorer Robert Scott penned the mantra which became infamous for epitomising the complete and undying devoting a leader should have for their people, regardless of any hardships and dangers:

'For God's sake, look after our people.'

Sadly, the British military of recent years has somehow managed to let this code fall to the wayside.

I remember even now, as if it were yesterday, when on my first day whilst reading through as many files as I could on the Sprs within my troop, Sgt Brown politely asked if I was ready to give a talk to the assembled troop. To introduce myself.

The dreaded first speech by a junior officer to his soldiers.

The first time where you stand out in front of them and introduce yourself, setting you out as their commander, their leader. Trying to come across confident but at the same time not cocky, stern but not ridiculously so, wise and worldly but also humble, bearing in mind the vast operational experience many of them will have compared to your total lack of it, it is a tricky sell to make or pull off.

Whilst being escorted through a small maze of rooms and corridors that made up the main vehicle hanger, where most of the kit my troop used was stored, I was informed by Sgt Brown that despite having the largest troop in the regiment, I would only be briefing around a dozen or so soldiers. As the rest were away on various assignments. Having only a handle of my soldiers at a time was something which I would become very used to as the months went by, due to the amount of times they would be trawled in 'ones and twos' on random last minute tasks set by RHQ.

We walked into the small troop brew room, in which lay a number of aged and worn sofas upon which my Sprs rested and chatted. The Sprs from my troop that were in camp on that day had been herded into there by the JNCOs and now they all looked up as I walked in, dozens of eyes fixing onto me.

I'd thought about what I was going to say and came to the conclusion, having written down a few bullet points beforehand in order to give my mind some direction to follow (thank you, RETCC), that I needed to speak only for a few minutes. To introduce myself, make it clear how much I was looking forward to working with them, that I knew the troop had a good reputation and that I wanted it to continue, what my role was going to be, that my main focus was to look after them and lead them, and that they could come talk to me about anything.

How well it went, or how well they perceived it, or me, is not for me to say and I've honestly never had the courage to ask. All I know is that after a few minutes of talking, and informing them that I'd soon be having interviews with all of them in order to get to know them, I then scuttled back to my office and went about creating myself a role within the troop. That, at least, wasn't as hard as I thought it to be.

The reason being that from the first day I turned up, to the day I left, the pace of life within 21 Engineer Regiment was absolutely hectic and it simply never slowed down.

It is a commonly stated fact nowadays that junior commanders, especially Royal Engineer troop commanders, are the busiest they have been in years, although sadly often not with the type of work they signed up to do, senior officers regularly commented to me on how the workload they faced as a Troopy was nothing to what Troopies are doing currently. I believe that this is because that the Army has forgotten that when a troop has nothing planned for a set number of days, known as white space, on the calendar, this is a good thing and it should be left as so. In my experience as a troop commander, as soon as my chain of command realised that an individual was not tasked with any specific assignments over a couple of days, they would inevitably find something for that person to do, despite the indignant and infuriated outcries from the NCOs and me.

Whereas I quickly realised, upon first arriving within the troop, that when some 'white space' appeared in the troop calendar occur, then it should be used as a period of time to give the soldier some much needed rest and an opportunity to see their family. At most, they should only assist with light work such as the maintenance of equipment and vehicles. Soldiers and officers do need rest at times, sadly the RHQs dotted around the country, and overseas, have seem to have forgotten this. Much to the chagrin and despair of soldiers and officers suffering under their yoke.

When I was going through my training at RMAS, I first came across the phrase 'gapped', which meant a post or position did not have anyone in it at the current time. When this usage came into being, it was seen as the epitome of taboo and all efforts were immediately made by all concerned so that the post could be filled as quickly as possible. Less than two years later, when I first took command of my troop, I discovered that this phrase had now changed from being the most taboo of all phrases to perhaps the most commonly accepted. Meaning that on discovering that a post or position has no individual to fill it and to take on its responsibilities, the British military now accepts this as the norm and it is perfectly common to find units with dozens of 'gapped' posts.

This is not helped by the simply woeful recruiting campaigns run by the Army, which have been completely outshone by the RAF's and Navy's efforts in recent years. Meaning that soldiers and officers who already have their own plates full with their own duties, are now expected to take on a number of additional jobs and responsibilities at the same time. I first discovered the depth of this issue when

I learnt the different roles my troop would now carry out as part of the regiment.

My troop, Support Troop (aka 7 Field Troop), was comprised mainly of Drivers and Plant Operator Mechanics (POMs) whose duties included operating the regiment's consignment of transport and engineering plant vehicles. As such, they were constantly in demand as they enabled the rest of the troops, and squadrons, within the regiment to carry out their own roles. On top of all this, we also had to keep enough manpower so that we could carry out our own duties; such as checks, maintenance, field engineering training and deployments.

A sign of what Army 2020 was going to be like was within my first week in work, it was made clear to me by talking with my various Sprs and NCOs that although each person within the troop carried out their assigned role day to day, they typically also had to do the work of two extra men as there were simply not enough soldiers for the tasks set by RHQ.

During an OCdt's time within RMAS, it is reinforced time and time again that one of the most important skills an officer must learn is time management and ensuring that their soldiers are given enough advance warning of future tasks, so that they can best prepare for them. This is stressed to such an extent during officer training that if an OCdt has appeared not to leave enough time in their orders for their soldiers to conduct administration and preparation for their future task or mission, often as not the DS would severely reprimand them and make them rewrite their orders all over again.

But, upon arriving within the field army, I realised that the amount of assignments (aka trawls) that we were tasked with every day that required instant action, and the subsequent assignment of soldiers, who were typically sent away for a number of days at the very least, with little or no time to prepare for beforehand, was unbelievable. I forget the amount of arguments I had with my 2IC, and higher chain of command, over the sudden requirement to send for instance, a driver to Salisbury Plain for a number of weeks or to Canada to operate a crane for four months. Usually, as an officer's task is to look after their soldiers and do as much as they can to develop them, this typically meant that the individual concerned then had to be taken off the Adventurous Training (AT) package, for instance, they'd applied for months ago, and had to say goodbye to their family again. Usually only just having just recently returned to the UK after a previous lengthy deployment; I forgot how many marriages and relationships failed due to the unceasing demand for personnel to be deployed at the last minute on menial official RHQ trawls.

Sadly, in the end I would usually have to give way as the pressure from senior officers increased and assign the soldier to this sudden and last minute trawl; this would then leave both me and the soldier concerned feeling annoyed and disillusioned with the Army.

Time management for anyone, especially a commander in the military, is essential and if it is not managed correctly, it can cause no end of frustrations and problems. The reason being that due to the amount of individuals and varied ranks within my troop, I constantly had to keep an eye on the report tracking timeline which was printed out and hung on my office wall so I could check what reporting period was coming up and what I needed to write for it.

Keeping track of my manpower was also vital, bearing in mind the amount of soldiers I had, and this was done by the online 'Manpower Tracker', in combination with my troop's yearly training calendar. Simply nothing happened before my SSgt or I checked the Tracker to see what individuals were where and for how long. It was a terrible faux pas for a Troopy to tell their chain of command that 'Cpl so and so' would be available for a trawl but only then find out that the individual concerned had been previously loaded onto a course that was occurring over the same date.

A very quick way to lose one's credibility.

The British Army, more so now than ever, loves meetings and coordination briefs. Meaning that aspiring troop commanders must be aware of the importance of these meetings, for it is often their only chance to demonstrate to the SNCOS and officers within the squadron, that they know their business.

That means predominantly having spoken with the troop SSgt so that you both go into the O Group with the same view on the relevant topics and don't offer conflicting advice when asked by the higher chain of command, which can be very embarrassing.

Having a full understanding of the questions that will likely be sent your way, usually through having spoken with the chain of command previously, is of the utmost importance, as is being able to answer the queries in an accurate and articulate manner.

Aside from the frustration of not being able to have an impact on where my soldiers were sent a lot of the time, I also struggled with the infuriating emphasis the military puts on bureaucracy and seemingly endless minor checks. To an extent I kind of expected it, but I for one severely struggled with the importance my chain of command put on issues which just made no sense to me. Such as having the correct and up to date posters around my buildings, ensuring that all of the trees within the barracks had had their registration plaques correctly nailed on, checking that all the chairs in the various offices were NATO registered, or attending mandatory squadron and regimental lectures which run for hours in classrooms or in the gym but taught us nothing.

Constantly I found myself struggling with my own frustrations at the chain of command's bizarre hierarchy of importance and the self-loathing I had due to the amount of time I had to devote to such miniscule and petty tasks, but the confusion and exasperation of my soldiers was simply something else altogether. Within my troop I had a liberal scattering of brand new Sprs and a collection of experienced, capable and battle scarred NCO, and they for one struggled with it more than I did.

It was very difficult, if not impossible, to put effectively across to a keen young soldier just out of training, or to an experienced NCO with numerous overseas combat tours under his belt, that it was suddenly of the utmost importance that they complete an online computer course on office desk safety or due to regimental direction they'd get formally punished. Especially, when I didn't believe what I was saying myself.

Initially, when I first arrived within regiment, I would look at the forecast of my day and naively think that I had plenty of time to not only do my required paperwork for the day, but also perhaps even to visit the gym or have a brew with some of the lads in the hanger. No sooner than making the first cup of coffee and sitting down at my desk, I would find out that regimental intranet was not working for some reason and no one could say when it would be back on, the OC suddenly wanted a meeting before lunch on the Cpl grading board, that there was an all ranks brief on pensions running after lunch, I was needed to do an armoury inspection at 1500 as the Troopy who was meant to do it had been called away and finally, due to the lack of men in the troop currently, the run through for the OC's inspection on Friday would have to take place last thing today. Oh, and by the way, the paperwork that had been submitted to the 2IC had been returned, red penned in different areas this time and it all needed to be back in close of play today.

This occurrence of having a seemingly empty day suddenly fill out with all manner of distractions also applied to the distribution and workload of my troop, as usually, despite having fifty soldiers under my command, I would usually only have a handful available at any one time.

My three Sgts would be employed running the POM desk and the Automated Bridge Launching Equipment (ABLE) detachment, our main bridging system. Whereas my three Cpls would be either running the JAMES account, which was our military vehicle management system, manning the camp guard staff or working within the QM's department. Out of my six LCpls, one would be assisting with the ABLE, two would be handling the MT department, one would be working within the regiment's gym, another would be on exercise and the last would be in charge of handling the Sprs. Five Sprs would be on sick leave, ten would be deployed in support of UK and overseas exercises, three would be on AT, thank God, four on leave as they'd just returned from months away, eight would be working with the other squadrons in the regiment as they didn't have enough Sprs of their own and that would leave eight Sprs spare. The last eight would then be busy with driving duties, vehicle maintenance and other minor tasks that occur as part of the daily running life of the troop.

That would be the pattern of life for the entire two years I was employed within 21 and I have no doubt that it has continued since, not exactly a vast number of men for a troop commander to command. Especially so, as bearing in mind that I had the largest troop in the regiment but typically had the least amount of soldiers available in camp day to day.

For these reasons alone, my soldiers and I were always desperate to do whatever we could to get away from the barracks and do things that we actually enjoyed and wanted to do, as well as getting away from the monotony of regimental life. Be it AT packages, military exercises, university courses, trade courses, sports competitions, and overseas deployments; simply anything that was of interest, a challenge and was enjoyable.

One of the biggest problems behind all this was that 21 Engineer Regiment was an 'Adaptive Force' regiment, a new branding meaning that we as a regiment were not preparing for any particular tour or deployment, thus we had no single objective or aim whatsoever. As such, we got tasked with every single trawl and demand that came our way and thus the regiment blundered on, taking on jobs that were as minute and nonsensical as they were annoying and frustrating for the soldiers and officers that had to answer them.

Whilst in the office, I quickly found myself, as well as the other officers and NCOs I knew, simply drowning in paperwork. As all ranks within my troop received their annual and midyear reports at all different times, and before serving the soldiers their reports I'd have to submit the paperwork to my 2IC for approval, I quickly became tied to my desk.

I hated it. Especially as I hadn't been informed to any great extent about these obligations, or the importance of them, during all my months and especially in during the months prior to the military training.

Thank you Army 2020. I mention this not in self-defence, but in the interests of strict truth.

My complete thanks goes to my long suffering Squadron 2IC who wearily, and at times angrily, returned my submitted reports and documentation to me, liberally covered in alterations written in red pen. Getting a piece of paperwork 'red penned' was to become a necessary evil as, especially in the early stages, my written work was simply woeful. This was due to a delightful and frightful combination of my own errors when it comes to written work, such as unintentional repetition or errors, and typically because I usually had never been taught, seen, or even written, such a report before.

This often resulted in me receiving a number of additional punishments in the form of weekend duties. Typically arising from substandard paperwork or, to be honest, forgetting that I also had some regimental responsibility or duty to carry out.

The ironic thing I was to discover about military writing, known as MS (Military Secretariat), that aside from every unit and sub unit within the British Army having their own particular preferences to how SJARs, for example, should be written, all forms of official personnel reports have to be written in a particular form of military code.

Meaning that although each report is written in plain English, it is not possible to state if an individual, say a Corporal, is absolutely useless, overweight and is not worthy of their rank. Instead, one must write a report that appears to be a glowing testimonial to the character of the individual concerned, but contain key phrases and hints that indicate poor levels of performance or character, obvious only to those who have spent years writing and grading such reports.

As such, I was to incur no end of near panic attacks and sky high levels of exasperation at my own supposed inability to produce the required standard of paperwork and my chain of command's tendency to seemingly accept one particular paragraph on a report one moment but then after receiving the report for the third or fourth time, would suddenly decide that something was wrong with that paragraph after all. All of my paperwork would also have to be completed in conjunction with the normal day to day duties and responsibilities of a Troopy. Meaning that it was not humanely possible to just focus solely on the paperwork as I also had a very large troop of soldiers, and a full fleet of vehicles to manage.

My own lack of knowledge or experience in constructing military paperwork, combined with my infuriatingly forgetful memory, led me to some truly unpleasant times whilst within regiment; not ideal.

The importance of being computer literate also cannot be underestimated and future commanders must accept the fact that units, large and small, do everything online nowadays and aspiring leaders must hone their skills accordingly. This is also not helped by the fact that without access to a military computer, known as a 'DII Terminal', one simply cannot do their job. The computers themselves, and the systems they run off, are famously slow, out dated, cumbersome and cause no end of frustration and limitations to the personnel that use them. Especially as none of the YOs in 21, myself included, had ever really used them before arriving at regiment.

Simply, all files and records that the army now uses are online and if the computer or systems don't work, nothing can be done; I have known entire regiments to cease to work or function because the computer system has gone down for some unforeseeable reason, running from just a few hours of forced idleness to a number of days. It amused a great many of us, over drinks or at mealtimes, to think that if an unseen force wished to completely take away the British Army's ability to operate, they needn't worry with expensive nuclear weapons, but merely to throw a spanner in the works of our antiquated computer system.

Heaven knows how we, the mighty British military, ran an Empire and beat the Germans in two world wars without the benefit of having such a computer system like DII. We all recognised the benefits of having a good electronic system in place, but sadly the Army runs off one that was bought 'off the shelf' and for the cheapest possible price, which resulted in it causing more problems than it solves.

Thanks.

It sounds hilarious but when an individual, such as a Troopy or troop Staff Sergeant, has a dozen tasks that they must complete by the end of the day or all hell will break loose, and their computer suddenly decides not to work, life quickly becomes a living hell.

A significant issue with the computer systems that the British military runs off, aside from the slowness of the programmes and the scarcity of the computers themselves, is that the actual programme designed to handle the administration and career tracking of individuals, known as JPA, is simply woeful. One would imagine that any system that is designed to record every single aspect of an individual's career, in an organisations that has tens of thousands employees, as well as important personal data, future career aspirations and suchlike, would be advanced, simple to use and reliable.

Not so much.

JPA was to cause me, and my soldiers, endless dramas and headaches, for a number of reasons, most of which stemmed from the confusing and bizarre way in which the programme runs. An antiquated system that takes months to slowly get used to and to understand its peculiarities, which are known in the military as JPA-isms. It is simply a pain in the ass for all that use it. As such, in order to improve the ease, speed and effectiveness of handling its personnel's careers, the British Army simply must upgrade to a better system. It just cannot afford to expect to keep up with the 21st century and still runs its administration through a system that is rumoured to have been copied from a hotel booking programme.

Future soldiers and officers would do well to prepare for dealing with this aged system and learn its various intricacies, I would strongly recommend speaking to serving personnel or at the very least buying a step-by-step book on it. Ideally, the numerous soldier and officer training institutions within the British Armed forces will devote more time to teaching military personnel how to deal with the computer programmes on which their entire career progression will depend, but as that would probably require additional funding or manpower, I am doubtful they'll do it.

Importantly, aside from learning how to avoid the various pitfalls, irrational processes and bizarre workings of the JPA system, officers must also learn how to teach their soldiers these lessons, as well as teaching them valuable tricks such as what expenses they can claim for, or how to best display their online career profile so as to best assist with them progressing up the career chain.

As for the Army's current computer system, at the time of this publishing, a new digital system has been introduced – one can only hope that it proves an improvement on the past incumbent.

The end result of all these inbuilt challenges and irregularities was that I always counted my lucky stars that within regiment I had a home to go to during the week, a place to forget my paperwork for a night and to chat with the other junior officers within the regiment; the Officers' Mess.

Sweet sanctuary.

In some parts the Officers' Mess is the same as it has always been since the conception of the British Army, such as riotous parties, host to outrageous characters and situated in far flung places around the globe in which officers have found residences. But in other parts it has changed dramatically.

The Officers' Mess in 21 was the centre of life for the regiment's officers, especially the bar. The place in which the 'Living in Members' (LIMs) of the Mess, typically the troop commanders, lived, ate and socialised when the working day was over. It was home for us during the week and we treated it as such. For aside from the ability to retire to one's room at the end of the evening and relax, or to have drinks in the bar with fellow officers, it was also a place of rest and a chance to garner knowledge and experience from the other members of the Mess on issues and situations that arisen during the day.

During the weeks and months we spent living together in the Mess, all of the YOs learnt the importance of relying on each other, trusting in each other's confidences and that we couldn't possibly survive without the support and advice of the others. This resulted in extraordinarily strong friendships developing very quickly and some truly blinding and memorial parties and games taking place where we all let off considerable steam; such as Mess Rugby, Beer Bridging, Mess Polo, Indoor Rifle Ranges, Urban Assault Courses and Beer Pong.

Beer Pong, the most recent arrival in the charged and boisterous atmosphere that occurs when YOs decide to settle into a serious drinking session, has been quickly adopted from our Colonial Cousins from across the Pond and assimilated into the British Army with gusto. Often far from simply clearing a table and getting some plastic cups, the Beer Pong table has often become a central focus piece of the Officers' Mess bar. As I was to discover whilst overseas on a course in a Rifles' Mess, where I found the officers had even gone as far as making a bespoke solid oak table inlaid with brass, purely in the pursuit of Beer Pong. There were even regimental silver goblets for the sole use of the players.

The most famous and memorable of riotous games I ever saw created in the 21 Officers' Mess were 'Mess Wizards' and 'Come Drink With Me'.

'Mess Wizards' required individuals, typically at around 1am, and after many fortifying drinks, to step out into the garden or car park and fire flares and fireworks directly at each other, whilst yelling wild incantations and hexes at the top of their voices. The first time I tried this, I held the firework the wrong way round and shot myself squarely in the chest, thank heavens I was wearing a rather fine chequered Charles Tyrwhitt shirt as protection.

These battles would range from a couple of individuals standing twenty yards apart like old school pistol duellists and blasting away at each, to most of the Mess spilling out of the doors and causing absolute havoc as dozens of rockets and flares bounced off the combatants, buildings, parked cars and surrounding trees. The last time I saw this game being played, at least one tree in the garden had been set aflame. Great fun.

During these occasions, bearing in mind our missiles often as not rebounded right up into the night sky with a subsequent deafening and multi coloured explosion, and that our Mess was situated on a hill that overlooked the entire barracks, the regimental Guard shift wisely decided never to venture up to us and investigate the sounds of battle issuing forth from our secluded hilltop.

'Come Drink With Me', which was styled loosely around the reality television show, was the result of many weeks without a single Mess function, due to regimental tempo, and significant levels of stress for all Troopies within camp. As such, each LIM within the Mess that Tuesday night, these type of events are always held on a Tuesday night, as there is typically no PT on a Wednesday, just sports, which we could all easily tackle whilst hung-over, was tasked with decorating their room in a style unique to them. As well as providing suitably relevant alcohol and to be in appropriate fancy dress at the appointed hour, ready to receive the other LIMs into their room.

Luckily, I was the first room to be visited and so everyone was in a reasonable state when they arrived. I'd styled my room in the manner of an English Country Squire and aside from filling my room with flags, patriotic music, some fruit cake sent to me by my mother and a liberal scattering of cigars, I also had a significant stock of whisky on tap. As there were around eight LIMs visiting and it wouldn't do any good to any individual to be accused of being frugal or, even worse, stingy.

After around half an hour, with the whisky in full flow, I was then asked to leave my room whilst all of the LIMs gave their opinions, all of which were formally recorded on a mobile phone for future reference, on my room, overall hosting skills, alcohol on offer and general bearing. Each point and view was heatedly contested by all right from the start.

Upon finishing in my room, sadly the subsequent recording of the discussion on my score was lost in the ensuing carnage of the evening's festivities, we moved up the corridor to the next room. Ryan, a brilliant officer who'd spent many years previously serving as soldier, had taken on a Continental theme to his room's decorations and had laid on a fine spread of wine and savoury treats.

One can easily see the effects the diversity of alcohol and food that we consumed throughout the evening was bound to have on us.

From that point, the evening crashed along in fine old style and by the time we had reached the seventh room, it had descended into simply delightful carnage. Cast iron furniture was being hurled along the corridors, people were wrestling in rooms, crashing into and knocking over all and sundry, dogs were running past barking with ladies' underwear strung between their ears and a truly bewildering and vile collection of drinks was being passed around.

The Officers' Mess had completely cut loose.

The next day was the only time during my entire time spent whilst serving at 21 that upon turning up for work, feeling rather worse for wear, SSgt Dixon saw me, bellowed with laughter, and then swiftly ordered me to return to my bed and not to come back until I had fortified myself with a stout lunch first.

A great evening, and one that will always be remembered by those who took part in the festivities. It sounds silly, and it was, but stress relieving functions like that allowed help us all to relax, bond and generally go slightly mad in the confines, secrecy and security of our Mess.

Great fun was also had whenever a Troopy was deploying out the door onto an exercise in the field. The reason being that as we were always so short of kit and equipment that often as not, it took the combined efforts of all the Troopies within the Mess to send one YO out the door fully stocked. Much akin to a girl dashing around to her friends' houses borrowing all and sundry so that she can go to a party suitably dressed.

It used to be a common joke that each Officers' Mess within the Army, especially the Engineers, should have a life sized manikin in a glass cage situated in the bar, fully kitted out in all the equipment, with appropriate doctrine, manuals and forms, that a YO would need for deployment, with a brass plate over the top of it, and a hammer dangling nearby from a chain, stating 'Break in case of Exercise!'

The Officers' Mess is far from unique in regards to the efforts its members make in seeking solace, tension relief and forgetting about their daily working routine for an evening. The Sprs of 21 were also far from shy in demonstrating their feelings about the tempo of regimental life and the workload they also faced. Typically, this would arise whenever the squadrons were confined to barracks for an evening, usually in the form of collective punishment from RHQ for some infraction or behavioural control measure, and when the sentence was first passed, all Troopies in station would hold their breaths and wait to see what form of protest the boys took.

Perhaps the most memorable of occasions where the lads took it upon themselves to 'self-destruct' and get 'completely mingmonged' was when a mayoral visit was taking place over the weekend and no one had been allowed to leave the barracks and see their families or have a drink in town, laughably in an attempt to make sure that the VIPs would not come across any hung-over soldiers. As such, despite the many rumours and mutterings that made it to the ears of the Troopies and SNCOs within the regiment via the Jungle Drums, the visit went ahead and regimental history was made by a few fool hardy, suicidal and truly commendable Sprs.

The mayoral party was being escorted by a host of senior regimental personnel through the camp, along its main road which bypassed the accommodation blocks of the Sprs who lived within regiment, the afternoon sun was shining, the birds were singing and the Sprs of 21 had decided to protest.

Upon turning a corner in the road, the view of the front of one of the accommodation blocks opening up to the mayoral party and their escorting officers, the entire group was treated to the site of a dozen roaring drunk Sprs, doing naked press-ups and deep squats on the grass by their accommodation, being cheered on wildly by soldiers leaning out of nearby windows.

Unfairly denied their freedom at the last minute, forced to stay behind doors, unable to see their loved ones and kept out of sight of visitors, the collective decision had been made to protest in the only way they knew how. The time honoured tradition of British soldiers getting blind drunk and capering about in fine old style, letting the future versions of themselves deal with the consequences.

It is not recorded in the annals of the regiment of how the visitors took this sudden view of Sprs dressed only in their birthday suits, many of whom were not in the finest of physical conditions, capering around wildly gesticulating with their arms, legs, and other appendages.

Far from being punished, which turned out to be a series of mundane tasks and report back parades, I believe, it was the opinion of many within the regiment that the ring leaders of the 'Naked Phys Session' should have been put up for promotion.

There was also much discord between LIMs and Living Out Members (LOMs) whilst I lived and worked within the regiment. Generally, it came down to the fact that the officers who lived in Army housing just outside of camp, with their families, were simply loath to allow any increase in funding to make life more enjoyable for those that lived within it; cheap skates.

Meaning that it was us who had to suffer due to their meanness and this always angered the YOs that lived in the Mess. As surely the senior Captains and Majors, who lived out in the local Army housing estates, aka 'The Patch', were also years ago once young officers too and surely once shared our views on spending money on upgrading the Mess, such as paying more for better food, so that our lives would be more enjoyable?

This fiscal tightness was always point of contention between junior and senior officers. Typically, they also demanded that all official Mess parties were to be held on the weekends, which we were all compelled to attend, despite the YOs often having all made other plans weeks previously. It was always difficult and expensive for our other halves or our friends to travel up and see us in Ripon, all because the senior officers on 'The Patch' didn't want to go home to their children tipsy on a week day.

Whereas we had to suffer because of their selfish and blinkered ways, giving up the majority of our precious weekends, often being forced to sit next to, and drink with, individuals we tried to avoid during the working week, let alone the weekends.

Bastards.

We were often asked incredulously by senior officers why we didn't drink during the week, 'like they used to back in the day!', and why so few of us made it to parties on the weekends. Instead we often inundated the Adjutant with letters requesting our removal from the party guest lists so that we could escape from the barracks for the weekend and see our loved ones. Often our response to these queries as to why we didn't party all night, every night, was that we were simply so damn busy, and under constant pressure throughout the week. Typically, with handling our troops in conjunction with the constant stream of incessant and irrational demands from RHQ. Thus, we rarely drank for fear of having one beer then turning into a 3am frustration and anger fuelled binge, and thus leaving us hung-over and less than productive for the morning after.

It was also not long after I joined my regiment I realised how sacred meal times, as well as occasional informal drinks were. Meaning that be it a one hour's break for lunch, or four hours spent drinking gin and having a BBQ at the end of the day, any time we had to relax and chat were cherished by all.

Subsequently I also then learnt how much of a faux pas it is for individuals, regardless of rank, to discuss work, or 'talk shop', at these events. We all spent hours and hours each day working with each other, as such, the times when we could leave all that behind and just chat to each like normal human beings were very rare and highly valued indeed. This made it even more cringe worthy when some thrusting and priggish officer, junior or senior, would suddenly lean across the table during breakfast or over the beer pong table in the evening, and start asking after work or official policies. Upon seeing or hearing this, immediately any officer in the immediate vicinity would subtly roll their eyes and move away from the crawler and go speak to someone more sociable and interesting.

The moments afforded for officers and soldiers, to move about in a relaxed atmosphere and talk as normal human beings are especially rare, so it's crucial not become one of those frightfully dull and robot minded individuals that, when everyone is relaxing and having a good time, talks about deadlines and office politics.

Do not.

Annoyingly, senior officers also showed a disappointing tendency to become two faced in the fact that they would actively encourage mess functions and punish YOs who didn't attend Mess functions but would then also punish them if they turned out worse for wear next morning. This made many YOs, including myself, extremely bitter.

Although the YOs did have opportunities at times to strike back at the senior officers, in the form of 'Gnoming'. This took the form of a large brightly coloured garden Gnome, typically made out of clay which sat atop our bar in the Mess, as well as many other around the UK. Whenever we felt like having a party at an officer's house, and none in our own Mess, a small group of YOs would creep round to the house on the 'Patch' one night, leave the Gnome on the doorstep, knock on the door and then run away.

As soon as someone from the house opened the door and saw the Gnome, and the accompanying note, which was hanging around its neck or from its fishing rode, written by the Officers' Mess, they were honour bond to suddenly plan and organise a party for the Mess the following night.

Typically these were always carried out in good form, and the ingenuity of the husband and wife who suddenly found themselves obliged to organise a party for half a dozen YOs within twenty four hours was fantastic; parties were often themed and typically upon arriving at the house for the party, weighed down with bottles and gifts for the house, the visiting YOs would have to complete a challenge before gaining entrance into the party.

Also, the youngest YO, which was once me, would have roughly one hour, upon arriving in the house, to find the Gnome, which the hosting couple would have hidden somewhere in their house or in the garden. If it was not found in time, thankfully I found my Gnome hidden in the dog food bin, the Officers' Mess would then be obliged to host their own party at short notice. The Gnome would have to be found whilst concurrently playing all manner of drinking games, such as Beer Pong or Laser Obstacle Course, and the pressure was on for it was common knowledge that the hosting family would have used all their collective genius to hide the idol.

Infamously, these Gnoming parties are sometimes aimed at the grouchiest and surliest senior officers, whom the collective YOs would bait like so many eager young hounds dancing around a grizzled and ill-tempered old bear. Their reactions to finding the Officers' Mess Gnome on their doorstep were sometimes priceless. One particular individual who was Gnomed, an OC who was known to be particularly surly, came up with a hilarious defence against the horde of energetic and boisterous YOs who were suddenly now coming to his house, his cave, the following evening. When the YOs from the Mess turned up outside his house the next night, at the time appointed on the note they had written and left around the neck of the Gnome, they found the house locked up and lights off.

What they did find however, was that outside in the garden, were two sofas, a couple of cases of beer, half a dozen bags of hot Indian and Chinese takeaway and that a television had been pressed screen first up against the nearest window, with a note pinned to the front door:

'You bastards aren't getting into my house; drink and eat your fill, then bugger off.'

By all accounts, the YOs then went on to have an absolutely smashing party in the front garden of the OC's house, clearing up all their mess before they left and leaving the OC and his family to slumber in peace; and the OC no doubt finally breathing a secret sigh of relief at hearing the welcome news that the YOs eventually retire into the night.

Alas, despite the fact that the boarding school attitude of high jinks, drinks and tricks still prevails strongly within the various Officers' Mess's in the Army, there are also many parts and aspects of the Mess which have changed not for the better.

The general attitude of the Officers' Mess within the British Army these days is very much that although it is indeed a place to eat, sleep, relax and have fun during the week, when time allows, typically as soon as work permits, everyone leaves the barracks as early as possible on the Friday and doesn't come back till late on the Sunday evening.

This is very different to what regimental life is like in overseas barracks, such as those in Germany, as due to the distance between the personnel of the regiment and their families, usually back in the UK, most stay in the Mess on the weekends and much more of 'lived in feel' exists within the Mess. Typically it is only those who are having someone visit them at the Mess, or are working through the weekend, or a simply too hung-over to anything productive, are the ones who stay in the Mess over the weekend in a UK barracks.

Additionally, sadly, the food that was served within the Mess was simply awful; this problem arising from the 'Pay as You Dine' (PAYD) system. The curse of the 21st century British military.

Up until a few years ago, all officers and soldiers within a regiment or battalion would pay a set amount each month towards their feeding by their military chefs; this meant that the chefs had a significant budget to work with during the month and at the end, they often had a large amount left over which could either be used to create extravagant and delicious meals or save up for the next Mess function.

But, sadly, this has now changed and officers and soldiers, for the most part, now pay individually for each meal and as a result, each bean, drop of gravy and leaf of lettuce is weighed up by the PAYD civilian chefs and their accountants so as to ensure the maximum possible profit for the catering company employed by the unit.

The combination of poor quality food, in often very small amounts, along with the demise of the truly beloved military chefs, is perhaps one of the biggest flaws or conceptions in the formation of Army 2020.

Unlike most of their modern day civilian counterparts, military chefs actually care about the quality of the food they produce and they used to have a good budget to utilise for the benefit of their clientele. Nowadays the budget for the chefs is much smaller, the chefs are also mostly civilian chefs of an inferior standard to their military counterparts, and as such, the quality of food is usually dire. There are indeed still some excellent dining facilities that still exist within some units in UK, the chefs at the Land Warfare Centre and at 1 RSME Regiment being worthy of particular note, and there are even a few regiments which do not have PAYD yet, but I daren't say where they are just in case the catering contractors find them.

It can be said that within Army 2020 it is just as hard to find a bad military chef, when you are fortunate enough to find one in the first place, as it is to find a good civilian chef.

Meaning though they do exist they seem to be few and far between.

Initially when the PAYD system and its civilian chefs arrived within some UK barracks, it was very enjoyable. But, as soon as the probation period was over and it was agreed by the various military HQs that the PAYD contract would be pushed out to all other military units, the standard of food dropped considerably. This phenomenon was perhaps best explained to me whilst I was on a language course at Shrivenham Defence Academy, which thankfully generally always has a good standard of rations served up, and I got chatting to a chap who'd seen PAYD first arrive and its subsequent decline in popularity amongst all ranks.

'It's as if you were starting to date someone and they were just perfect; did anything that you wanted, couldn't do enough for you, all they were concerned about was making you happy and as such you rightly thought they were the best thing since sliced bread. But, as soon as you were committed to them, updated your online profile and told your friends, they suddenly became total drags and would only offer up the bare minimum and would raise pure hell if you queried them about it. And you couldn't leave them as all hell would break loose and it would no doubt become extraordinarily expensive and complicated to get rid of them.'

PAYD is excellent example of how in order to save money, the British military had bought into a contract, thinking it was initially on to a good thing but quickly realised that what they had now bought into was much worse than anything they'd had before; as well as costing much more in the long run. It is impossible for an Army to have fit and healthy soldiers if you do not provide them with sufficient nutritional substances.

I, as well as most of the officers and soldiers I would come to know, spent significant parts of our incomes on providing ourselves with sufficient food whilst living in the Mess in order to maintain a healthy and nutritional diet, as what was provided by the PAYD chefs was usually of inferior quality and quantity.

The scrimping and bean counting attitude of the various companies that have been hired by the military to provide the meals are always personified whenever soldiers or officers deploy out of the gate and require food from the Mess for their lunch. These always come in the form of packed lunches, known by one and all in the British Army as 'Horror Bags'. A brown paper bag containing a stale and feeble sandwich, a packet of crisps, withered fruit and a bottle of water. How on earth is that meant to be a filling and nutritious meal?

After my time at RMAS, I don't think I ever ate a 'Horror Bag' ever again as not only do they typically taste vile and are not filling at all, but they are also typically very unhealthy. This, aside from issues with pay and the frustrating workload and directions from HQs, are the most spoken about gripes in the British Army, by both officers and soldiers.

Armies have always marched on their stomachs, and always will, but sadly it is clear that the British military is not able to march far on what is provided to them by PAYD.

All of these issues are commonly known and frequently cynically laughed about by those serving within the military. From the poor quality of food, nonsensical priorities of higher command and the numerous ways in which we are limited and restrained by red tape and contractual obligations to civilian companies.

Months into my service within 21, whilst drinking in the Mess one evening, a senior officer spontaneously vented in one phrase all of our pent up frustrations and exasperations at the numerous ways in which the military makes life needlessly difficult for itself:

'Royal Engineers of 2020, we could do it, but it'll probably be crap!'

This laughingly summed up our attitude towards how difficult, time consuming and expensive it often is for us to not only train effectively for future conflicts and interventions, but also how difficult it is for military personnel to create, fix or build the simplest thing for themselves, especially annoying coming from the Royal Engineer's point of view. Meaning that any task however small, such as, say, the construction of some smoking shelters within the barracks, soon becomes overly complicated and an absolute nightmare for the officers and Sprs involved with it.

In the end, in this particular case, the smoking shelters within the regiment were indeed built but in the end, due to a technical oversight, the roofs leaked when it rained as the holes had been drilled into the wrong parts of the corrugated material.

Personnel can't even do repairs on their own military houses on 'The Patch' or play areas for their children as the various contracts the host units have signed up to won't allow anyone, except the assigned expensive private contractors, to touch them. Meaning that instead the repairs are done by expensive sub-contractors which aside from taking far longer are done to a typically poor standard.

A far cry from the days when the Army could, and would, 'look after its own'.

A lot of this stems, in many soldiers' and officers' opinions as well as my own, from when the British military lost 'Crown Exemption'. Meaning that it was no longer able to conduct training and activities within its own set of rules and regulations. This means that instead of being allowed to be able to conduct its own affairs and train its personnel as best as possible to their own desired standards and regulations for future conflicts, the British military now has to run itself like any other civilian company. Much to the chagrin of all ranks.

The only issue being that it's not a civilian company, it's the British Military.

It's involved in the most dangerous business of all, and must push its personnel as much as possible and thus best prepare them for life threatening situations, if only Whitehall would realise this.

But aside from the irregularities of contractual obligations and losing 'Crown Exemption', due to the high tempo of regimental life, which we will all expected but could never truly prepare for, despite the months and months of previous training, I also quickly gained some very rewarding insights as to how best command my troop.

One of the trickiest things to manage when talking with soldiers, especially when there is a touchy subject involved, is actually getting the soldier to feel confident enough to open up. With some individuals, regardless of rank or time spent in the military, this might be almost instantaneous or could only come about after many weeks of working with them.

An excellent but less conventional technique I found for making it easier for soldiers to come to the office was actually to have a dog present, although one must be aware that some soldiers do not like canines. Meaning that upon knocking upon the open door and seeing the troop commander or the troop SSgt look up from their mound of paperwork from behind their desk, most soldiers are well within their rights to be slightly nervous.

But having a Spaniel or Labrador, for instance, relaxing and farting quietly in a corner of the office whilst chewing happily on a toy, which would then jovially head over to snuffle at the feet of the soldier in the doorway, often has a remarkable effect of putting the individual at ease. Unless they have a fear of dogs, that is.

No one, simply no one, likes going to their boss's office, even if they are about to be rewarded for some particularly good work that they may have done, as there is always something akin to the feeling of being told to the go the Headmaster's Office. Thus aside from always leaving the door open, except when it had to closed when a sensitive topic was being discussed, I found that I when I had a soldier come to my office to discuss something, I would often have to discuss a range of completely different topics before the individual concerned felt confident enough to broach the key topic.

Not unlike a doctor who has had a patient come to their office, clearly having a matter that needs urgent discussion, but must ask about all and sundry before the patient finally opens up.

The most hilarious, and memorable, case of this 'Oh, and just one more thing, sir....' approach by many visitors to the troop office, happened not to me but to a brother officer and it highlighted the way in which often, a soldier just needs to talk to someone about what is concerning or worrying them. The very opening of the discussion turning out to be the very tonic the soldier requires.

An officer is busily writing away at his desk on a Monday morning, a heap of paperwork and inbox full of emails staring him in the face, when suddenly he hears a knock at the door and looks up.

'Ah, good morning Spr X, what can I do for you?'

'Good morning sir, I was just wondering if I could talk to you about something?'

'Of course, please come in and have a seat. Close the door. Now what's up?'

Over the next ten minutes or so, the Spr and Troopy make polite conversation in the quiet seclusion of the office, with the Troopy asking genially after the state and health of the Spr's family, friends, as well as how he's finding life in regiment at the moment.

After a while the conversation slows down, with nothing of consequence being spoken of yet, and it becomes clear to Spr X that now is the time to talk about the issue he has, but the Troopy realises that the Spr may need a little prompting still.

'Is there anything else that you'd like to chat about Spr X?

'Well sir, there was one thing....'

'Do go on, I'm all ears.'

'Well, I've always thought that I might actually fancy men.'

'Oh right. Well that's absolutely fine....'

'I know that sir, so over the weekend, I spoke with a mate and he let me shag him.'

'Right....'

'I didn't really enjoy it be honest.'

'Right....'

'And then I let him shag me.'

'Right....'

'I didn't really enjoy that either to be honest.'

'Right....'

Spr X pauses for a second, clearing gathering thoughts and then smiles suddenly.

'Actually, I don't think I fancy men after all to be honest boss, thanks for the chat.'

Spr X then stands up, salutes and then smartly walks out of the office.

The Troopy stares bemused at the door, smiles at the peculiarity of Monday mornings, and Sprs in general, and then returns to his work.

Aside from the humorous incidents and stories which often present themselves in the troop office on Monday mornings, the seriousness of recognising when an individual, regardless of rank or age, has an issue which they need to discuss with someone cannot be overstated. I often found that from noticing that a Spr had something on their mind, I would quickly arrange a private chat with them, this often being the two of us in the privacy of the conference room fortified with a couple of brews, and then simply encourage them to talk. Some persons would come out straight away and say what was bothering them, others would require a good few minutes of polite and friendly aimless chatter before then shyly indicating what the issue or problem was.

A lot of the time I found that aside from wanting to be told a solution, individuals often just desperately wanted to talk to someone about their problem, nothing more, the sheer relief of 'getting it off their chest' was enough and very little else was needed. Too often talks such as these have been ruined by the other person trying to come up with a solution and imposing on the individual concerned. An easy trap to fall into. Regularly I would have to remind myself that the Spr I was talking to didn't necessarily want me to tell them what I thought the solution was, they just wanted someone to talk to.

Whenever one of my Sprs would politely knock on my door, or come up to me whilst I was walking around barracks, and ask for 'a quick chat', I would drop everything that I was doing and go for a brew with them; always careful to show the individual that I was listening, that I was taking on what they were saying and carefully summarising what appeared to be the issue at hand.

Helping someone to help think a problem through, often demonstrating commonality to them by mentioning how I'd come across a similar problem or situation in the past, and being careful not to express my own views whilst slowly establishing the facts and by letting them find a solution, with some careful steering by myself when needed were perhaps the best ways to not only to help solve the problem, but also to make the individual concerned feel not only comfortable but glad they spoke to me about their problem and concerns.

The amount of times I, as well as simply every other NCO and officer that I knew, would have a soldier, or officer, to be honest, come into their office and spin a yarn of such hilarity, outrageousness and illegality that we'd often be torn between speechlessness, and side splitting laughter.

Usually resulting in the following statement once the office door had been swiftly closed:

'Cpl, you definitely shouldn't be telling this to people, most of all me. But on that note, for God's sake please keep talking!'

It must be said that having worked with the British Army and a full range of its personnel, I can say that I never come across another organisation that is more accepting of the different personalities, preferences, religions and life style choices of the individuals that make up its workforce. I have had the pleasure of working with soldiers and officers who have been straight, homosexual, bisexual, and transgender, to name but a few, and not once has their sexual, or even religious, orientation had any form of negative impact upon them.

In fact the Army, and the British military as a whole, goes out of its way, through its many publications and online forums, to promote its acceptance of all personnel, regardless of their religion or sexual preference. Helped in no small way the fact that British soldiers are still the delightfully crazy, eccentric and erratic breed they always have been.

I myself have been fortunate enough to work with personnel within the Army who come from a range of different nationalities, countries and cultures from across the globe; British, Dutch, Italian, Irish, Ukrainian, Indian, Ghanaian, South African, Fijian, Chinese, Jamaican. Nepalese, Danish, and more.

The different countries, backgrounds and cultures that soldiers and officers in the British military come from not only mean that often there is a wide and fantastic variety of individuals throughout its different units, but they are also often a number of solutions and ways of working out a problem on offer that are not often always entirely conventional, but are still as effective at solving said problem, as well as they are at creating greater unity between ranks.

For example, most units across the Army have strong contingents of Fijian soldiers within them, a truly great nation, and they bring their strong sense of tribalism and loyalty with them. After spending considerable time within my regiment, I was to learn how the close ties that exist between Fijian soldiers, as well as their tribal hierarchy and loyalty, can be, and are, used to solve any issues or problems that may arise. Especially if there is a falling out between soldiers, Fijian or otherwise.

One day whilst in my office I learnt that an altercation had taken place the night before between two British and Fijian Sprs, escalated due to the fact that alcohol had been consumed and blows had been exchanged. Now bearing in mind the Army's hypocritical attitude towards brawling, in that too often, in my view, scrapping between soldiers is blown out of all proportion and sends out the wrong message to all ranks, the individuals who had seen the incident take place became concerned that RHQ would be made aware and the two combatants would become embroiled in a lengthy and potentially career damaging disciplinary hearing.

'I'm looking for a criminal....'

'Get your own! It took me years to get this lot.'

So, as a Fijian had been involved in the fight, and he was the one in wrong, the Regimental 'Head Fijian' was called for by the Sprs who had witnessed the brawl. The reason being that each unit in the British Army has its own senior tribal Fijian member, often a member of the tribal monarchy back in Fiji, and who is often used to unofficially oversee the discipline of the other Fijians present within the unit.

A few minutes later, bearing in mind this took place late at night, midweek, the 'Head Fijian', who shall remain nameless, arrived upon the scene, a four man room, which was in ruins as a result of the tussling that had been place between the two large, and drunk, Sprs. After hearing from the assembled witnesses what had taken place, the Fijian solemnly considered the facts, found the drunken Fijian Spr to have been at fault and then ambled off to find him.

Mere minutes later, the rather bruised British Spr was sat on his bed, nursing his wounds when all of a sudden, the Fijian Spr, less than fifteen minutes ago his brawling partner, loomed in his doorway and practically threw himself at his feet, tears in his eyes, begging to be forgiven and for peace to be restored between the two of them.

An entirely nonconventional solution to the problem I agree, and one which relied heavily on discretion, respect and understanding, but one that worked perfectly and to the satisfaction of all concerned. Meaning that everyone within the troop knew that when a problem arose, I would be content to allow it to be solved in the correct way, not just merely the official way.

I quickly came to realise, whilst serving within 21, the highly tuned sense of social justice that most officers and soldiers have. Whilst the humour of the British serviceman or woman is still as dark, twisted and deviant as it has always been, never did I see it turn into any form of bullying or persecution. In fact, I have also never before seen such an effective and genuine support network exist between groups of such diverse and independent individuals.

Meaning that although each and every soldier and officer I knew had a typically coarse and blunt sense of humour who would make ribald comments about all and sundry if the opportunity arose, they would also draw together and close ranks in support of a colleague that needed them. It would be unprompted and in an instant.

Often have I seen soldiers and officers, often the youngest and most inexperienced in their groups, have perhaps the most severe and heart rending of tragedies happen to them or their loved ones, and yet somehow they manage to deal with it so effectively and professionally, leaving me absolutely astounded as to their fortitude and professionalism.

Each and every time it is discovered that an individual, or their family, was hurting in some way, every effort would be made by that individual's section, troop, squadron, or even regiment, to provide whatever help they could.

Be it an issue involving a sick family member, severe financial issues or a whole range of complex and intertwined problems, I always saw the group draw around the individual concerned and aside from shielding them as much as required, they would also offer whatever help and assistance was available.

Although absolutely no one is safe from some form of ridicule or jovial mockery in the workplace, and rightly so, it was always tailored to the individual and current situation. This was epitomised to me when I attended my first regimental social function.

I was in the process of creating the final guest list for the party and I couldn't understand why a certain individual's name wasn't coming up on the nominal role, even though I knew they were attending, but after speaking with one of my NCOs, I was informed that the individual concerned assumed a different name on the weekends. When I looked at him quizzically from behind my desk, the Cpl informed me, with a huge grin on his face, that the individual concerned dressed up as a woman on the weekends and even went as far as taking on another name. When I asked what his wife thought of it, I was informed that not only had his wife known of the soldier's habit long before they were married, she now even helped pick out clothes and shoes for him whilst shopping.

Having not met the individual concerned before, I now very intrigued as to what form the evening would take, bearing in mind the military sense of humour's ability to make fun out of the slightest thing and how the individual would fare socially.

The evening soon arrived and after an hour or so, the tables littered with cans of beer and the karaoke in full flow, I spotted the cross-dressing soldier.

A short hairy man, with a bulging belly, a five o'clock shadow spread across his chin, was walking around the hall chatting happily with all ranks, clearly something of a local celebrity. This might have been helped by the fact that he was wearing a knee length bright purple sequin dress, stretched tightly across his belly and hairy legs, accompanied with stiletto high heels, a can of lager in each hand and wearing a truly monstrous blonde wig. Best of all, he had volunteered to speak in front of the assembled regiment and give the breakdown of the evening's events. As he tottered across the cleared dance floor, the disco music muted for a few minutes, the hall erupted in wolf whistles and cat calls and true to form; the soldier winked and blew kisses back to his assembled fans.

It was certainly an evening, and lesson in equality and inclusion, that I won't forget in a hurry. It also most definitely wasn't a topic covered on the military Equality and Inclusion course that I volunteered for a few months later.

As a matter of fact, I believe the British Army is ranked as one of the top ten organisations for acceptance and equality in the Stonewall organisation, a group dedicated to promoting equality and diversity within the workplace. Although many of the comments and remarks, as well as pranks, that are made and carried out within the British military might turn a civilian HR representative's hair white, the British Armed forces, in my opinion, now has perhaps the most adaptive and effective acceptance policy within existence.

My view of it is that in the British Army, it does not matter to anyone who an individual goes to bed with, who they pray to, or even what they eat, but as long as they do their job well, can give and take a joke and are a team player, they'll be accepted by all and sundry.

We once had, at great cost, a drama troupe of actors come to the regiment, 'all ranks above Cpls must attend!', who played the role of a range of different soldiers and officers who proceeded to get themselves into various supposed mishaps through various faults such as racism, sexism, and alcohol. After they had finished their play, around half an hour, they then made the mistake of asking the assembled audience a few questions on what they had just witnessed. Needless to say the resulting replies caught them all off guard and resulted in most of the personnel in the room laughing quietly behind their notebooks.

'Who has ever felt they have been persecuted due to their physical makeup?'

A Corporal, who stands well over 6ft and looked like he could win in a fight against a building, puts his hand up in the air.

'Yes, I have.'

'Oh really? Do explain.'

'Well, recntly I had to have a vasectomy and now all the lads say I should get an extra minute on my PFA run time as they think I should now be classed as girl. What do you say to that?'

The room subsequently erupted in laughter.

Later on, after another scenario had been acted out before us, the leader of the troupe posed the assembled ranks another question:

'As you've seen what can happen when someone is called a bad name, and how it can make them feel, what are your thoughts on insults when addressing someone?'

A burly Commando trained Sergeant with a strong Northern Irish brogue replied from the back:

'Today I called one of my guys a 'Wet Pants' because he was being mince and not doing his job properly, what is your take on that?'

'Well, if you called me that, I'd feel persecuted, a bit hurt and probably wouldn't feel confident enough in talking or working with you. What do you think that would make me?

'Aye…, that would indeed make you a Wet Pants.'

The room subsequently erupted in laughter again. Money well spent there, Army 2020; well spent!

Within the British military there is wide spread annoyance at being taught leadership approaches and attitudes that should be carried out in the workplace, despite the fact that the military has already been practising them for years. Well before some civilian office guru had put catchy names to them. From respect and tolerance in the workplace, to guarding against bullying or introducing flexitime, all of these have existed within the military well before the civilian workplace took them on.

Typically these incidences of labelling long standing practises with new titles would come about as some senior officer was angling for a good comment on their annual report, or some rabid doctrine had been pushed out by Whitehall, and then all of a sudden, all junior commanders within regiment would be trooped sullenly out of their offices and would be made to sit and then taught subjects or command styles they already knew and had used.

I believe that never have I seen bullying or intolerance within my time within the military as whenever an individual is found to be, say racist or homophobic, the retribution, usually carried out by their peers, is swift and fierce. The reason being that within any group that relies on effective teamwork and comradeship, none more so than the military, everyone is aware that although a robust sense of humour and thick skin is essential, anything that threatens the cohesion or effectiveness of the group is not tolerated and is quickly removed.

That is not to say that such persecutions did not exist in the British military in the past, as they did, such as the abuse that took place in Camp Bread Basket, or still go on in some units, as they sadly do. But what is excellent about British military personnel is that in a good unit, they quickly learn if something is having a negative impact on the team or individual, and are often even quicker to address the problem.

One leadership aspect, or policy, that in my opinion, should be introduced into the British Army, the exact execution of it depending on the culture within each separate sub unit, is '360 degree reporting'. Where a subject gets their subsequent performance evaluated by not only their higher chain of command, but also by their subordinates.

Too often have I seen officers and NCOs who have led their soldiers perfectly and developed an outstanding and effective working relationship with them, receive negative reports from their senior commanders as they have a warped view of the individual concerned and haven't thought to ask the opinion of the soldiers whom the individual commands. Whilst officers and NCOs who have turned out to be truly dreadful commanders, almost despised by their subordinates, receive excellent reports from their chain of command as they, again through not checking the honest opinion of the personnel they are in charge of, have a mistaken opinion of the commander in question.

Very frustrating.

Additionally, when an issue arises or simply needs addressing, the importance of 'going for a brew' with someone cannot be overestimated. As it is a time honoured approach that combines British military personnel's seemingly limitless appetite for hot drinks and their desire to solve a problem quickly and effectively. Meaning that the individuals concerned, regardless of rank, can go off and, over a cup of tea or coffee, discuss and resolve the issue at hand.

It may sound simple, or perhaps needlessly overstating an obvious approach, but too often this is not used within the Army nowadays. Often an issue has arisen which could have been easily solved 'within house' but instead has been needlessly complicated, made public and prolonged, exasperating and annoying all concerned.

'Within house', a common phrase meaning keeping an issue behind closed doors within the troop, or any group, regardless of size. Being able to keep a handle on an issue and involve as few people as possible is essential to not only quickly solving issues and demonstrating to individuals that they can raise an issue with you without fearing that you'll run straight to your chain of command and broadcast their personal problem, but also does wonders for protecting the image and reputation of the your soldiers. As, of course, protecting your troop's or platoon's, image and reputation within the regiment, as well as doing as much as you can to promote it, is, or at least should be, every officer's priority.

Annoyingly, there will be a number of times where commanders, both officers and soldiers, feel let down by their subordinates. Sometimes deliberately and other times accidentally. Times such as this are where the skill and leadership of the commander involved comes to the fore, where they really earn their pay. The reason being that it is down to the commander to decide on what action to take in regards to the offending individual, and this knowledge comes from getting to know and understand their soldiers.

A good commander, be they a junior troop commander or weary Staff Sergeant, will know what punishment is appropriate to the individual concerned. Be that a softly spoken reprimand expressing disappointment in the soldier, taking away the individual's weekend through additional duties or turning red in the face and giving them the loudest and angriest verbal bollocking they have ever had in their life. But nothing is worse than awarding the wrong form of punishment. From crushing a newly joined soldier, thus taking away his fledgling confidence and trust in his leaders, to letting the troop scallywag get away for the umpteenth time with nothing but a slap on the wrist and thus sending the wrong message to the rest of the soldiers within the troop.

I also found it good practise, whether I was going to give a slight reprimand or hand out heavy punishment to an individual, that before I launched into my tirade, or not, as the case sometimes was, was to ask the soldier if 'there was anything going on that I should be made aware of?'.

Meaning that I wanted to know, and that I'd be relying on the soldier's good graces and trust in me, if there was anything happening, say at home or back in the accommodation block, that had been having an adverse effect on his performance in work. If the answer was a 'yes', I'd then look into what was happening and how it might be resolved, if a resolution was needed. Whereas if the answer was a 'no', I knew that I could go straight into the bollocking without fear of the soldier suddenly bursting into tears and admitting that he was being bullied or that he was going through a divorce with his wife.

When giving someone a telling off, especially if it is a severe one, try and plan what is going to be said beforehand. Meaning that it is very important, if it is indeed possible, to have a discussion with an NCO, ideally their Sgt or SSgt, and determine what is going to be said, by whom and in what order. This is so that the bollocking is then given in the swiftest, most efficient, logical and professional manner. There are very few things more embarrassing or awkward than a poorly executed verbal dressing down.

Tearing someone a new one, or talking to them in quiet but cutting tones, is never easy or enjoyable, and never should it be, but if it is required, a leader, especially an officer, should always remember that is it part of their job.

Their soldiers don't want a friend, they want, and need, a leader. It is lonely at the top, and that is the way it will always be, although there is always confidence to be gained from knowing that what is about to be done, or said, is the right course of action.

Or, in the immortal words of the intrepid explorer Ernst Shackleton:

'Loneliness is the penalty of leadership, but the man who has to make the decisions is assisted greatly if he feels that there is no uncertainty in the minds of those who follow him, and that his orders will be carried out confidently and in expectation of success.'

It is often embarrassing to see junior officers, especially green troop commanders, attempt to copy their NCOs and shout and yell at their soldiers. At times like this often the individual concerned simply 'switches off' and secretly smirks at the YO who is trying to imitate a NCO.

Unless a serious punishment and verbal debriefing is required, typically it is the NCO's, in extremis the troop SSgt, who turns red in the face and makes the soldier feel like dust beneath their chariot wheels. Not the troop commander. As one of my Sgts once said to me:

'Troopy, why do you bark yourself when you have your own dog?'

A good officer can punish a subordinate, soldier or officer, without ever raising their voice or swearing. The reason being that when an incident arises where the officer must shout and swear, everybody stops and listens.

This is especially important if the individuals concerned are deployed out into a dangerous area or situation and instance obedience means the difference between life and death to all concerned. Something akin to hearing one's parents swear for the first time.

I would say that perhaps the most important thing for any junior commander to get right is to get the basics right. Meaning that you simply must fully know and understand your soldiers.

Meaning that a commander must be able to talk with their subordinates in a way that makes them realise that their leader knows them, understands them and has a genuine interest in them. From knowing of their family and their hobbies, to their own personal beliefs and aspirations. This is especially important in the military where individuals can easily be made to feel unappreciated, like just another name and set of numbers in their commander's nominal role. The smallest gesture and effort by their chain of command can swiftly change this belief.

This approach can be started off best by simply being able to, when standing before them on the parade square, walking past them in the corridor or squatting underneath their basha from the wind and rain in a dark woodblock, address them by name and ask them a few questions on topics unique to the individual. Family, hobbies or their own particular career are usually the most effective. Care must be taken in ensuring that the soldier does not feel like they are getting asked bland or 'out of the box' questions, else they will shut off and turn into automatons.

If this is done correctly and soldiers feel like their officer has a genuine interest in their welfare and has gone out of their way to get to know them, they will then move heaven and earth for that officer, as they feel confident that their officer will do the same for them. When this is achieved, it is like no other experience I have ever come across and is not one that can be forgotten.

You get the best from others not by lighting a fire beneath them, but by building a fire within.

I would say that asides from this approach working extraordinarily well for me, as I was treating, or at least trying to treat, soldiers the way I would expect to be treated by my chain of command, it is not anything new and commanders of all ranks would do well to examine history's leaders, from Joan of Arc, Garibaldi to Michael Collins, to see what people can do when properly led. As well as what they will, or won't do, when improperly led.

What was also a lengthy learning process for me during my time at 21, and in other units afterwards, was to learn that it is unwise to expect all one's subordinates to excel at the same things or develop equally in the same environment. It is all too easy at times for commanders, young and old, to dismiss an individual due to a poor performance in one area and not actually realise that although the person, or persons, concerned may not have performed well in a certain aspect or test, it is extremely likely that they may excel in something else, or via another way.

As such, it is always down the commander to realise where their subordinates' areas of expertise lie, bearing in mind they may be varied in the extreme, and then to allow the individuals to progress in their given fields as much as possible. As Albert Einstein once said:

'Everybody is a genius. But if you judge a fish by its ability to climb a tree, it will live its whole life believing that it is stupid.'

PT sessions with my soldiers, be it a rapid 8 mile jaunt with 30 kilograms packed into a bergen, a heart rending sprint session or an hour long circuit in the regimental gym, were perhaps one of the quickest ways for me to start earning my troops' respect and proving that I was tough enough to lead them.

The military will always be an alpha male organisation and soldiers will, accordingly, follow a leader who they feel is tough enough to command them and is worthy of their respect. Conversely, it is also the quickest way for young commanders to instantly lose respect of their soldiers, if they cannot keep up with them.

An officer should always be first, be the fastest, the strongest and the most motivated, but without being overbearing. If an officer, especially a YO, finds themselves not being able to keep themselves with the fittest of their soldiers, whilst being able to chat comfortably or easily verbally encouraging the weaker members of the group, then significant extra work is required in order for that officer to develop as an effective leader of soldiers.

The actual place of the officer within PT lessons is always tricky in my experience. Should the commander be up with front runners, showing that they can run as fast as them whilst still being able to chat easily and confidently or beat the rear, encouraging those at the back, as the group is only as fast as slowest man?

I believe it is a balanced mix of the two. Meaning that you can't be seen as an arrogant prig who forgets everyone except his fittest blokes, but also not the one who covers up their own lack of fitness by running with the slowest in the group. In short, a commander must be able to move between all members of their unit whilst on PT, encouraging one and all, whilst alienating no one.

Aside from proving one's fitness and fledgling command ability, good communication between all ranks within the troop, especially the Troop management, is essential. The most common form of effective and quick communication between individuals, especially within the troop during my time as its commander, was the distribution of mobile phone numbers and having shared chat nets. Although it may sound crass or perhaps overstepping the line into familiarity, having soldiers feeling comfortable enough to contact you directly, especially if a serious incident suddenly arises, does wonders for quickly solving issues and keeping the matter 'within house.'

Although commanders must be aware of the importance or significance of what they write in messages to their soldiers, as not only could a flippant comment come back to bite a naive commander, as what is written in a text can be, and is, taken as a direct order, it could also become the source of ridicule amongst a commander's soldiers.

Communication within the regiment between different troops, squadrons and departments is also a very tricky beast and often it takes individuals a long while upon first arriving within their unit to find out what is the most effective way of communication with the other members of the regiment. Due to the military's utter reliance on computers, YOs have it drilled into them throughout their training and first few months in their unit that they should avoid emails at all costs and simply talk with people. It sounds simple enough but one must factor in a number of issues which get in the way of this approach. Such as the distance between individuals on camp and after walking to their office, only finding that they are not there and no one knows when they'll be back. Or eventually finding said person and after chatting with them, the person then, because they have so much else on their place, forgetting what you told them and thus the work doesn't get completed as there is no email for them to refer back to.

The solution, I found, was to fire off an email to the person or department in question and then walk over to them and discuss the email I had just sent them; following the audit trail. This way I was forcibly engaging with the individual concerned to recognise the email whilst still having that vital face to face interaction key to any work between individuals.

Ensuring that soldiers' good work, be that doing well during an OC's vehicle inspection, passing a trade test or cutting their teeth during a particularly savage troop level attack, is recognised and highlighted by their commander, should also always be carried out. For it reinforces success.

Although no one in the military does their work purely for the sake of recognition, and if they do they are quickly recognised and dealt with accordingly, it is important that commanders do not fall into the classic trap of the British military and minimise good efforts done by their subordinates. All personnel, from any workforce, like to know that their chain of command realises when they have worked hard and rewards or commends them appropriately. If nothing else, it makes them want to work with them further in the future.

Many YOs seem to feel, whilst going through their training, that the best way to go about earning the trust, confidence and respect of their soldiers is by loud and dominating statements and gestures or acts, whereas in reality this is actually earned by dozens of little acts each day. It is in fact the small acts, not the big ones, that are usually the most effective and simple way of proving to soldiers that their commander has their best interests at heart.

From getting a tired and disillusioned Corporal out of the Guard shift, to putting the newest Spr onto a ski course despite the fact that he has never skied before, who then goes on to become the best skier in the regiment, to finally getting two NCOs onto P Company or just simply letting some of the blokes off work an hour earlier than usual as there is no work left for them to do. The various ways in which a commander can show a genuine, and balanced, care for their subordinates are many indeed.

Overall, despite my difficulties with getting to grips with the paper trail and attitude of my chain of command, I did love my time within 21 Engineer Regiment. For although I had a chequered time with dealing with the vast amounts of reports and admin that came my way, as well as adapting to RHQ and their incessant trawls and demands, I simply loved working with my soldiers and the chances I had to get away with them.

Working with military personnel, especially my own soldiers, turned out to be one of the most enjoyable and rewarding experiences I was ever to have.

Looking back over my time as Support troop commander, 7 Headquarters and Support Squadron, 21 Engineer Regiment, I realise how fortunate I was. In that I can honestly say that I had plenty of opportunities to practise my command of soldiers whilst deployed in the field. From leading small groups of men on bizarre trawls such as taking on the role of hunter forces for SF personnel in the wilds of the West Country, to commanding dozens of men and vast fleets of vehicles whilst enabling entire regiments and BGs to advance across the plain. The opportunities I had to practise my own command style and lead in the field, both as infantry and as engineers, were many and varied in the extreme.

I was also not just restricted to standard conventional military field exercises in my attempts to do exciting and interesting things with the regiment. From such activities as skiing, boxing, sailing and shooting, it seemed that as long as I could find the time and the soldiers, I could almost do anything I wished. As such, I quickly realised that as I thoroughly enjoyed being away from my regiment as much as possible and having the opportunity to command my soldiers, without any outside interference, every officers' dream, it became clear that it was best for me, as well as my chain of command, if I was out of the office as much as possible.

Such as planning section attack lanes that ran over five kilometres in the rough rolling hills of Sennybridge and marshalling my sections through each serial, where I watched with great enjoyment as each JNCO demonstrated his ability in managing his section and successfully attacking an enemy. Being able to look upon a group of eight soldiers work their way through the initial bursts of enemy fire, taking cover in the thick and dank ferns and then find a route around via the dead ground to a position where they could assault the enemy, usually via a bitingly cold stream or utterly filthy debris ridden trench. Then, under the effective and dominant control of the section commander, assault and clear the enemy position in a fury of thrown grenades, bursts of machine gun fire and harsh commands. Only to then regroup after the savagery had passed, bodies and equipment soaked with mud and sweat, their breaths hanging damp in the air, helmets strewn with bracken and sloping over foreheads, cigarettes hanging from rueful smiles, and then prepare to move off and continue their advance.

To seeing my troop of Sprs in single file, with me just behind the front man, stealing quietly through the early morning mist of a Norfolk wood, like a group of predators on the hunt, weapons held ready, each and every one of them poised to dash forward in an instance to attack the enemy if ordered. Having had to navigate through countless woodblocks and waving fields of wheat, nothing guiding us through the darkness except for the occasionally referred to map and compass, hurriedly glanced at under the soft red glow of a cupped torch, mile after weary mile in complete silence. Until we then chance up on the unsuspecting enemy, huddled in their defensive positions, lone sentries; poorly concealed glows of cigarettes marking some of their positions.

Then as per their troop orders, given hours ago, without a word or murmur, the different sections silently splitting up along their different avenues of march under the command of their Cpls, forming up in their various positions, ready to pour suppressing fire onto the enemy, or leap out of a drainage ditch, mere yards away from their targets, and attack. Bodies squirming rapidly on the ground as a section snakes its way through an overgrown field, masked by the tall wet grass, getting closer and closer to their designated fire support position. Individual soldiers flitting between the trees, like dark menacing spectres, feet softly padding between the twigs and branches scattered on the ground lying in wait to break the stillness of the morning with a sudden 'snap!' caused by a careless footfall.

Gazing out from my perch hidden in a thick patch of bushes, overlooking the entire scene, waiting for the drama of battle to unfold and disrupt the quiet of the morning with the sounds of fighting. Then nodding at my signaller who is looking up at me, a flare held carefully in his hands, ready to signal my troop to unleash its collective fury at the unsuspecting enemy.

As I look at my watch, the time comes for H-Hour and I nod affirmatively to my signaller who then gently aims the rocket at the sky and pulls the cord. It billows up in the sky in a burst of flames and sparks, soaring over our heads and bursting in the dark predawn sky, illuminating the tableau the battle is about to unfold in with a bright red flickering glow.

Whoosh!

The field and surrounding area erupts with harsh light from the gun barrels of my soldiers who are scattered around the contact zone, figures dashing and running around, half lit by the blinkered flare lights and half hidden by the all-enveloping darkness. Voices coming across harsh and loud.

I peer at the scene closely, following the antics of the lead assault section as they run forward, throw themselves onto the ground in their fire teams, getting closer and closer to the enemy positions, using every inch of dead ground, the control of the LCpls over their individual fire teams just incredible.

Soon after what seemed hours, but were only minutes, passed and the smoke clears, calm settles over the field of battle and I'm standing in the middle of the organised chaos of collecting my troop back together again. Bringing them in from their scattered final positions, ascertaining if there are any casualties, and getting them ready to move off again.

Then, as we wind our way to the pickup point where our vehicles patiently wait, distant miles away in the folds of the countryside, the enemy then counterattacks us with concentrated IDF and dispatches half a dozen individuals to keep my last section under fire. Now I must move my troop back whilst under fire, a fighting withdrawal. Keeping the enemy at bay but managing my three sections like chess pieces. One is keeping the enemy at a respectable distance, one is getting ready to provide cover when the section in contact gets the word from me to withdraw, with the third and final section providing flank protection.

All the while keeping myself calm, thinking of not only the next move I must make as the commander, but the one after that. Keeping an eye on all the moving pieces of my scattered troop, giving loud but confident orders to assist the movement of my sections, all the while pausing to crack an occasional joke and politely refuse an offered cigarette with the machine gunner who is lying at my feet.

I love my job.

Then, weeks and months later, what seems like worlds away, the collective roar of mighty engines sound in my ears and belches of thick dark smoke herald the arrival of the main column of my engineer vehicles and my plus sized Engineer troop at the BG crossing site. A martial combination of Mad Max style vehicles, my drivers laughingly referred to their trucks as War Rigs, and the quiet professionalism of highly trained soldiers about to start their task.

Seeing my Sprs and NCOs buzz around a task site, especially one as important and complex as an ABLE crossing site, the ABLE bridge system costs millions of pounds and being so rare it is typically a Brigade level asset, always gave me a deep sense of satisfaction. Also, if I'm being truthfully, a pang of concern as I was always worried the damn thing would develop a fault and break.

Looking back it was amusing to see how much I, having openly admitted straight from the start that I'm one of the only Royal Engineers who doesn't get that excited over bridges, would almost have a slight sense of childish delight when I saw all of the pieces of my troop's equipment and soldiers come together from across vast distances and difficult terrain and then throw their resources and efforts together in a careful amalgamation of muscle, technical expertise and steel. Soon resulting in a bridge, running from one only a few metres to one well over thirty metres, successfully crossing a gap or obstacle and allowing units to cross and continue the fight.

Sadly though, no matter how much I enjoyed training with my soldiers, in groups both large and small, the time eventually would always come when we would have to pack up and return to camp. Initially bursting with troop pride and with the deep profound professional satisfaction of a job well done, only for us to then again face the strange beast that was an Adaptive Force Regiment and its numerous and nonsensical 2020isms.

An increasingly frequent 2020ism which we came across was the focus in which the higher chains of command in the British military now appear to now put increased emphasis on statistics, at the expense of actual training of their officers and soldiers.

It was often farcical when it comes to the mandated training, known as MATTs, of the soldiers and officers within a regiment, as typically there is simply not enough time, or even personnel, spare within the calendar year to actually train the personnel. As such, due to the heavy focus by HQ's on official regimental statistics, the completed online registers are often than not rigged so as to appease the chain of command, with the end result being that the squadron or company will have appeared to have carried out all of its required training and thus gets its clean bill of health at the end of the year.

Regardless of the fact that everyone, from SNCOs and troop commanders downwards, are fully aware that the figures are mostly always smoke and mirrors as that due to the amount of military personnel that are already occupied with trawls sent downwards by HQs, in order to accomplish an annual classroom assessment an individual upon walking into the room is typically presented with the following statement:

'Here for the CBRN training? Right, sign here and you can go.'

I personally know of at least one squadron that went from having less than ten per cent of its personnel having been able to carry out their annual MATT training, to one hundred per cent, in only the time it took for the exasperated Ops SNCO to tick all the boxes on the online regimental MOSS spreadsheet. The reason being that, despite their best efforts, they'd simply been unable to carry out any actual MATT training throughout the year as there had no personnel available to actually teach due to them all being away on various trawls and assignments. It seemed that everyone knew except for those within RHQ.

Significantly, it is unfortunate that for many soldiers and officers within the Army now often never get to go the ranges and fire their rifles except for when it is time for the annual marksmanship assessments, and when the relevant qualified personnel are available to take them. Aside from being a serious disappointment, it is also a significant concern for junior commanders that their soldiers, as well as themselves, often simply just don't have the time to practise their marksmanship.

On the subject of training, when deploying soldiers onto field exercises, often extremely trying and in truly unpleasant parts of the country, with accompanying dismal weather, I quickly realised that due to the current political climate that exists among many of the higher tiers of Army HQs and their political masters, it was also pretty much impossible for NCOs to physically motivate, or chastise, offenders within their troops or platoons.

Once deployed out the gate and operating on their own, now relying on the collective physical capabilities of the troop, when it becomes clear that someone, say a junior Spr, is becoming lazy and letting the side down, the desired outcome by all ranks, except the offender, is usually a robust and loud one way conversation with one of the troop

NCOs. In extremis, having a 'private physical exchange of views' out of sight, typically behind the closest Land Rover, albeit this end result typically occurs only in extreme circumstances.

The reason being that there is often no place, or desire, for the filling out of official regimental punishment paperwork (known as an AGAI) once away from one's unit. For the section or troop, being the epitome of an alpha society that they are, always responds best to swift and appropriate physical chastisement, not officialdom's paperwork (typically known as AGAI 67). The desire for RHQ to poke their noses into any section or troop business, sniffing after any non-official resolutions to lapses in discipline, is another curse of Army 2020 and pisses off everyone, officers and soldiers alike.

The attitude of maintaining discipline in the field being summed up in one perfect and common phrase:

'Black eye, not AGAI!'

The fact that NCOs, the physical backbone of any unit, cannot be known, at least by RHQ, to physically motivate or chastise, when the situation calls for it, their soldiers, always a key reason for NCOs in any military, is a severely negative point of today's British military. This official, and weak kneed, approach to reprimands within the Army sends entirely the wrong message to all those in the chain of command. Meaning that as individuals are not allowed to be physically reprimanded all NCOs and officers live in fear of the RMP turning the incident into an episode of a low-rate crime drama. Even when both individuals concerned, and even the rest of the troop or platoon, accept the punishment handed out as appropriate and don't want any outside interference of any sort.

On the subject of unit identity and effort, I cannot state enough, whilst the troop, or any collective size of soldiers, are deployed as a group, of having a separate, if possible, living area for your soldiers.

Having had the chance to have my troop live and operate away from other units, be it in a different room of a building or half a mile away in an abandoned warehouse, was vital to achieving not only unit cohesion but also providing my troop with a sense of unity and oneness. Ever since I first discovered the importance soldiers and officers put on obtaining an accommodation area separate from everyone else, I endeavoured to achieve it wherever I went. This, at times, allowed me at times to create separate facilities for ourselves such as troop cinemas, gym areas, construction yards, BBQ fire pits, which were very good for warming everyone, especially if the weather was particularly crisp, up in the morning before work started, and relaxation/smoking areas.

Whilst deployed away from barracks as an independent unit, it always struck as funny how that whilst a group of soldiers working within barracks may not be the most enthusiastic for PT sessions, whenever I deployed with them outside of the wire, I found that whenever they could, my soldiers would throw themselves into impromptu phys sessions. Even my laziest and most docile soldiers would, say during real life support to an infantry battle group, take every opportunity to either life weights, do CrossFit sessions or go jogging. I've never had the phenomenon explained to me but after seeing it for the first time, if I knew we were going to be left to our own devices for lengthy periods of times, I would always try bringing some gym kit along with us.

Fantastically, I was delighted to also discover that the British Army, as well as the wider military, simply loves all forms of sports. One only has to name a sport, not matter how obscure or select, and it is highly likely that the British Army already has a number of teams that participate within it.

Annoyingly, when it comes to planning an AT expedition for the first time, it is generally a bit of a nightmare for the YO in charge of it. The simple reason being that planning a training package or sports expedition of any kind within the army typically involves following a series of processes and procedures that are totally unique to the military, and make no sense to anyone who has planned a similar trip previously in the civilian world.

Also, due to the workload that commanders, especially YOs, face within Army 2020, the planning and execution of the expedition must be done in conjunction with every day works; meaning that a YO must be able to concurrently run their troop or platoon, handle the various tasks assigned to them by HQ and organise, for instance, a seven week ski trip to Austria and France.

This is always compounded by the fact that typically the YO concerned has probably never planned such a trip before, and has to deal with the various pitfalls and irregularities of planning said expedition whilst dealing with the various pitfalls and irregularities of being a junior officer in the Army.

Typically, regardless of what is being planned, from a week's AT in Wales, a sailing expedition along the French coast, or a Nordic skiing competition, the biggest challenge the planner will have is often just simply finding the soldiers to take on the expedition.

Meaning that as each and every regiment, battalion, and sub-unit is so busy with life within Army 2020, there is usually almost no one spare to actually fill the spaces on the expedition. I cannot remember how many excellent and well planned trips had to be cancelled because the officers and NCOs in charge of them simply couldn't find the personnel to take on them. Or where they found some spare personnel but found that the soldiers had no interest in taking part. I once saw a Spr turn down two weeks free snowboarding in France because he didn't like the idea of the long drive out to the Alps.

Well, you can take a horse to water but you can't make it drink.

Usually, in order to find half a dozen individuals required to fill the bare minimum amount of spaces, an expedition leader would not only have to search their entire squadron or company, but more often than not, their entire battalion or regiment. Even when there individuals who were willing, and also suitable, for the trip planned, difficulties always arise as no sub-unit can comfortably spare even a single individual. Within Army 2020, one cannot please all the people all time. As such, whenever an individual goes away on an AT expedition, or even a military exercise trawl, the unit in questions has to deal with the hit and subsequent drop in manpower.

As a result of all the headaches that come about from the planning the various ATs and expeditions that land in the lap of newly arrived YOs, many become determined never to plan one again. To take part in future expeditions, yes, but not to be the organiser.

The various processes, forms and applications that must be filled out and completed in order to allow a military sports expedition to go ahead are legion. What also makes these harder is that aside from the delay in contacting the various people required to agree to the finances and suchlike, there is also no recognised step by step process for organisers to follow. Also the range of forms, applications, submissions and organisations one had to apply to simply made me, for one, want to jump out the window and go live feral in the bushes for a while.

From JSATFAs, diplomatic clearances, Sports Lottery memberships, regimental Public and Private funds which had to be applied to, different insurance policies, ticket booking procedures and transport acquirements, there were so many pitfalls for a naïve YO such as myself to fall into.

Although, once they were made, I seldom made them again but the whole process was made needlessly painful and frustrating because of an apparent lack of a coherent guide. The reason being that everyone else is also typically so busy in regiment with their own affairs that it is rare to find someone who can offer effective and comprehensive advice for any length of time. Often they simply could not be found, didn't answer their phones or seldom answered emails.

But, despite all the problems and difficulties I encountered when planning, carrying out and closing down various sporting expeditions, being able to take my soldiers on AT trips was a dream come true.

Meaning that as soon as I realised how important it was to make my soldiers actually enjoy their time within the military, as well as trying to gain them as many useful qualifications and experiences as possible, I did all I could to ensure that they could escape from the clutches of peacetime regimental life and its incessant trawls.

Also, if I'm being completely honest, planning my first AT expedition was my first introduction to the possibility for officers and soldiers to not only enjoy themselves on sports trips entirely paid for by the military, but also, if I'm permitted to demonstrate a slight mercenary mind-set, for them to earn substantial extra pay, which goes a long way, as any military commander in history knows, towards maintaining morale within the ranks.

'Troopy, the 2IC wants to speak to you in his office.'

'Really? Righto, I'll be over there in a second.'

Oh fuck, what have I done now?

After this brief exchange of words, and worried thoughts, I found myself one early Monday morning, only a few weeks into my job as troop commander and frantically trying to take on all the new information and responsibilities that were coming my way, walking slowly, although I wanted to scurry but I didn't want to be observed by others in such an undignified state, over to my 2IC's office with my heart in my mouth.

'Ah, morning Henry, yes, come in, take a seat. Let me see now, oh right – what is your PFA time?'

'My PFA time? Well, the fastest time I've run is 8.23. I never seem to get down to that vital 8.15 time; though I fare rather well on the press ups and sit ups.'

'Right, well that suits rather fine. You've been chosen to lead the regiment's Alpine team in this year's competitions in Austria and France. Feel up to it?

'Of course!'

This was my first experience with leading a team outside of regiment, an overseas competitive event at that, and my head was agog with the sense of adventure and panic about how to organise the bloody thing. Especially where to find the time to do it, bearing in mind that each and every waking hour of my life so far was already taken up with learning how to do my job as a troop commander.

Having skied in the Alps when I was younger on a number of occasions, I was confident in my abilities to get down mountains whilst having two planks strapped to my feet, it was just that I simply had no idea how one went about planning a military expedition to that part of the world. I knew even then that it wouldn't be as simple as it is typically is in Civilian Street - calling up friends, getting the names, getting the money, booking the flights, hotel and kit, then flying out there. The difficulty would be in finding out exactly what strange military processes and procedures I would have to jump through and how to best do them.

Firstly, I'd have to find the men. Thankfully, this proved remarkably easy as during my initial speech to my troop I'd stated how I intended to get them away as much as possible and as this was my first attempt at fulfilling my promise, they all leapt at the opportunity.

Word had also spread rapidly throughout the regiment and soon I had a steady stream of individuals walking into my office and politely enquiring if there were still nay spaces.

After a few hit and miss attempts, I stumbled across the best way of finding out whether an applicant would be a suitable member of the ski team, especially whether we'd get on over working together for seven weeks in the mountains. I would contact their officer or SNCO and ask one question:

'Is he a good bloke?'

If I received a positive reply to this question, the individual would be placed on the provisional nominal role; after a few days all I had to do was then tailor the list down to the key seven individuals. After reviewing all the names, and in some cases, skiing CVs, that were laid out in front of me on my desk, I became determined to have a team that I would enjoy working and socialising with, perhaps with a couple of seasoned skiers thrown in for good measure to lend me key advice and expertise when required.

Within less than a week of taking on the role of Ski Captain, the 21 Regimental Alpine team was born; aka 'The 21 News Team!'

The final list of names looked like something between a mixture of a police line-up, mixed online dating profiles and a reality television potentials list.

Stevie – A short chipper blonde haired and very experienced LCpl from the Medway area, already proven as one of my best NCOs within the troop. A LCpl who regularly comfortably handled vast amounts of tasks during the working week which would be normally be assigned to individuals of much higher rank. Always with a wry smile and humorous reply held ready in reserve to any question that may come his way; he was also eagerly awaiting the arrival of his first child, due in the next few weeks.

Mikey – A former infantry NCO who'd, after a number of years spent in Battalion, finally seen the light and joined the Corps. He had skied before and appeared to have a wealth of knowledge far in advance of his years, honed perhaps by the raising of his young son and daughter with his wife. Clearly one who I could rely on to reinforce discipline and control, however subtly, if required. He was also a fitness fanatic which I could rely on to do PT with whilst we were abroad, getting accidentally out of shape being a shared nightmare of ours.

Queenie – Stocky, cheerful and confident, he hadn't skied before but was keen to give it a go. Always appeared capable and at ease with taking anything that came his way. Clearly something of a jack the lad and the epitome of an experienced Spr, balancing typical squaddie humour with quiet professionalism and unassuming confidence.

Whitey – A dark haired, wiry, tall chain smoking Cpl. A cliché weathered NCO, who had come close to passing selection for Special Forces twice, narrowly missing out by a whisker each time. Full of experience, very capable; had done a lot of competitive skiing before and knew the area where we would training. Also another one I could use as a disciplinarian if needed, someone who I could rely on to back up my decisions and influence the more junior members of the team.

Riggers – Tall, gangly and shy; the newest Spr to arrive within the troop. He hadn't done any skiing at all beforehand but was keen to get involved. Would be an excellent way of welcoming him into the regiment and showing him what fun could be had courtesy of HMG; who knows, maybe he'll turn out to be a good skier?

Greeney – A calm and composed young Yorkshire LCpl, who had skied before and would always on hand to offer expertise when required. The perfectly matched combination of well-presented practical advice mixed with razor sharp wit and dry humour, always faultlessly delivered in the rich accent of one born and raised in the North of England.

Speedy – Good ole Speedy. Bursting with energy; he positively vibrated with enthusiasm when it became clear that I was going to put his name onto the list and take him with us. Couldn't do enough to help; from arranging vehicles to selecting stores from the gym to take and train with whilst in the Alps. Chomping at the bit to get another adrenaline buzz, to get away from the monotonous life of regiment and see more of the world. I think part of me brought him along purely for the devilment and entertainment he would no doubt cause.

With this motley crew in tow, how could we not succeed?

There were also a number of mistakes and learning points, some of them more painful than others, which I was to compelled to address during the following weeks when it came to the overall organisation and planning of the trip.

Principally, the fact that although I'd haggled and booked the appropriate amount of Euros from regiment and various other departments and organisations, I thought that my regiment would settle all of its Austria bills via bank transfers. Like many other regiments that I knew of.

Alas, no.

When we got out to Austria, with only the Euros in my possession were the ones intended to purchase the team's food and drink for the next five weeks, I found out that not only did the ski stores from which we were to purchase equipment want cash payment only, so as to avoid some local government charges, but that the regiment did not have an online account, unlike every other organisation in the world. So, with much wild exasperation, hair pulling and knee quaking panic attacks, I was eventually able, through the good graces and efforts of the regimental accounting department, to get the thousands of Euros transferred to my own account from RHQ and thus I could withdraw the cash needed to pay our bills.

All the while incurring horrendous exchange rate fees from the local ATMs, as well as being only to take out a few hundred each day due to ATM restrictions, and subtly trying to ask an incredulous RHQ why I hadn't been informed that the regiment didn't do online transfers. Did they not think it strange that I left the UK having only taken out the money intended for our food?

It makes me want to put my head in my hands as I think back to all of the bouts of depression, panic and worry that I had to go through over those past weeks which could have been avoided if I had only just asked someone at regiment if I should take the money for the trip out in cash before departing. I call this a perfect 2020 hindsight.

But I digress.

Despite these setbacks, all kit was eventually purchased, items paid for, bills settled and the team, despite, on occasion, its beleaguered naïve Second Lieutenant, was to have an excellent time Alpine ski racing in Austria.

Before we left the UK, after sorting out which skis we'd need and finding a place to store them, as the previous ski officer had left them slap dash piled in an old unlocked gym storage room, as well as getting money from the various departments and societies which were to fund our venture, the time soon came when we all packed our equipment and ourselves in the van and headed off.

It is worth noting that aside from spending considerable time finding out what ski equipment we would need to bring out with us, as well what we'd be buying once in country, that asking the advice of my NCOs of what miscellaneous items we should bring for the benefit of the team would pay dividends as time wore on.

Spending considerable amounts at a local bulk-buy warehouse before departing the UK meant that we ended up saving a lot of money once in Austria as we'd already brought key low cost cooking and washing components out wish us. From large sacks of vegetables, bottles of sauces, bags of pasta and rice, various tinned goods, all of it was eventually consumed and aside from helping to maintain balance the books, it also meant that we'd have a balanced and varied diet. No endless dishes of overcooked pasta with tinned Bolognese for us, military success has often largely depended on the diet of the troops and as such, I became determined that we would become the envy of the other teams and eat like kings throughout.

After much deliberation, we eventually drew up a list for various items which would help alleviate monotony and boredom amongst the ranks whilst we were in our chalet, having been warned of this phenomenon by other skiers. Principally, in the form of an Xbox, widescreen television, controllers and numerous shooting games. Over the coming weeks, tucked away in the warm seclusion of our chalet, the dark and windy night sky outside swirling violently with driven snow, fortified with numerous bottles of fine Austrian beer, my Sprs and I would battle for hours in exotic digital battlegrounds and many points of honour would be settled over violent and nerve wracking fire fights.

I was also keen to maintain an air of 'enjoying ourselves' where appropriate and not taking ourselves too seriously and to put this feeling effectively across to my team. For although we would ski like demons, when required we would also whole heartedly engage in the variety of alcohol fuelled parties and games the British military ski community out in Austria would in no doubt have in store for us.

'The English treat war like a game but treat games like war.'

With this in mind, I sported a strong Cheshire cat grin on my face whilst I typed up the final clothing list for my team in the final few weeks before departure, for aside from the mandatory appropriate skiing clothing, I also stipulated the following garments:

- Appropriate celebratory party Christmas attire
- The most outrageous coloured ski clothing available
- At least two offensive Fancy Dress costumes (must be able to ski in them)

It was a good sign of what was to come. Although, on the day we left, Army 2020, and its bizarre nonsensical ways, had one last treat in store for us.

For despite weeks and weeks of desperate please from me, we only finally got our ferry tickets after having to delay our time of departure for a couple of hours. This was due to the strange procurement system that the Army uses when it comes to such processes. Meaning that we had to wait for some obscure and far off department to confirm our clearance to buy such tickets, as we weren't permitted to book our own tickets, and then issue them.

This delay then resulted in a missed ferry and the team then having to fork out their own hard earned cash in order to get onto the next one. It always made us laugh to think how much our chain of command was always looking to critique our plans and processes, but seemed to be unable to examine their own state of affairs.

However, after many long hours later spent driving along vast European motorways and up perilous and twisting lonely alpine roads, we finally arrived in the snow burdened Austrian town of Neustift. Sat nestled between two great mountain ranges, snow lying scattered deep and thick all around, the games and adventurous were about to begin.

We soon found our chalet, run by an elderly and smiling HausFrau and unpacked. Each chap quickly taking a room and then moving to unpack the skis, all determined get to the slopes as fast as we could, like greyhounds in the slips, straining at the start.

It would not be feasible to cover all of what followed over the following seven weeks of competitive skiing but the following snippets cover some of the more memorable mishaps and adventures that the 21 News Team would end up having.

Having the privilege to tear down the snowy slopes and peaks of the Austrian Alps at truly terrifying speeds, the wind and cold tearing at our protective clothing and our eyes stinging with concentration as we swept along, knees bent, skies locked parallel to each other, our elbows almost skimming the ground with each rapid turn, was just incredible.

The tutelage that we received through our Austrian ski instructors was second to none and we were soon delighted to find out that our own instructor was a former Austrian Army officer, and a paratrooper at that, much to Speedy's chagrin.

This was because as due to our instructor's previous experience within the airborne forces and was thus a fellow brother paratrooper, it made him exempt from any ridicule from Speedy as a result of that bond which exists between all paratroopers. Even though he proudly sported a rakish ponytail throughout, a positive red rag to Speedy's bull.

We also soon we found that he would happily tell stories of his former military career spent crawling around the peaks of the Alps in the height of winter in exchange for cups of tea and hot chocolate when we stopped at the various restaurants along the slopes to warm our freezing bones.

It had also been made clear to all of us right from the start that protective equipment and clothing was essential during our time spent racing down the slopes, but it was interesting to see that although we received funding from our regiment for helmets, hand guards and suchlike, protective clothing was an entirely different matter.

'Protective clothing? Pfftt!'

Due to a random instance of fiscal meanness from higher ups, the only protective clothing the 21 News Team were to sport were some ageing wafer thin bright pink and purple racing suits that we had found rotting in a box in the old regimental ski store, as funds hadn't been cleared by RHQ to buy new ones, as we already had some.

Our race suits had no pads or thick layers of any kind, not even over the 'sensitive' areas and were more like all body condoms instead of professional racing suits.

They were simply hilarious to wear, so snug and tight fitting were they that there was no doubt as to what gender we were, except when it was really cold, and they made us stand out from the other skiers like bright purple and pink thumbs. Colours that even David Bowie might have hesitated to put on.

Although, looking back, we all found it bloody funny to wear them, bearing in mind the love of self-deprecation and eccentricity that exists within the British Armed Forces, and aside from making it easy to identify where everyone else was on the slopes, they also went a long way to creating a real and true sense of team identity.

We felt like the unfortunate kids at school who can't afford the new uniform and have to search for scraps in the lost and found bin; we loved it.

'Are you from 21 Regt?'

'Yes, why do you ask?'

'Well, I'm pretty sure I wore one of those outfits when I skied with them fifteen years ago.'

This was the conversation I had with one of the gate keepers, an ageing Royal Engineer Major, at the top of one of the slalom runs in the initial few weeks of skiing. For word had quickly spread about our team's attire, mainly due to the fact that you couldn't fail to notice us, and we were on the end of many barbed comments questions our sartorial and tailoring tastes. To which we all responded with suitable farcical indignation and queries about the questioner's heritage, reproduction organ size and state of their mothers' moralities.

The Alpine drinking scene was strong amongst all skiers out there at the time, military and civilian, and a number of planned, as well as impromptu parties, took place either at the famed bar of Neustift, The Dorf, or at the Umbrella Bar at the bottom of the slopes. It was during one of these parties that Riggers, our youngest and most inexperienced Spr, although who was quickly becoming one of our best skiers, thanks to the efforts of our instructors, was shot by 'The Drunk Sniper'.

It took place after a long week of hard skiing, the snow and wind had been severe throughout and all had now gathered at the Umbrella Bar, ready to enjoy their well-earned pints and steaming glasses of hot gluhwein. Everyone in the heaving bar was still in full ski gear, heavy boots included, but dancing along merrily to the techno 'Umpa' music that was blaring out the speakers. Some, mostly the males, were even trying their skills at a stripper pole standing in a corner whilst still wearing their heavy ski boots. Riggers, however, had discovered 'The Jager Train'.

A number of the powerful shots were on offer at the bar, around a dozen, and according to the bartender, it was the 'done thing' to down all the shots as quickly as possible; at least, that's what a real hard drinking, hard farting, hard fighting skier would do.

Riggers, never one to back down from a challenge, especially one when surrounded by his grinning peers, mistakenly bragged in front of all of all the assembled 21 News Team that he could handle such a number of shots, 'no problem'. Needless to say that after swiftly and professionally downing each shot, we all knew that it would not be long before they would make themselves felt. A few minutes later I quietly sidled up to him and subtly suggested that aside from drinking some water, that he refrain from any more alcohol for the night.

Riggers, still talking coherently but clearly slightly unsteady on his feet now, turned and commented piously that he wouldn't touch any drop all night. But then, after a pause, uttered one of the most feared and powerful phrases known to the British Armed forces:

'On my eyebrows....'

This famed military utterance means that if the individual then goes back on their word, they will shave off one of their own eyebrows as punishment. The only step further than this is the 'Robocop', where an individual than has to shave off half the hair on their head and keeps it that way for at least a day, before then typically shaving off the rest of their hair.

I immediately gathered a few witnesses from the team, who were all now rather unsteady on their feet but their eyes quickly became sharp and alert as they realised what was in the offing, and made Riggers repeat his statement to them all. Brilliantly, not a few minutes later, he apparently then forgot all about his promise as the wave of raw alcohol hit his system, aka being shot by 'The Drunk Sniper' and was recorded on film happily and merrily tucking into a pint of lager by the bar.

I patiently waited till the next morning to call him to account.

As the sun rose over the towering peaks that surrounded the tiny Alpine town in which we slept, I got up from my bed, albeit slightly shakily, as it had been a rather heavy night for me too, as the team had earned their night of excess and an officer must always lead by example. After putting on the kettle, I then went about rousing the team from their slumber. Ten minutes later, all sat around the kitchen table with cups tea held in their great paws and nursing truly potent hangovers, the team watched as I formally called for the setup of a 'Kangaroo Court'.

Great evil smiles broke out amongst all the unshaven, bleary eyed individuals present, including Riggers, as he'd promptly forgotten about the promise he had made the night prior, as they watched intently to see who I would call to the stand. Quickly, but with the great formality these situations and proceedings require, I called Riggers to the fore and highlighted the great crime he had committed the previous night. But, as the British military being a strange but fair beast, I allowed Riggers to choose his own defence attorney and a few minutes to prepare his case; after many frantic and urgent mutterings between Riggers and Stevie, the individual chosen by Riggers as his lawyer, I called for the defence to begin.

After an impassioned, but in the end futile, plea by Stevie on behalf of his client to the assembled jury, who the other members of the team, who were now all sat around the table like so many sharks around a wounded swimmer, I was then given the chance by the appointed Judge, Whitey, the most senior NCO present, to give my final evidence for the prosecution. My ace card was then flourished, in the form of the short video showing Riggers making his promise and then subsequently breaking it a few minutes later, and the jury were left to make their verdict.

Although he was swiftly found guilty on all counts, including lying to his officer, by the assembled group of his peers, the unfortunate Spr was given the option of carrying out his sentence immediately and shave his eyebrow himself or, delay it but accept that he would be pounced upon by the rest of the team at some point and forcibly shaved. Very wisely, after only token resistance, he opted to take his own eyebrow — deemed by all present to be the wiser of the two choices.

This was perhaps the finest example I had seen of not only the Army's infamous 'Kangaroo Courts', but also what happens when a code or promise is broken by an individual, regardless of rank. Always fair, properly presented and swift but, inevitably resulting in, appropriate, punishment for the offender.

On the subject of alcohol, a significant worry of all of the team captains during our stint in Neustift which loomed over all of us was the concern of maintaining discipline whilst our soldiers drank. As that due to the availability of drink, intense unit rivalry, close proximity all soldiers and officers worked and lived together, as well as the fact that everyone typically drank at the same bar, the Dorf, it was looked like it was going to potentially difficult to stop our soldiers fighting. As ever, discipline is always at the fore front of priorities for any aspiring commander and thus all troop commanders present soon found themselves, as the days and weeks progressed, standing at the bar or pool table and watching over their soldiers drink and dance around, like so many mother hens keeping a concerned eye on their chicks.

An interesting point of note was that over the course of the evenings we spent drinking in our own chalets and in the various bars throughout the mountains, the various troop commanders learnt, some by instinct and some by trial and error, when to know to leave the party. Meaning that some nights it was fine to drink and celebrate all evening with our Sprs, whereas in others it became clear that, in order to maintain our positions as disciplinarians, an early exit would be prudent.

A gentleman always knows when to leave the party.

But, we needn't had worried as the discipline of all of the soldiers and officers was fantastic throughout and even though we all drank like fishes, there was no trouble between units, in fact most had friends in the other teams. Hilariously, the only people who started fights were from the Commando team and they just fought each other.

The competitive nature of soldiers and officers is always worthy of note and plays an important part throughout an individual's military career, regardless of the setting. From challenging the youngest or most naïve Spr, whilst deployed in the field, to attempt the 'Twenty Four Minute Challenge', which involves eating an entire 24 ration pack in twenty four minutes, including the packets of beverage powders and seasonings, to a Para Staff Sergeant declaring to his troop upon arriving in Afghanistan that he will only eat rations, no food from home, else he'll allow the youngest Spr to Baboon him, thwack his bare backside with a pole.

Surprisingly, the soldiers, and their officer, of The 21 News Team were no different. Meaning that due to the slight monotony, i.e. after the skiing had finished, as the days went on, we quickly found ourselves challenging each other to a series of last minute, but typically quite funny, tests and challenges; all of which were taken on with an equal air of deadly seriousness and utter farce.

The combination of countless hours spent shooting Nazi zombies on our Xbox, battling over chessboards and of playing pool in the Dorf meant that our skill levels quickly became quite high, especially Speedy and I. Looking back on it I suppose that it was inevitable that, given the degrees of competitiveness and friendly rivalry that existed within the team, we would eventually go head to head.

It finally occurred during a celebratory team meal at a local steakhouse, paid for by the money I had saved from the collective team funds, after perhaps one or two steins of lager than was necessary, that Speedy loudly challenged me to a combination game of Xbox death matches and a final game of pool in the Dorf. The loser would then 'go in the clogs'.

The gasps and surprised yells of amusement and surprise from the other team members sat around did nothing to drown out the seriousness of the challenge that had just been thrown at my feet by Speedy, who was grinning at my blearily over his frothy glass of beer, for 'going in the clogs' was a serious penalty to consider, perhaps even more so than 'eyebrows'.

In the Dorf, that delightful sprawling wooden alpine bar which has numerous rooms and booths, a dance floor, games areas and a well-stocked bar, also hosts a pair of ski boots which were nailed upside down into the dark wooden panelled ceiling by the bar. Whenever a skier had lost a challenge or competition, local tradition dictated that they then had to be helped into the boots, hang upside down, whilst surrounded by a wildly cheering crowd, swinging pints of beer and chanting, and then be forced to drink whatever evil cocktail their opponent could think of. The owner, and head barman, of the Dorf had a number of distasteful and odious looking bottles of murky alcohol sat behind his bar and was always more than happy to create a suitably disgusting drink when required.

The long short of it was that, after a number of closely fought Xbox shooting death matches, and a truly cataclysmic game of chess and pool, Speedy was helped, screaming and laughing in equal measure into the boots and his grinning troop commander, cheered on by the rest of The 21 News Team, then poured almost half a pint of raw Austrian alpine spirit liquor down his face and into his mouth.

Although, due to the amount that I had drunk in celebration of winning the challenges and not being put at the mercy of my soldiers, especially Speedy, my aim was slightly off and as the liquid was clear, most of it went into his eyes and nose before it reached his jawline. My accuracy was also not helped by the fact that Speedy was bucking and jerking from his upside down position like a freshly landed marlin.

'Speedy? How'd that taste?'

'Taste it Boss? I can fucking feel it on my brain!'

Although not all of the weeks we spent speeding our way down the snowy mountainsides, or celebrating at the bottom of the slopes, were without mishap, we were to be one of the few teams which was not to suffer any broken bones, as I was to abruptly discover one afternoon whilst having an end of the day pint with Stevie at a bar halfway up the slopes.

My phone rang and only a few seconds I was to discover that Mikey, having decided to go ahead and meet us at the bottom of the mountain, had been skiing along in his fine old style, only to have a heavily overweight German tourist to crash into him at full speed. The German, thanks to years of beer and bratwursts, bounced off the ice and was not harmed, pausing only to insult the unconscious and sprawled figure that was Mikey, before then hurriedly skiing off like the coward he was.

Mikey, on the other hand, was unconscious for a number of minutes and was only revived after much shaking and coercion by passers-by. But, we needn't had worried, as after a frantic drive and visit to the local GP, we were informed that he'd only had mild concussion and as long as he didn't drink any alcohol and got plenty of rest, he'd be skiing in a day or two.

So after thanking the elderly GP and giving Mikey a day's forced bed rest, the team then met him the next day at the bottom of the slopes and proceeded to celebrate his survival by a prolonged stay at the Umbrella Bar, all of us recommending different drinks which we believed would best speed up his recovery. My ardent recommendation was regular doses of good whisky.

What whisky cannot cure, there is no cure for.

Unfortunately, due to another injury, which turned out to be much more serious, which happened to Queenie, and Stevie's wife suddenly giving birth, a number of days later I was compelled to send two of the team back to the UK. Now, considering that I'd made sure that all of the team had a number of insurance policies taken out, both civilian and military, just in case a compassionate or injury case occurred, it was an absolute nightmare for me and the rest of the team in trying to get one of our policy holders, civilian and military, to pay for the flights. In the end, throwing their hands up in exasperation, both Queenie and Stevie ended up paying for their own flights, much to my chagrin, back to the UK. It was a learning point for me, as well as the team, that aside from taking out every insurance policy possible before we left for our skiing, considering how high the risk of serious injury is whilst out on the slopes, we also needed, for the next time, to double check what processes we'd need to follow and who we'd need to call in order to activate the relevant policy if someone got injured.

A good learning point on what an organisation say they'll do, and what they'll actually do come the hour – look after our people.

After the first night out the team had when we first arrived in Neustift, I also quickly learnt to lock the door to my room as if it was left unlocked, else at the end of the night the rest of the team would come in and wish me a good night, often swaying quite heavily and burping happily. More often than not also very kindly offering me some choice scraps of their takeaways, before shambling off to their own beds.

Aside from having to lock my door in order to avoid any uninvited, but none the less friendly, late night callers, I also discovered that if I didn't, come the morning, I'd usually also find a number of extra coats piled on top of me or my luggage. These additional garments, which still continued to be 'collected' as time went on but were left outside my locked door instead, were the result of a number of visits to the local 'Gentlemen's Club' by various members of my team, who shall remain nameless. The reason being that as upon leaving the establishment at the end of the night, usually the worse for wear, they often took not only their own coats but also any which they thought I might like.

The collection of coats, which continued to grow despite my protests, I think they actually increased the more I protested, was a testament to not only the different views my team must have had on what they thought I wore in my spare time, but also the varied and strange clientele that must visit such 'establishments'. Bright purple parka jackets, knee length leather trench coats, white fake fur lined gilets and much more, all used to lay scattered on the floor by my door like so many dog's toys each Saturday and Sunday morning.

When the team weren't throwing themselves at terrifying speeds down the slopes killing each other via the Xbox, partying in the Dorf, collecting garments from suspicious establishments or getting run over by Teutonic tourists, I also led them in boxing and running sessions. Determined that not only would such sessions help the team bond, but they'd also ensure we didn't run to fat whilst operating in our Alpine hideaway. Plus, soldiers are less likely to get into trouble after a full day on the slopes and then a lengthy session of boxing and running whilst wearing conditioning masks, contraptions designed to restrict the oxygen intake. Generally, their only wish is to crawl wearily and gratefully into bed. Having brought out a number of pads, gloves, ropes and other paraphernalia with us, after most days I'd be able to drag down at least two or three individuals from the warmth of their rooms and put ourselves through a heavy sparring and technique regime, followed by the obligatory three mile run through the dark streets.

The looks on the faces of local skiers and inhabitants as they saw our little pack of runners, suddenly emerging from the night's gloom, wearing hoodies and our conditioning masks, running at full gallop, sounding like a herd of hippopotamuses in labour as we struggled to breath, were priceless. The fact that due to constant exercise over the seven weeks, on and off the slopes, we were all as fit as butchers' dogs and would be able to give anyone back at regiment a run for their money during PT sessions.

Morale, always the key factor to bear in mind and to ensure gets maintained, was constantly at the back of my mind and

I realised as time went on, and Christmas leave was drawing closer, that my team, as well as many of the other teams, were beginning to show signs of missing their families and thus something was needed in order to put them in the right frame of mind for their final few weeks. It was clear to me that above all, my team of hardened skiers and hairy arsed Sprs, tough as nails and brave to a fault, needed to have a Christmas party.

As silly as it sounds, after telling them my idea one morning over breakfast, as it was my turn that day to make the tea and cook the sausages and eggs, the smiles that broke out all around the table indicated me I was on to a winner. Suggestions and recommendations soon came thick and fast, the 21 News Team Christmas Party was a goer.

After picking an evening to host our event in our chalet, I sent word to our instructors that Mikey and I had both fallen ill and wouldn't be able to ski that day. As soon as the rest of the team had tramped off to the slopes, Mikey and I then swooped off in our van and set about securing supplies, all bought out of our collective regimental funding that I'd been carefully hoarding for the decorating of our kitchen and the preparation of our Alpine Christmas dinner. Many Euros later, with shopping bags bulging with clinking bottles, various meats, vegetables and sauces, we stumbled out of our van and set about turning our flat into own version of Santa's Grotto. After two or three hours of cleaning, chopping, boiling, decorating, wrapping and tasting, we were ready. As the rest of the team arrived, weary and red faced from a day on the mountainside but eager to see what we had prepared for them, their wide grins and cheerful voices told Mikey and I that we'd done a suitable job.

Brightly coloured wrapping paper had been used to make not only been used to make streamers, wrapping for the 'pass the parcel' and placemats, but also rather fetching

Christmas paper hats. Within minutes of arriving everyone was walking around sporting hats that not only varied in size, due to my rather slapdash work with scissors, but also were either too big and fell down over their eyes, or were too small and perched on their heads like Turkish Fezzes. As we showed them to their seats, the table positively groaning under the weight of boiled, roasted and fried vegetables, bottles of wine and spirits, tins of chilled lager and hams and chicken crisped from the oven, we then doled out ladles of steaming hot gluhwein into tea cups and handed them round so as to warm up their chilled bones.

With the Canterbury Cathedral Choir belting out carols from a speaker by the oven, we quickly settled into games, essential to any festive gathering, principally the 'pass the parcel'.

I was especially proud of this particular parcel, as I'd bought a gift unique to each team member and had wrapped them in a particular order so that the right gift went to the right person. As I sat with my hand on the stereo pause button, stopping the music, after a suitably nerve wracking period of time had passed, and watched with a smile on my face as each individual got to open up a layer and the roars of laughter that greeted their particular bespoke gift.

Some individuals got small miniature bottles of local spirits, to which they all downed with vigour immediately, with loud cheering and banging of the table by everyone else, others got little handmade chocolates, which were immediately eaten with much smacking of the lips and satisfied sighs, Riggers, the youngest member of the team, got an empty bottle of washing up liquid.

Hours later, after all of the alcohol had been drunk, all the food had been eaten and all the drinking games had been played, the table an absolute mess of scattered plates and glasses, all of us slightly cross eyed and very merry, we stumbled off into the night and swirling snow, determined to continue the festivities in town. Later on it was surprising, as well as very funny, to find how many other soldiers came up to tell me, once we'd reached the Dorf and started drinking with the other teams there and jovially talking about our team's Christmas party, they were all rather jealous and had berated their own troop commanders for not organising parties of their own. It was a party to remember.

Also, because on the way back from town afterwards, Mikey famously drunkenly mistook a ramshackle wooden hut by the side of the road for a bus shelter and sat in it for a while to catch his breath, only to realise, after it was too late, that he was sat in a local farmer's dung heap.

On the subject of funding, and the bonuses that can be reaped if it is saved and spent in the correct manner, the importance of the team leader, whether whilst on a ski tour, sailing around Croatia or on a Battlefield Study in Poland, taking command of all of the supplied funds and keeping it all in a centralised account, cannot be over exaggerated. Thus the spending of the team, or group, can be strictly monitored and it ensures that no one goes over budget and thus has either to fork out of their own pocket or have a very embarrassing conversation with the regimental accountant when back in the UK.

It also means that money can be saved in a number of ingenious little ways and thus allows for financial safety nets, if accidental damages must be paid for, to be be created. Such as in the form of an impromptu Christmas party, special team dinners out in the town or an 'end of tour' bonus in which everyone receives an equal share of the remaining funds. Managing this is achieved by carefully collected receipts, usually ones picked up from the discarded pile at the checkout counter at supermarkets, which 'officially' prove that said funds had been spent on approved items.

Following in the mantra of Julius Caesar:

'The sinews of war are infinite money.'

Those glorious weeks spent skiing in Austria, and then in France almost straight after, in the Divisional Skiing Championships, were my first independent command, away from my SHQ and RHQ, and I loved it, relishing the various challenges that came my way.

Relying on only my fledgling command ability to inspire and lead my team, treading that careful line between comradeships but not becoming over familiar and thus undermining my leadership. It was a time that was often filled with considerable amounts of stress, bearing the initial hiccup with our funding, and challenges that weren't exactly covered in the weeks and months of my RMAS and RETCC training. I got to know my men, learned what motivated them, who they were as individuals and what made them, and I was always immensely surprised and proud when they shared their jokes with me and let me know, in their own individual ways, how they saw me as an officer and if I was worthy of their loyalty and trust.

Perhaps the best example of the latter point, amongst all of the other excellent aspects I was to witness, was when I had to call out a drunken SCNO who, along with his gangly pubescent acolytes, was verbally, and just short of physically, abusing my men in the Dorf one Friday night. Clearly drunk and in an ugly mood, he, in a complete disgrace to his rank and position, was clearly spoiling for a fight and was doing all he could to cause trouble with any other soldiers he could find. After quietly escorting my blokes out of the Dorf, we found ourselves in the takeaway next door and whilst ordering our portions of 'Gyros', the drunken SNO suddenly spilled through the doorway and started pouting abuse at us. Funnily he appeared to take particular exception to my red trousers and thick tweed coat.

The mood within the small takeaway joint quickly turned sour and I struggled with keeping my Sprs from launching themselves at him and his cronies, their regimental and personal pride deeply wounded. After perhaps thirty seconds I'd gone over to the bald, portly, foul breathed SCNO and asked if he'd like to have a word with me outside; where we could discuss the issue at hand between ourselves.

I opened the misty glass door and stepped out into the cool of the night, walking slowly across the trampled snow to the middle of the small town square, my hands thrust into my pockets and my ears listening to see if the SNCO had followed me out.

He had.

I walked perhaps twenty yards out into the open and then slowly turned to face him, his face twisted in a sour expression of hate and within seconds of me asking why he was causing trouble with my soldiers, he launched into a high pitched and vulgar tirade against me. Highlighting my accent, clothing and rank as reasons to why he apparently so vividly disliked me.

Perhaps less than a minute into this one way conversation, his face less than a hand's span from mine, his foul and alcohol laden breath crashing against my senses like a wave, I knew that he wouldn't listen to reason and that I'd have to fight him in order to settle the issue.

Whilst he was still leaning in close to me, his voice of hatred resounding loudly off all the surrounding buildings, I slowly shifted my feet in a comfortable position where I could easily hit him without fear of slipping on the cobbles and took my hands out of my pockets. As I did so, his piggy eyes glanced down and saw me slowly getting into a boxing stance, albeit hands still hanging loosely by my side; a flash of panic danced across his face.

Taking a depth breath, fully aware that I'd probably have to report, and justify, my actions to senior officials later on, I quietly but confidently told him that unless he stopped his verbal assault and shameful behaviour, I'd have at him.

Now bearing in mind that he was at least twenty kilograms heavier than me, mostly pudgy fat from what I could tell, and fuelled up on alcoholic belligerence, I knew it wouldn't be an easy fight and that I'd have to watch out for the classic tactics typical of angry drunk bullies; the bear hug, the head butt, spitting and the wild haymaker.

But after only a few seconds of silence, like all bullies when faced with someone who is not afraid of them, he went red in the face, swore at me once more and then turned around and slunk off into the night like the coward he was.

Breathing deeply in order to calm myself down, sucking in great draughts of that deliciously cool mountain air, I looked around the empty town square and saw that less than six feet behind me, stood silently, were three of the SNCO's young soldiers, clearly in a position to jump me if their drunken champion had had the courage to fight me in the street. But more importantly, I saw that behind them, waiting quietly like wraiths in the gloom, were each and every one of my Sprs.

They'd seen the SNCO's lackeys slink out of the takeaway joint after me and cunningly take up position behind me, ready to pounce and restrain me whilst their SNCO flailed away. My blokes had then quietly followed them out too, and had got into position to leap to my defence in the fight had started.

Although there were many muttered comments afterwards between us as to the disgrace of the SNCO and his soldiers, as well as to how cowardly they had all proved to be, no words were mentioned as to my Sprs having followed me out into the night and got ready to fight with me if required. I knew that they had had my back, and they knew it. Nothing more needed to be said.

After countless highs, some lows, and some exceptionally noteworthy victories and triumphs, our skiing adventure eventually came to a close, but I will always remember those days and weeks I spent in the mountains training and leading my men. My Sprs.

21 News Team, assemble!

***

I first became interested in sailing, especially along the Adriatic Sea and the Dalmatian Coast, after first reading a book called 'Eastern Approaches' by Fitzroy Maclean which covered his escapades, amongst others, along the Eastern European coastline and its hinterland in the 1940s. A delightfully eccentric and adventurous individual who was initially a diplomat in Paris and then in Soviet Russia in the 1930's, as well as personally exploring vast tracks of Russia in his spare time, always one step ahead of the paranoid Soviet security forces, and subsequently then becoming a member of the Long Range Desert Group (LRDG) and SAS in the North African Desert. His wartime career then culminating in taking on the position of chief British military liaison officer to Tito's Partisans in the Balkans.

After reading his accounts of working and living with the Communist Partisans, I was hooked on venturing into that part of the world myself, especially if I could do it aboard a boat and explore the numerous islands scattered along its coast. From reading of him operating throughout the length and depth of that stunning and savage Balkan countryside and islands for months at a time, relying only on his wits, charm and personal example, as well as a grasp for different languages and cultures, to survive, I soon became determined to follow in Fitzroy Maclean's footsteps and have my own adventure there, perhaps similarly courtesy of HMG's purse strings?

From the early stages of the conception of the venture, to actually getting my regiment to approve my proposal and then plunging into the depths of despair and frustration that was actually getting the expedition to a successful fruition, it was in no doubt a long slog in getting my crew and I to Croatia. Indeed there were many times I was convinced the trip would not go ahead.

Organising a sailing expedition was an entirely different beast from what I did for carrying out the ski training in Austria, as the skiing was classed as 'Individual Military Training' and was technically in the same class as, for instance, carrying out an infantry exercise in Catterick training area, whilst the Croatian sailing was an 'Adventurous Training' package. Meaning that there were a whole range of new forms, processes and sources of funds for me to address and deal with. The same principles, but different rules.

But, in the end, after remembering many lessons learnt from my ski planning escapades, we finally boarded the plane which would take us to Split airport and subsequently had an adventure of a lifetime, which would thankfully go on to produce a steady stream of memorable experiences and laughable occurrences and no small number of white hairs on my behalf. Snap shots of our adventures along the Dalmatian coast upon the 'HMS Lost At Sea', as it became known by those who sailed upon her, often come to my mind and perfectly capture the bizarre situations my crew and I often found ourselves in. From impromptu rapid catastrophe aversion tactics, to farcical situations which almost had no apt way of description due to their bizarreness, our life atop the Adriatic ocean waves were certainly not dull.

Such as finding out, when we had first dropped our anchor in the cool and clear depths of a sheltered Croatian bay on the first day of sailing and were preparing all to dive in and relish our sunny nautical freedom, that Spr Ampong, a Ghanaian, and one of the most intelligent soldiers I have ever come across, couldn't swim.

So, after a brief pause for incredulous looks and laughter, the remainder of the crew, Obi, Taff, Mick and I, came together and thought of an appropriate solution. As none of us could be bothered to dig out one of the life jackets, all of which were buried deep in one of the galley cabinets, we then jumped into our dinghy and motored to the closest island where we then purchased a shiny pink plastic football.

All of us then motored back to the boat and instructed Spr Ampong to put on a spare t-shirt. Once having done so, we stuffed the ball underneath it and promptly shoved him overboard, resulting in an almighty splash but a smiling, and more importantly buoyant, Spr Ampong. This arrangement proved very satisfactory to all concerned and was adhered to throughout the rest of our holiday whenever we fancied a dip. I forget the amount of times where we'd all be swimming lazily around our yacht, at some harbour or anchored out in an idyllic bay, and another yacht would pass and inevitably slow down as all the crew would peer over the side in order to get a better view of Spr Ampong, who would be happily paddling alongside, appearing to all and sundry to be nine months pregnant.

On a separate occasion, narrowly saving our boat from certain wreck and ruin upon the savage rocks of a nearby shoreline was certainly an experience that I did not envision in the early planning stages, but one I certainly had to contend with. The event came about after a number of days at sea, and the crew and I were beginning to think that we knew a thing or two by this stage, always a warning sign, we dropped anchor just offshore from a gorgeous island that was reputed to have an excellent nightlife and prepared ourselves for the night ahead. As the sounds and smells of various members of the crew showering and their overpowering cologne wafted up from below, Taff casually remarked to me as I lay on the bow, sunning myself, that the yacht still appeared to be moving.

I sat bolt upright and glanced around, my sunglasses falling my nose and my book dropping from my hands, and glanced around.

We were indeed moving.

Clearly our anchor had not bit sufficiently into the sea bed and we were being slowly pushed by the waves of the bay towards the nearby rocky shoreline, a few hundred feet away. Calmly I padded over to the wheel, smoothly hoisted the anchor and then started the engine, determined to gain some more sea room away from the rocks before dropping our anchor again.

As the strains and roars of the engine echoed throughout the calm bay, everyone else present in the area quietly preoccupied with sleeping on their moored up Gin Palaces or lazing on one of the shore bars, it became clear we were still moving towards the rocks, the propeller was not working for reason.

Having not have had this happen before, I glanced around slightly frantically as I saw that we were fast approaching the shore and that if something drastic was not done urgently, within the next few minutes or so, our vulnerable little vessel would be washed up against the rocks and her white pristine hull peeled open like a tin of sardines.

Not exactly a message I wanted to pass onto RHQ back in the UK.

Ordering Obi, by far the most experienced sailor aboard, to take charge of the wheel and engine, I stripped off down to my shorts and went over to the starboard side. With one final glance at the rapidly approaching rocks, the sounds of waves crashing against them resounding in my ears, I launched my best attempt at a swan dive and knifed into the water.

With the water thankfully as clear as gin, but the sea salt stinging my eyes and hindering my vision, I swam urgently underneath our yacht and drew up next to our propeller. Although I could hear the wining of engine through the water, clearly trying it's hardest to move the propeller blades, they weren't moving; they appeared to be vibrating violently.

Lungs beginning to burst under the strain, I peered as close as I dared to the strangely immobile metallic blades and through the emerald water, I suddenly realised there was something wrapped around them. A length of carpet!

As I eagerly thrust my hands forward to unwrap this menace, ears beginning to ping and lungs burning, I had a moment of clarity and pushed myself off the sea bed, the yacht having only a few yards of sea water beneath her at this point, and burst back out onto the surface, face turning towards Obi at the helm.

'Have you turned off the bloody propeller?!'

'Oh right boss, forgot about that! Yep, it's off now.'

With my brain flooded with fears of my yacht being torn apart, causing thousands of pounds of damage that no doubt I would have to pay and the subsequent punishments, however unfair, from RHQ, as well as the relief of narrowly escaping having my hands chopped off whilst trying to unravel a blockage from a propeller that was trying to move at maximum speed, I once more plunged back under the water.

Mercifully, with the engine now still, I frantically clawed my way back through the water to the propeller and in double quick time, thankfully managed to unwind all seven feet of the beige household carpet that had somehow wound itself around our propeller. I then popped back to the surface, the yacht less than ten feet away from looming wreck and ruin, and ordered the engines full steam ahead. Counting my lucky stars, I was greeted with the sight of seeing our yacht triumphantly surge through the water, leaving the rocks far behind its frothy wake, not unlike a young lady lifting her head proudly and elegantly striding away from an undesirable suitor at a party.

If Taff had not brought the movement of the yacht to my attention when he did, or the carpet didn't unravel as easily as it did, the yacht would have been torn open upon the rocks, we would have found ourselves abandoning ship and seeking shelter on the shore. But, it didn't and so in fine old British military fashion, we all promptly went ashore and got drunk, laughing about it.

I for one raised a private toast to Poseidon that night in the fervent hope that no more incidents such as the one we'd just encountered would come our way whilst sailing around on the briny deep.

On a different note, one day we once found ourselves moored up at some minute sun kissed island, doing morning PT after particularly heavy evening in which I'd introduced my crew to a number of drinking card games I'd learnt at university, accompanied by pure coincidence with us just having just replenished of our drinks cabinet. After upon completing a series of punishing burpees and skipping rope routines, trying to rid my body of its toxins, I decided that it'd be a good idea to run up the small mountain which the entire island rested on and purchase ingredients for the crew's breakfast at the village at the mountain's peak. The alcohol residing in my veins may have still been affecting my thought process at this point.

Thirty minutes later and positively pouring with sweat, legs staggering step by step up the savage incline, the early morning sun already beating down upon the brows of Spr Ampong and I, we began to think that our decision may have not been the wisest and perhaps we should have just visited the shop in the harbour that sat opposite our yacht.

But, thankfully, the gods were slightly on our side and when we finally reached the summit, and we thankfully found the delightfully crumbling antiquated village that sat atop it. We were also greeted with an absolutely stunning panoramic view of the Adriatic Sea which lay all around us, and the countless sun kissed islands that lay scattered upon it, forming a simply stunning archipelago. Thankfully, also, the local shop was clearly used to thirsty and hungry and potentially hung-over sailors, due to the Royal Navy's presence in the surrounding waters years ago, and was well stocked to suit the demands of our stomachs.

261

After much Kuna swapping hands and careful packing of our new stocks in precarious plastic bags, the locals on the island were then greeted by the sight of the two of us hurriedly running back down the hill, for we so dearly wanted our breakfasts, trying vainly to soften the tread of our flapping feet in case of the bags splitting due to the undulation whilst the precipice which was the road that led back down to the harbour was doing its best to make us run full pelt back down the mountainside.

One particular morning later on in the expedition, just before we were to head off on our longest leg, instead of its typically calm and gentile blue, the sea had become a violent moving mass of turbulent dark waves and thunderous white horses, whilst the clouds had turned an uncharacteristic stormy grey and the wind was blowing gustily. Obi and I looked at each other over breakfast table, holding onto our cups of coffee as they slid about dramatically with each jostle from the waves against the boat, and decided that today was the day for some real old fashioned sailing and to see what kind of sea legs our leisure tub had.

After much of battening down of the hatches, stowing away of provisions and putting on our rough weather attire, t-shirts and shorts, we set full sail and shot out of Hvar harbour like a cork out of a bottle and went forth to do battle with the waves and wind. As our bow ducked and heaved to meet each great moving mass of dark water, the waves marching solidly towards us from across the horizon, spray washing over the yacht, the port side of the deck was almost in the sea, so much so was the yacht leaning over as a result of us putting on every inch of sail we had in order to best catch the wind.

It was a surge of pure adrenaline to stand there at the wheel, legs braced to count for the slippery and sloping deck and to keep my balance as the yacht bounced and crashed against each wave, the salty seawater washing over me in great cold sheets. Whilst also watching with a keen eye over each and every stitch of sail that we had, ensuring that nothing was snared and that we didn't slow down in the heaving seas. All the while catching scattered glimpses of other vessels that were dotted around the heavy ocean, some cautiously close hauled and relying on their motors to get them across the water safely to harbour. Others, like ourselves, were letting out every spare yard of sail and coursing hell for leather along at full speed, like grey hounds charging after a rabbit, revelling in the rush of it all.

Much to Obi's and my amusement was seeing Spr Ampong first poke his head out of his cabin, minutes into our tumultuous journey, calmly view the stormy seas all around him, the clatter of opening cupboards and the crash of items as various locks burst open and their contents to the floor resounding from behind him, then smile bravely at us, retreat back inside for a few moments and emerge sheepishly sporting a life jacket. I wasn't too sure if it was an indication as to his doubt on my sailing talents or his fear of falling overboard; needless to say Obi and I both politely asked, over the roar of the fierce wind, if he'd like one of us to fetch his football for him as well.

Due to the previous night's excesses, both Taff and Mick were both fast asleep in their joint cabin when we'd first left our moorings and only emerged towards the end of our journey, Taff spending most of his time lying on the deck, head cautiously poked over the stern, regularly but violently contributing to the nutrition levels of the Adriatic. Pausing only to give a ghoulish smile and a brief thumbs up as we all took it in turns to take pictures of him in his agonised state.

It was a happy, relieved and rather soggy crew that arrived in harbour that afternoon. Some greatly pleased at the speeds we had achieved and the sensation of having faced some good stormy weather, others appeared to be more concerned with setting their feet on solid earth for the first time that day.

Finally, early on in our nautical wanderings, I'd decided that the crew would take turns at taking on the role of galley chef for each evening meal that was taken aboard ship. These quickly became fiercely competitive and as the chef for the evening triumphantly, or, as the case was sometimes, sheepishly, bore the evening's rations up out of the galley and laid on the dining table, every crumb was intensely scrutinised by the prospective diners. As we found ourselves poised over the evening's offerings, knives and forks held ready in hungry anticipation, there were always a variety interesting of remarks and recommendations made by those present, as usually the wine and rum had been flowing freely for a long while before dinner.

Needless to say the abundance of fresh fruit, vegetables and meat on every island we came across, as well as the excellent selections of local spirits and beers, all made for some excellent meals.

Despite the rigours and pains of getting the expedition off the ground in the first place, finally having the chance to explore the length and breadth of the Dalmatian coastline in the peak of summer was, to me, was a dream come true and was worth its weight in gold. Especially fantastic was the sailing past of islands and fortified towns that I had read about time and time again in numerous books. Eastern Approaches being only one of the many novels and accounts that I had eagerly devoured in which the Dalmatian coastline and its populace featured.

Croatia was perhaps one of the most stunning countries I have ever visited, with its people charming and polite almost to a fault and it was a once in a life time experience to be fortunate enough to sail along it's fabled coast, to revel in the mesmerising beauty of its scattered islands, bays and ocean waves.

The simple delight of waking up every morning, the early morning sun's rays pouring through my cabin window, our yacht gently rocking against its moorings, in idyllic and timeless settings such as Hvar and Split, or many of the surrounding stunning islands which were scattered around the Adriatic like crumbs on a blanket. The cool sea breeze and the slow warmth of the early morning sun creeping over the horizon whilst I walked over to stand at the prow of the yacht, quietly yawning and stretching languidly. Only to then take a leap and plunge into the refreshing emerald depths, the cool waters washing over me as I propelled myself down to the soft sand of the sea bed, before then rising to the surface and spending a good long time lazily swimming around with not another soul in sight, just the gentle aching cry of the far off sea birds echoing across the water.

Am I really getting paid to do this?

***

Thankfully, my wanderings outside of regiment with varying sized groups of Sprs were not solely overseas and I was lucky enough to also get the chance to dabble in some domestic adventures, and sometimes arduous, pursuits.

Aside from its truly stunning countryside, from streams and fields, to woods and hills, Ripon and Yorkshire as a whole, is also very fortunate to have amongst its populace a number of individuals, a hearty combination of ex-military and civilian, who are excellent fishermen, shots and guardians of the land and the wildlife that inhabit the area.

In combination with the extensive amount of land in which 21 Engineer Regiment, as well as the other surrounding northern military units, trained in and the desire of so many of the locals, civilian and military, to see the wildlife to prosper and develop in a controlled environment, upon arriving I was to find out that 21 Engineer Regiment had an excellent relationship with the local shooting society. The Ripon Shoot.

After my chain of command found out about my childhood experience in both fishing and shooting, I was soon put in contact with the headman of The Ripon Shoot, an ex-infantryman, and I was subsequently kindly invited along to the next meal the club was to host.

A number of weeks later, with my brogues neatly polished, tie carefully arranged and tweed coat finely brushed, I found myself one crisp and cool evening nervously stepping out of the taxi and into the welcoming lights of a local pub, the sounds of a content crowd happily chatting and laughing wafting out of the open door. Throughout the evening, after being genially introduced to all and sundry by my host, as I knew simply no one there, ranging from grinning and grizzled career game keepers drinking local bitter, to recently retired staff officers with a military pedigree as long as my arm jovially swilling whisky, it became clear that not only would The Ripon Shoot wish to extend an invitation to me to its next shoot, but also to as many Sprs that I could bring along with me.

As a courtesy to the regiment, all costs, which are typically met by the paying guests, would be covered entirely by the club.

Now, bearing in mind my attitude to getting chaps out-of-the-door and doing something rewarding away from the confines of the barracks, as well as something new and exhilarating if it could be managed, I positively leapt at this opportunity like a salmon after a fly. Upon returning to my office the next day, I sent out a carefully worded email, although I wish I'd printed out a copy of it as I made it deliberately farcical and pompous, to all my contacts within the regiment. They were principally all the YOs, some tame senior officers and SNCOs, and the email stated than a shooting opportunity was available and that'd I'd be soon taking as many men, experienced and novice, as I could, for a free day's pheasant shooting in the wilds of Yorkshire.

Due to the rarity of the opportunity, the offers soon came thick and fast, and some truly experienced shots came out of the regimental woodwork to not only kindly volunteer their services in organising the day with me but also for any potential future developments. Weeks later we even came within an inch of setting up a regimental clay pigeon shooting team, but we were ultimately foiled by the fact that no one had the time to spare.

By this point I'd learnt a thing or two with regards to planning and carrying out an exercise, which this venture was to be classed. In order to obtain regimental permission and funding, for I'd suggested that the regiment, as a courtesy, would at least pay for a bulk load of cartridges, and I quickly got to grips with my nemesis, i.e. damned paperwork.

A week or so later, towards the end of the pheasant season and the countryside all around echoing with the sounds of far off shotguns and the happy barks of men and dogs, I ushered my fledgling team of would-be shots into the waiting regimental transport and drove off, in a belch of petrol fumes, to meet The Ripon Shoot.

To their credit, as we arrived at the woodland RV and poured out of our vehicle, the men and women of The Ripon Shoot could not have been more welcoming. Within minutes my Sprs, young and old, novice and experienced, were cheerfully shaking hands with their escorts for the day and flasks of spirits were already being flourished and offered from deep tweed pockets.

The weather for the day could not have been better, healthy doses of warm sunshine, interspersed with intermittent light showers, and as we tramped through the thick woods and twisting paths of the local training area, Spaniels and Labradors panting happily at our heels, I thought that if nothing else I'd managed to take some of the Sprs out of their hangers and offices for the day and given them an insight, and interest to a world and sport that a lot of them would not have thought of venturing into previously.

Well worth the effort and paperwork in my opinion.

At the end of the day, after a number of drives, smoking cartridges and hours spent standing thigh deep in bogs and puddles, fighting with thick gorse bushes and briar patches of thorns and bracken, my team of Sprs were stood around grinning like school boys after a day's successful absence from school pillaging a local apple orchard. Guns still smoking in their hands, eyes flushed with what they had experienced and at least a dozen different game birds lying at their feet, a testament to the hard work and coaching of our kind hosts from The Ripon Shoot.

The success of that first day was such that, after many months had passed, thus allowing for the shooting season to open up again, I was kindly allowed to not only take up another group of Sprs to shoot with the club, with an even greater amount of success and enjoyment, but also a small team of family and friends from Ireland.

I only hope the relationship, and exchanges of goodwill, between 21 Engineer Regiment and The Ripon Shoot have been allowed to continue and flourish. Aside from field sports, such as shooting and beating with the local shooting and conservation societies, thankfully due to the Army's love of sports, even more so if the sport is arduous, I was also able to create and lead a team of Sprs from the regiment in perhaps one of the toughest trials of strength, determination and cunning; boxing.

The British Army has long been a fan of this pugilistic sport and richly awards any souls brave enough in body and in mind to step into the ring and take on an opponent, typically in front of a large crowd of their peers, with not just their own, but also their regiment's, pride at stake.

With my fledgling experience in the ring from my time spent getting the seven bells knocked out of me in Cairo, Leeds University and at RMAS, and after finding out that the regiment did not have a boxing team when I first arrived, I took on the challenge of creating a regimental boxing club.

For the first and perhaps only time, in my career as an army officer, I found that when I first approached the regiment for permission for me to start this particular venture, far from inundating me with paperwork requests and carefully thought out financial predictions, officers and soldiers of all ranks suddenly fell over themselves to flood me and the new boxing club with money, time and recruits.

Perhaps the three rarest commodities to any commander.

I was massively helped by not only the deep routed love the British Army has with boxing, but also in the form of a surprising alliance with the current Regimental Second in Command (Regt 2IC) at 21 Engineer Regiment. A fearsome man, having risen from Spr to Major, soon to be Colonel, a towering and powerful figure standing well over 6ft, bald as an egg and with eyes that glared fiercely, sleeves sporting both the Commando and Paratrooper flashes.

He was not a man to be dealt with lightly and was known to often leave senior military personnel quivering and stumbling as they left his office, having been found wanting in some detail or trait. Even Lucifer himself would have thought twice before disagreeing with him.

Bizarrely, he and I ended up getting on quite well.

With his help I quickly found that money had been found for not only for all brand new training equipment, but also for a top of the line boxing ring. The club was to be given ownership of one of the empty hangers within the barracks and if I could find outside civilian clubs that would like our team to come and train with them, then the more the merrier.

Now, all I had to do was find my team of would-be fighters.

In my various trawling throughout the regiment, I was to discover that conducting boxing training, including sparring, would not only turn out to be a great way to get to know some of my soldiers at a more personal level, but also a way to prove to them my own courage and discipline. For to step into the ring, touch gloves with an opponent, whilst surrounded by a crowd of soldiers who all knew me well, took no small amount of courage and I hope that it showed to them, even if only on a minute level, that I had courage and was willing to toe the line when required, thus hopefully gaining me a few grains of respect.

It was also perhaps the only opportunity in the military for a soldier to be able to legally hit an officer, and vice versa. Great fun.

Thus I'm not sure whether it was down to my skill of command and leadership or lack thereof that meant that from when I first announced my idea to my troop one morning and subsequently saw a forest of arms shoot up in response, to the first sparring session we had in the hanger, the team never lacked for volunteers. All of whom eyed me during our training sessions, grinning at me as much as I grinned at them.

After a length of time had passed and I had issued out the word to the others squadrons and departments, I found myself standing in a large hanger, now the official home of the boxing team, in front of just over a dozen individuals who were all keen to embark on becoming fledgling boxers. Aside from my own experience within the ring, I also had plenty of luck in the form of a number of regimental PTIs, including one from my own troop, aka Cpl Hodge, who were all keen to lend a hand wherever they could.

One of our best instructors, a weathered NCO who claimed to have taken part in at least twenty official boxing matches, and going by how well he taught our team we were all inclined to believe him, was by his trade an army chef and had been sent our way by the head army chef (aka Q Spoons) in the barracks.

Again, showing all of us that a man's chosen trade was in no way an indication as to his toughness.

With the emphasis being on fitness, as well as skills and techniques within the ring, we set ourselves the challenge of three phys sessions a day (although only one on Friday) and all the volunteers, and instructors, who stuck with the programme for the following few months, were an absolute credit to their cap badge and made me proud to be a Royal Engineer.

Conducting no holds bar boxing training also turned out to be an excellent way for me to measure someone's character. For initially I simply couldn't believe the amount of people that came forward at the start of our training regime, all full of bravado and displaying plenty of talent on the pads and skipping rope, but when we then started stepping into the ring and going the rounds with each other, the loudmouths (of all ranks) almost immediately all dropped away.

I also saw that rare spark in men, Sprs young and old, that meant even when they were beaten, weathering a multitude of powerful blows that had hammered their bodies and sporting numerous bleeding wounds, they still wouldn't give up and continued to walk back into the ring, gloves raised.

Cometh the hour, cometh the man.

As such, as the time drew closer to the RE Boxing Night at Brompton Barracks, quite the event in any regiment or battalion social calendar, I was left with a team of quiet, but confident and brave individuals who I knew I could not only train with and trust to step up to the plate when required, but who would not falter when it came to a task or challenge within their troop in the future.

An excellent opportunity came our way, weeks into our training programme, by which we were invited to come to a boxing club in Teesside and learn what we could from the fighters who trained there. The gym, a converted church, was headed up by an ex-serviceman, heralding from the Green Howards I believe, who upon leaving the military, had decided to give something back to his community and offer a chance for the lesser advantaged younger generations to develop themselves and potentially help them keep to the straight and narrow.

Needless to say, nerves were tense as the 21 boxing team piled into its transport and headed off to Teesside later on afternoon. For we'd no idea of the talent we were about to face and although we were all confident in our abilities, we still weren't sure how we fare up against these inner city fighters.

We arrived after an hour or so and after being welcomed into the gym/church, we were all immediately struck by two things; that although the facilities were minimal and in places slightly worn, they were all enthusiastically used by all club members. And secondly, the variety of ages that were present. After being shown around by our kind host, the gym owner, we learnt that for almost all of the individuals present, from plucky boys to looming young adults, typically their options were either to come to the boxing club after school and train, whilst being schooled by adult figures they could look up to and respect, or while away their nights on the inner city streets and endure the resulting risks.

Having started up the club purely out of the goodness of his own heart, all subscriptions were collected only when an individual could contribute, as the surrounding area had high levels of unemployment, went straight back into the club and to obtaining new equipment for the trainees, the ex-soldier had saved dozens of kids and teenagers from a potential life of crime and misery and had instilled in them not only a respect for others, but also for themselves.

A true local hero.

Although we did not have long to ponder on these thoughts and musing for we were all soon heavily engaged with the training programme that the club's boxers went through each evening and it was gruelling to say the least; the dedication and enthusiasm of the members more than making up for the sparse facilities. The evening was also to become unique for me as it was perhaps the one and only time I have suffered such a sound thrashing in the ring that I threw in the towel towards the end of the match.

It all unfolded when towards the end of our training session, by this point having gone on for well over an hour, at quite a fare pace at that, we were taken to a backroom which held the ring and were invited, one by one, step into the ring for three rounds and face the local prize fighters. What was to unfold however was something we hadn't seen or heard of yet, in that one of our boxers would go two rounds with the same opponent but for the third round, where they are truly beginning to tire, a fresh opponent would be swapped in and they'd have to face them for the final round.

The reason was that, and it was sound reasoning too, when a boxer has gone two full rounds, they are understandably very tired and make mistakes, thus highlighting to their trainers what they then need to work on in the future.

After two bouts had taken place, boxers from both the 21 team and the local club acquitting themselves well, I was then asked to step up and take my turn in the ring. By this point, of no small consequence, the room had filled up as all other training had ceased and all boxers, civilian and military, had turned up to watch the matches.

My opponent turned out to be an absolute giant, imagine a young Hereford bull with arms, but I knew that as long as I didn't let him corner me, I could hopefully dance around him and make my skill make up for his superior strength and weight. As such, all went relatively well during the first two rounds, with me dancing around him, throwing jabs at his head to make him bring his arms up and then pummelling his stomach, then dodging away urgently as his great fists shot back in retaliation.

Although I'm not sure as to how much real damage I did to him in the end, for he looked like he'd walk off a blow from a charging elephant, I was confident, come the end of the second round, that I'd won the rounds on points. I then stepped back to catch my breath, which was rather heavy at this point, having spent entire rounds hitting the equivalent of a side of beef, and looked up to my new opponent as he stepped into the ring and donned his gloves.

I was in trouble.

He was young, perhaps eighteen, but long limbed and well-muscled; I knew that not only would I have to get in under his long arms in order to be able to hit him, but it'd be bloody difficult to do so as he looked like he clearly knew his stuff. With my soldiers, and the club's full complement of boxers, now stood around and yelling advice (to the both of us), the bell rang and after walking in to the middle of the ring and touching gloves, we both set about getting to grips with each other.

His trainers were clearly a credit to their craft for as with almost every jab that I threw at him, he brushed aside, with pretty much every hook that I launched he ducked and with every feint I sent his way, he ignored most. All the while I was dodging his own heavy blows, which hurt like Hades, whilst trying to catch my breath, keep my chin down and keep away from him whilst still being able to suddenly make full use of any advantage that came my way.

Perhaps a minute in, which can feel like a lifetime to anyone who has stepped into the ring, with my breath coming in short gasps and my legs feeling shaky, I dropped my guard for the shortest of moments, hands lowering slightly as I gulped down air, a habit I've always struggled to shake, and as quick as lightening he threw a beautiful straight right jab at my face. It thundered between my gloves and smashed with full force into my face. Now my nose, which in the past could always be relied upon to stand up to any length of punishment, having been through any number of fights already, including a bare knuckle throw down at a Cairo house party, simply exploded. Blood spouting in all directions.

For the first time ever, I was out of the fight. As I was knocked back, senses reeling, struggling to keep my balance, eyesight spinning, nose leaking claret like a fire hydrant, I raised my gloves admitting defeat and conceded to the referee that I could fight no more.

I'm glad to say that despite the battering that I took, after a few seconds, I remembered to shake my opponent's hand after my eyesight had returned to normal, for it really was an excellent punch.

As I climbed out of the ring, annoyed that I'd let such a blow through my defences but at least happy I'd made it as far as I did, especially in front of such an audience, one of the club instructors said to me, whilst offering me a tissue to stem the flood from my ruined nose, a phrase which not only put a smile on my bruised and bloody face, as well as reminding why I loved such a sport, but also summed up his tactic in previous fights were he too had let punches through his guard:

'Don't worry, if any blows got through when I was boxing as a lad, I just blocked them with my face.'

That visit to the boxing club in Teesside was truly a humbling experience for all of the team, not only for the fact that our best fighter, in the fight after mine, was taken apart by their best boxer, all of sixteen years old. For it showed that despite being disadvantaged, in any number of areas, it just went to show what could be achieved by someone who was willing to spent time and effort in order to better the lives of others.

Sadly, a few weeks later, I was forced to withdraw from the running of the regimental boxing team, as well as the training, as my workload had steadfastly grown to a terrifying amount during my absences, spent in the delightful seclusion of the boxing hanger, and I found myself unable to juggle the responsibilities and duties of my troop and the boxing training.

It was a sad moment for me to tell the small team of tough boxers I'd help train, as well as their PTIs, over a number of weeks that I'd not be going towards the big competition with them.

But, thankfully, a saviour was close at hand in the form of Rob, my old diving partner who'd been posted to 21 with me, who was a truly accomplished boxer and a complete terror in the ring, and he took the reins from my begrudging hands.

The team then went on to a range of successes at the RE boxing night and I roared as loudly and proudly as I could as each one of my boxing team confidently stepped into the brightly lit and blood stained ring.

The perfect accolade summing up those who have the courage to step into the ring, whatever the circumstances or situation, was in my view written by former US president Theodore Roosevelt:

'It is not the critic who counts; not the man who points out how the strong man stumbles, or when the doer of deeds could have done them better. The credit belongs to the man who is actually in the arena, whose face is marred by dust and sweat and blood; who strives valiantly; who errs; who comes up short again and again, because there is no effort without error and shortcoming; but who does actually strive to do the deeds; who knows great enthusiasms, the great devotions; who spends himself in a worthy cause; who at the best knows in the end the triumph of high achievement, and who at the worst, if he fails, at least fails while daring greatly, so that his place shall never be with those cold and timid souls who neither know victory nor defeat.'

***

The Nijmegen Marches, the largest endurance marching event in the world, officially started in 1908 by members of the Dutch Army, are a true challenge of endurance to any soldier or officer. Twenty five miles each day, for four days in row, in the baking heat of the Netherlands summer. It is the most famous competition of its sort, with perhaps thousands taking part each year, many from military units from across the globe, of all sizes.

Would I be interested in leading a group of soldiers towards it? 'Yes sir, I would!'

When this gauntlet was thrown down before me whilst I was in the final days of the exercise in Salisbury Plain, which turned out to be my last training exercise with 7 Support Troop as, after almost two years I was coming to the end of my with 21 Engineer Regiment, I remembered that DanDan had taken part in the Marches when he was a junior officer and with that suitable incentive, as well as the challenge of completing one hundred miles in four days with a small team, I immediately got to work.

By this point in my career I'd taken soldiers on exercises to France, Germany, Austria, Poland, Croatia, to name but a few, and thus I knew a thing or two about how to organise one of these affairs. Especially at short notice, as the qualifying marches, in Scotland, sadly, were mere weeks away and I'd need to act fast in order to guarantee victory.

Aside from a sudden, but ultimately excellent and fitting, final test of strength and wills in South Wales in the form of a hybrid Troop deployment shortly afterwards, this venture was to be my last chance to lead a small unit of soldiers from my regiment in an infamously arduous environment, in a truly independent command environment.

Of course, the farce started almost immediately as when I eventually returned to 21 after completing the exercise in SPTA, where my troop and I had been overrun by the force of bulletproof Guardsmen in desert robes, I set about casting around for a team of half a dozen individuals, potentially some from the local Reserve units if I could, and to get us all onto a training programme that would prepare ourselves and our feet for the many miles we'd have to tackle.

Everyone I had spoken to about the Nijmegen marches had stressed the importance of numerous practise marches, as these would not only toughen the team and lessen the chances of injury, but would also help gel everyone together and create a modicum of team pride and identity.

'No. Not allowed. The regiment can't spare the soldiers to go off on separate training. You'll just have to get them all to the qualifying marches in Scotland and go from there. Crack on....'

This was the message eventually passed down to me from the various departments within 21's RHQ, because as per normal, all squadrons were too inundated were trawls that no spare time or manpower could be created. Also the local Reserve squadrons could only release up to three individuals between them, and they couldn't come across and train with us on a weekday.

Fantastic.

But, as with most things, this was nothing new and within a few days I'd managed to create a team of hopefuls. Some jumped at it willingly for a laugh (Bear), some I jokingly said I'd accuse them of physical weakness they didn't take up the challenge with me (Speedy), some did it for the chance to see Dutch girls in their summer clothing (they shall remain nameless) and some did it for the half dozen days spent in Holland, getting paid to march and then drink beer afterwards (everyone).

But before we could bask in the glorious Dutch sunshine, surrounded by thousands of military personnel from around the world and then try and drink them under the table in the evenings afterwards, we'd have to qualify first. Thus an equivalent area around the city of Nijmegen, thus meaning as flat as a pancake, would have been to be found in the UK. So I was little surprised when I found out where the qualifying marches were to take place.

Garelochhead. Scotland.

A place so desolate, bleak, isolated, windswept, cold, wet and filled with soaring highland peaks and mountains that it was reputed to be twinned with Mordor.

I decided that perhaps it'd be best to break the news to the lads once they'd been officially signed onto the venture, confirmed when their names were posted in regimental standing orders and therefore attendance became compulsory, before breaking the news to them. A credit to their uniform, they all loudly complained, blustered, laughed and then good naturedly clambered into the transport and went with me up to Scotland. Due to distances and time restraints, the Reserve Sprs drove up separately and met us there.

Hours later, the terrain outside the foggy windows of our van gradually changing from windswept and rain sodden gloriously green North Yorkshire countryside to even more stunning Scottish highland lochs and valleys. The journey, although a bit long, was a real treat in itself.

Except when our SatNav took us into the heart of a Glaswegian slum estate by mistake.

Once arriving in Garelochead training area, an army camp that time has forgotten, later that afternoon, we met our Reserves comrades and were pleased and surprised to find one had been a Regular beforehand. After throwing our sleeping bags onto some empty bunks, I decided that the best thing for the team to do before we started our thirty mile march tomorrow, the day after we were to march twenty, bearing in mind this was the first time that the team had all been together in one place, was to go into town and have a curry and a few beers.

I was careful to make sure that lads all kept their receipts so that returning to their units, they could claim back the price of their meal, as well as the subsequent fast food meals on the return journey southwards afterwards. My burgeoning JPA and my military financial know-how finally coming to the fore.

The next morning, a fine drizzly Saturday as ever there was, we lurched out of our ageing bunks, many of the team loudly questioning how I'd convinced them to spend a precious weekend in some forgotten barracks in the Scottish countryside, and after picking up our patrol sacks which were all stuffed in equal measure with food, painkillers and bandages, we went outside to form up with the hundreds of other people who were taking part in the event.

Royal Marine Commandos, British Infantry, Dutch Infantry, Army Cadets, Air Cadets, American soldiers, charity teams and dozens of civilian competitors all lined the roadway in the barracks in a ponderous column, waiting for H-Hour and to be allowed to start.

Now, it must be stressed, that in order to qualify to go towards the marches in Nijmegen, a team only had to complete each of the two marches, thirty miles, and then twenty miles, respectively, within the given time. It was not a race; teams were not competing against each other and were told at great length not to push themselves and go to fast.

Despite this, it didn't stop all of my team agreeing, both Regulars and Reserves, after having walked less than a mile, that we should march as fast as we could and be the first to cross the finish line that day, the common argument being:

'I don't care where we come in tomorrow's march, that's only twenty miles, but sure as hell we should be first today. That'll show these other units and civvy bastards a thing or two'

Again, how could I not but agree with them?

We subsequently set off at a fierce pace, not running but striding confidently and soon were steadily overtaking team after team, both military and civilian, and after an hour or two, we found ourselves at the front. Or so we thought.

As we dutifully followed the undulating thirty mile route laid out for us by the event organisers, bypassing large turbulent grey lochs, scattered and lonely highland farmhouses, fields of wet and doe eyed cattle and countless looming green hills, the team's morale grew very high indeed. For our feet were bearing up fine, we were trotting along at a fair old pace and we were positively eating up the miles.

Then, perhaps at the fifteen mile point, we rounded a corner and saw off in the distance a small straggling group of what looked like middle aged male ramblers, all wearing brightly coloured clothing and ambling along with apparently not a single care or worry in the world. Are they a team?

Surely not. Perhaps just some of the local old chaps going for a stroll. Hmm, they are following the same route as us; they can't be in front of us! It can't be.

They were.

It only took us a few minutes to realise that this collection of motley geriatrics were the final team standing in our way of coming first and so after girding our loins, we bent our backs to the task and set about overtaking them, for surely a team of fully fit soldiers would have no difficulty in outpacing a group of old men?

Well, mile after weary mile, we chased them. Each time as we thought we'd gained on them, we'd then see them disappearing around the next corner, just tantalising out of reach, like the rabbit in Alice in Wonderland, always just moving out of sight. It drove us all mad but it was also astounding to see how fast a pace that these elderly highlanders could maintain, despite their advanced years.

But the pace that we set ourselves in trying to beat this aged team soon began to take its toll. The blisters. Dear God, the blisters. I'd never had anything like them, or had anything like them since. For although always having had good feet and never suffering more than the occasional blister due to a bad choice of sock, we all soon had rich crops of them all over our feet.

It came to the point where we, especially me, would pray that the blisters would just burst as the pain to a popped blister was less trying than one still intact. As we steadily plodded along, every now and then one of the team would suddenly cry out and stumble, another blister having painfully burst and subsequently filling their boots with blood and sweat.

Our feet became veritable seas of pain, every single one covered in open sores, with new blisters forming in the bloody remnants of old ones. At the end of the march, everyone had had at least half a dozen blisters form and pop, and form again, in the same spot, but on different parts of their feet.

Thankfully, our efforts were not in vain and at the twenty file mile point, we finally overtook the last of the team of elderly civilians. It was during our cheerful chats, with us out of breath and pouring with sweat and them composed and breathing easily, with them as we strode past, that we found out that all of them had taken part in numerous qualifying marches previously. At least fifteen times each. Their feet must have been made out of leather and oak.

Sadly, as we passed the last of the highland gentlemen, we realised that we couldn't drop the pace as the elderly civilians, aka 'The Geriatrics', would have then overtaken us, making all our previous efforts null and void. We simply couldn't allow that.

As I helped drive our team onwards, encouraging where and when I could, all the while trying not to yell too loudly as my feet were gradually torn to shreds under the onslaught of blisters, I found myself rallying all of them (as well as myself) with the following battle cry:

'We're not getting beat by those fucking geriatrics!'

Those thirty miles over the highlands eventually passed and it was a very happy, although pain ridden, team that arrived first back at Garelochead camp, singing 'Hurrah for the CRE' as we marched through the camp gates.

It was laughable to think that out of all of our would-be competitors, from British, Dutch and American soldiers, to teams of young and healthy adults, the most serious obstacle to us achieving first place was a group of half a dozen elderly Scottish gentlemen. They certainly showed us a thing or two.

With our feet in shreds, we stumbled back to our block and the room was soon rent with cries and expletives as we all peeled off our boots and remains of our socks. Our ankles, soles and toes were simply ruined, all soaked with blood and not one of us had a square inch of flesh that wasn't torn and ripped. We all gingerly washed our feet in the showers, whilst desperately trying not to fall over as we'd have struggled to get back up again. After hobbling to dinner, and taking on board vast amounts of painkillers, we crashed down onto our bunks and fell immediately into a deep sleep.

The next morning, Sunday, was agony.

The record does not go to show what place our team came on the second day but let it be said that after another twenty mile march, we certainly didn't come first a second time round. The weather was simply foul, the wind cut into us like a knife and the rain came down in freezing sheets throughout. Our feet were in bits and only a bizarre mixture of personal pride and fantasising about Dutch beer and sunshine kept us going to the end.

I'm proud to say that throughout the agony of those twenty miles, the blokes kept up a steady stream of jokes and insults, some aimed at the organisers and a great many aimed at me, and not one of them let their ruined feet get in the way of them completing their final march.

Looking back on the qualifying marches in Garelochead, aside from the brutality that our feet went through, most of the team all went on to return home and then subsequently place themselves entirely in the care of their girlfriends, fiancés and wives, (myself included), it was a brilliant opportunity for me to escape away with a small unit of soldiers and take on a challenge together.

Sadly, fate and Army 2020 had one last cruel twist in store for me when I returned to work on Monday morning. For instead of taking the team onto Nijmegen, and the subsequent beers, sunshine and challenge, in a few weeks' time, I was suddenly trawled to take a hybrid troop of Engineers to support a Battalion of infantry in their preparations and training in Wales for an overseas deployment instead.

C'est la guerre. Napoleon once said that 'a soldier would march a thousand miles for a piece of ribbon', summing up the importance of awarding medals for bravery or fortitude to individuals that have earned them.

But the miniscule dab of cloth with a bottle cap sized scrap of plastic attached to it that we received at the end of our second march in Garelochead was stretching that theory a bit far. It just went to show how much officers and soldiers are willing to push themselves for the sake of their own pride and that of their unit. Or as one of the team put it to me, as we stood looking aghast at the pitifully miniscule medals that the event organiser had handed me when we wearily crossed the finish line in Garelochead barracks for the final time, having completed the fifty miles in record time, before starting our journey back down south:

'Don't worry boss. Wounds heal, chicks dig scars, and pride lasts forever.'

***

'Those who don't learn from history are destined to repeat it.'

Upon first starting my fledgling military career when I first entered TA RMAS, I discovered that in keeping with this mantra, the British military regularly conducts all manner of Battlefield Studies across the globe. Taking groups to near and far previous battlefield, teaching its officers and soldiers important lessons from the past, good and bad, as well as highlighting the efforts and fortitude of their forbearers and opponents.

Now, as God's own history bore, this discovery simply delighted me.

As such, when I first joined my regiment, I delved straight into seeing how I could get my soldiers, as well as me, onto such Studies. For aside from creating the opportunities for soldiers to get onto something interesting and enjoy themselves, be it firing Vickers machine guns and WW2 Russian automatic weapons on ranges, to driving tanks or having dinner in various prestigious Officers' Messes across Europe, I also wanted them to learn what hardships and challenges previous officers and soldiers had faced in a range of varying wars and conflicts. Thus hopefully inspiring them and giving them motivation to do 'their bit' when the time came.

To my delight I also discovered that Battlefield Studies, through the guidance of some of my NCOs, could be used as a reward for individuals from my troop who had been working particularly hard and had, in my view, earned a reward and a short break away from regiment.

For the countries we were to visit were many, and often the Sprs that accompanied me, or those who went on their own, had not visited those parts of the world before, not at least at the expense of HMG. France, Belgium, Luxembourg,

Italy, Holland, Poland, Germany and Greece, to name but a few.

In the early opening adventures of getting my feet under the table of Battlefield Studies and learning the ropes on how to develop myself and those under my command, I was very lucky to chance upon a man whom I was to discover was the major domo of Battlefield Studies in the British military. A man known to one and all as 'Sticky'.

In my view, a truly fantastic and experienced Royal Engineer officer. Eccentric, driven, an avid student of history and an accomplished veteran of various African conflicts, as well as keen as mustard to teach as many officers and soldiers he could on the importance of learning about, and remembering, the lessons of the past.

After completing a course that he and his department ran where all the students of all ranks were taught how to plan and lead Battlefield Studies throughout Europe, I realised that under his guidance, I'd be able to offer my soldiers a chance to see some very interesting parts of the world, learn some excellent lessons and do something that wasn't exactly the norm.

France. The general playground and training area of the British Army for hundreds of years. Its rolling fields of wheat and grassland, as well as the cobbled paves and broad boulevards, have been graced by the treat of countless thousands of weary British military units and its soil has been blessed with the presence of graves of soldiers from a multitude of nations, both as defenders and transgressors. As such, there are many historical battles, both large and small, which serving personnel can glean valuable nuggets from and use for the benefit of their own soldiers and officers. The principle lessons from WW1 seemed to be don't trust artillery against barbed wire and if at all possible, infantry should be provided with all opportunities to use surprise, speed and cover.

Quelle surprise.

But it is surprising how often these simple and glaring facts seem to have been forgotten by commanders, past and present, or omitted in their plans, with severe consequences.

Over a number of Battlefield Studies, with 21 and with a number of mixed unit groups, I was to tread the fields and quiet lanes of areas whose names reverberate throughout history and are synonymous with slaughter, bungling and unwavering bravery and heroism. Cambrai, Arras, Amiens and more.

Aside from visiting these sombre and hallowed areas and learning what we could from them, and how to apply the lessons learnt to twenty first century warfare, we were also fortunate enough to visit and spent time in some of the fantastic towns and cities across France, and have some truly memorable occasions as a result.

Paris, after a wine soaked dinner in the former Officers' Mess in Paris, a building filled with deep carpets, glittering silver and imposing portraits, all ranks then poured themselves into taxis in search of the fabled Parisian night life. In our efforts to be first to the designated club, our extortions to our drivers to go faster and faster subsequently created full blown competitive taxi races down the Champs Elysees. Additionally, many hours later, after tumbling out of perhaps the only Irish bar in Paris open at 3am, after a long time spent drinking and carousing with the expat community, I looked up and saw one of my fellow officers talking loudly to a lady who was clearly one of Paris's infamous Ladies of Negotiable Affection.

What made the whole encounter all the more amusing that my friend didn't speak French and the Lady clearly didn't speak English and they were obviously talking at cross purposes, helped along in no small amount by the large amounts of alcohol they had both clearly consumed. For my fellow young officer was politely enquiring, albeit it slightly slurring his words, as to where the nearest nightclub was, having no idea what profession the lady he was talking to was in, whilst the lady was very loudly and clearly stating in her Parisian patois how many Euros each of her very select and nefarious services were.

After watching each of them talk to each other for roughly five minutes on the street, standing in the rain and light cast by the street lights, neither of them understanding a word of the other and getting increasingly irate at their counterpart, they both abruptly turned and strode away from each other.

This impromptu piece of street theatre, and example of two cultures meeting, left me simply helpless with laughter, leaning onto a lamppost for support and bent double, clutching my sides.

Or upon turning up one sunny morning to conduct a tour down a rural French river to look at the difficulties faced by Royal Engineers in WW1 in their attempts to cross them under fire from the German Army, only to find the local Mayor, accompanied by two local Gendarmes, turning up within minutes and very politely asking 'what the hell the British Army was doing in his village?'

I was out of earshot when this deputation had first arrived and it was only after finding out that none of the Battlefield Study organisers spoke French, only German, which would ingratiate any rural Frenchman, I was then called for. This was the first time I was to see how useful it is having an effective translator, as well as someone who knows about the culture and background of the locals, in order to help facilitate conversation and cooperation.

For after politely explaining to the Mayor and his escort that we were not in fact occupying his village in the name of Her Majesty Queen Elizabeth II, but were only learning about the efforts that were made by the Allies during WW1 against the Germans, he couldn't help us enough.

Indeed, ten minutes into our conversation, my GCSE French teachers would have been proud, he accepted an invitation to come along with us in one of our boats and we spent the afternoon talking about his previous career in the French military and the quality of the local wines in the region.

Crisis averted.

The Polish, potentially aside from the Burmese, are perhaps some of the friendliest and most welcoming people I have ever had the pleasure to talk and work with. When I was offered the chance to follow in the footsteps of the rapidly retreating German Army, and rapidly advancing Soviets, in the dying days of WW2 through Poland, I couldn't fill out the Battlefield Study paperwork fast enough.

The hospitality of the Polish people, urban and rural, was first demonstrated to me when our group were collected on the banks of one of the sprawling rivers that spread throughout Poland and were studying how the Soviets had crossed it despite all the obstacles put in place by the Germans, when all of a sudden a deputation of local civilians approached us and pointed towards a picnic area nearby.

Through the explanation of our local Polish guide, knowledge languages and culture coming to the fore again here, we suddenly realised that the locals had seen that we were British military and out of the kindness of their own hearts, had taken it upon themselves to bake cakes, brew coffee and lay on a picnic for all of us. Sitting on the sun drenched banks, lazily watching the ducks sun themselves out on the water in the afternoon heat, whilst feasting away on freshly baked Polish pastries and piping hot and delicious beverages, was not something to be forgotten.

We also had the pleasure of being guided around Warsaw and learning about the 'Uprising', as well as what followed after, and visiting the museum dedicated to those brave individuals who fought during that heroic but tragic saga of Polish military history. As well as being privileged enough to be invited along to a WW2 mock up battle between Polish resistance fighters and the German occupiers, accompanied by a range of working WW2 vehicles and weapons. From Halftracks, Bren carriers and vintage machine guns and to a very rare and fully functioning Goliath tank; it was a rare experience.

Especially as that particular morning all of us in the Battlefield Study were suffering from simply hellish hangovers and as part of the courtesy of the locals who had put on the display for us, they had also got a fully functioning WW2 Soviet field kitchen running and were dishing out bowls of some of the most delicious soup, and baskets of freshly baked bread, that I have ever tasted.

Within the towns and cities we ventured into whilst our coach load of officers and soldiers scribbled down notes on the titanic clashes that had taken place between the Germans and the Soviets we all discovered how delicious Polish food is and how much the Polish, like their British compatriots, love a good drink and night out on the town.

One of the benefits of going on these Battlefield Studies was that due to the number of overseas military officers and soldiers that work within the UK as part of the UN or NATO, we also had a few interesting characters with us whenever we ventured abroad as it was always good politics, as well as good fun, to invite some of overseas allies along with us.

In Poland we were fortunate enough to have along with us a very large, very friendly and very funny American Army Engineer. A true Yank, a friend to all the world, as well as being an accomplished Afghanistan veteran, he kept us all amused by a constant string of very dry and witty jokes predominantly aimed at himself and his country, especially when we were into our sixth or seventh pint of the evening.

'Euros? Oh, I'm sorry, can I pay with freedom?'

'Do you know my girlfriend, Lady Liberty?'

It was during one particularly good sojourn out into a rather large Polish town that my soldiers and I, for I'd managed to bring four of my Sprs out with me, under the pretext of an administration party, had to conduct perhaps the only British military strike operation that has taken place in a fully functioning strip club.

Whilst swigging down yet another large glass of good, but cheap, vodka in a local cantina one evening, I was startled by the sudden arrival of one of my Sprs who breathlessly informed me that allegedly Stevie had been, whilst walking drunkenly back to our hotel, supposedly dragged into a local strip joint by the bouncers. Now, knowing that Stevie was a staunch family man and wouldn't be likely to traipse into a House of Ill Repute, we leapt from our bar stools, made our way through the heaving crowd of the bar, comprised of locals and Brits all getting on like a house on fire, and ran outside.

Breathing in deep gulps of refreshing cool night air, we looked around, saw the strip club that had apparently swallowed up one of my Sprs and after issuing the briefest of brief QBOs in my military career to my assembled, although slightly swaying, gang of raiders, I led the charge straight through the belligerent club bouncers and charged into the darkness.

As I sprinted up the neon glowing stairs, thoughts of my passed out Spr being robbed blind by Eastern European gangsters running through my head, I burst through a set of closed double doors and into a den of sheer sin. Ladies walked around in pretty much nothing, or nothing at all, flashing their eyes, amongst other things, at prospective clients, sleazy middle aged lounge room lizards sat at a long tacky mirrored bar at one side of the room, eyeing all the local talent over their sticky cocktails and throughout the room were numerous open air booths with deep red cushions lining the outsides, and a single pole in the middle of each one.

My Sprs and I stood at bay at the top of the stairs, glancing round with haste from our position, hoping desperately to catch a glimpse of our missing comrade. Every second counted and the last thing I wanted to have to do was inform his wife that her husband had been drugged, robbed and then sold for spare parts on the black market.

We couldn't see him.

What we did see, however, was another one my Sprs, aka Ginge, sitting like the Roman Emperor Nero in one of the open booths, a broad grin on his face, a bottle of house imitation champagne in each hand and a six foot blonde wearing nothing but some strips of lace sat on each knee. He looked up, saw us, gave a thumbs up and then went back to nuzzling between the breasts of one of his beauties.

I dispatched one of my raiders to walk over and check he was okay and had possession of his faculties, as well as his wallet and passport. Upon hearing the affirmative and the subsequent assurance that he'd be on the bus the next morning in time for our departure to another region of Poland, I did what every sensible officer would do and left him to his fun.

Later on we found Stevie was in fact sprawled out fast asleep on his bed back in his hotel room, a case of mistaken identity it turned out. And Ginge, true to his word, was packed and ready to go for the bus that following morning, albeit smelling like a tart's handbag and grinning like a Cheshire cat.

Not to be out done, whilst we were sat on the bus that morning, all drinking gallons of tea and water in order to try and mitigate the effects of the local spirits we had all drunk the night before, our Battlefield Study leader did a headcount and realised that one young RLC captain was missing from the bus.

Within less than five minutes before we had to depart, things were getting a little tense and the general mood on the coach was beginning to turn sour against this young captain. If he couldn't handle his drink, then he shouldn't have gone out, much less than turn up late and thus keep the bus from departing and us from our breakfast, which was waiting us in our next hotel. But, with less than a minute to spare, suddenly he appeared through the crowds by the bus and leapt aboard and was immediately grilled by the trip OC as to why he was late:

'Where the hell have you been? We've been waiting for you! What do you have to say for yourself?'

Everyone aboard the bus, soldier and officer alike, Colonel to Private, ceased all conversation and craned their necks around their seats, listening with baited breath what this young buck had to say for himself.

'Well, sir, firstly my apologies for keeping everyone but, you see, I ended up having a threesome with two strippers last night and I only just left their bed ten minutes ago.'

The entire bus broke into a huge and rapturous applause and wild cheering.

***

Belgium, the home of the best beer in the world (except for Harvey's of Sussex, of course), the centre of fine dining, a shrine of classical architecture and the crossroads of Europe. A country which has felt the tread of armies more than most and its battlefields are seared into the hearts and memories of the entire British military.

Numerous times I was lucky enough to be paid to visit the length and breadth of that small European country where the fate of nations have hinged more often than the history books care to remember. From strolling round the fine winding streets and coffee shops of Mons, to seeing the glorious and heart rending spectacle of the 'Menin Gate' and the ceremony that occurs there each evening to honour those that fell in the savage fighting at Ypres, or striding over the green fields of Vimy Ridge and listening solemnly to the tales of the slaughter and the bravery of the Canadian Corps who fought there; there is much to be learnt, good and bad, from the history books and Battlefield Studies of Belgium.

These, sadly, one could say, are not just limited to WW1 but also extend to WW2 and what occurred there under the march of the German Jack boot and the tread of their Panzer tanks. Most famously was the Battle of the Bulge where Allied forces, principally American, fought off a fierce encircling German counter attack which was aiming to drive the Allies back into the sea.

As the savage and bitter winter ravaged the beleaguered Allied soldiers, week after week, it was only their fierce esprit de corps and dogged determination not to give in that kept their will to fight going. Epitomised by the reply given by the American commander when asked by the Germans to surrender his forces:

'Nuts!'

The importance of learning from the conflicts that have taken place in Belgium it also extends to many years previously, well before the events of WW1, where, again, the fate of Europe was decided on a Belgian battlefield; Waterloo.

It would be foolish to think that just because the soldiers who marched there fired muskets and not machine guns, that there are no lessons to be learnt from them and the battlefield they fought in. Such as the folly of fighting on two fronts at the same time (Napoleon), or the penalty of not using a combined armed battle group against an enemy and instead sending the cavalry in alone (Field Marshall Ney) or the merits of keeping one's soldiers out of site and range from the enemy's artillery until the last feasible moment (The Duke of Wellington).

The opportunities to get up to capers and bizarre but hilarious incidences were also plentiful during my numerous visits to Belgium and its various towns and villages; a particular incident that always springs to mind whenever I think of the gorgeous city of Ypres was when I was drinking with a number of officers in a bar by one of the city's courtyards one evening.

'Hey, Beeching, look at the ladies coming this way. I think they're going to come down and sit next to us!'

'No chance mate. You're ugly as sin, I've got my girlfriend back home and besides, you don't speak bloody French.'

'But you do! Come on, translate for us. Big us up. Look, here they come, play it cool, get chatting to them and see if they'll speak to us.'

Not subjects exactly covered in my GCSE and university French classes.

Aside from the various opportunities available to all ranks to travel across the length and breadth of Old Europe and examine the armed struggles that have taken place upon it, too much focus, in my view, is often given to the WW1 conflicts that occurred in Central Europe. More attention needs to be paid to the savage and cruel fighting that took place during both world wars in the Alps and in Eastern Europe. Seemingly chapters the history books, and past Battlefield Studies, appear to have neglected.

Thankfully though, through no small amount of cunning and guile, I was fortunate to also visit some truly infamous and varying battlefield sites where various Axis and Allied soldiers came to blows.

Best of all, Arnhem, the most famous place in British, as well as American and Polish, airborne military history, where in order to shorten the war, although the operation ultimately ended in failure and defeat for the Allies, the entire British First Airborne Division jumped in and around the Dutch city of Arnhem in order to try and seize the bridge that spanned the river Rhine.

The fighting that was to take place there between the men who wore the Maroon Beret and their German opponents was to become legend and enshrined in history books and films throughout the world.

Dramatized in the film 'A Bridge Too Far', the tragic story of the brave men of the British Airborne Division, roughly ten thousand paratroopers, equating to one eighth of the entire British Army nowadays, is littered with lessons to be learnt and remembered. Additionally, important lessons aside, many who went on the visit, and I was one of them, also just wanted to pay homage to the brave men that fought there.

At the end of the fighting, when the remnants of the British Airborne forces had either surrendered due to lack of ammunition, had been killed, over eight thousand dead, more than the total number of British Paratroopers currently serving in Army 2020, or had escaped back to Allied lines, the First Airborne Division never truly recovered. The lessons that were highlighted to us whilst we were guided in and around the city of Arnhem were legion.

Such as the dangers of relying on one single narrow road for advancing a large group of vehicles, such as the entire Allied Armoured advance; having poor communications between ground troops and aircraft; not having effective intelligence as to exactly what enemy troops would be in the area, an experienced SS Panzer Brigade and not low grade troops as was initially thought; not supplying the forward troops well enough; not bearing in mind how liberated civilians would hamper the advance of soldiers, comparable to the opening days and unforeseen difficulties of Op TELIC in Iraq; and many more.

Due to its history, especially with airborne troops, the city of Arnhem regularly receives hundreds of Battlefield Studies each year, from a range of militaries and as such, its various cafes, bars and restaurants know full well how to cater for hungry and thirsty troops. The hospitality and friendliness of the Dutch meant that after all of our touring, there was no doubt in anyone's mind, this particular Battlefield Study had over fifty officers and soldiers on it, with a good smattering of Paras, that good times would be had on the one night we were permitted to venture into the city.

The peak, in my view, was when my Sergeant Major, a thoroughbred paratrooper himself, suddenly grabbed me whilst I was outside a club in the early hours of the morning and excitedly, fired up on by a combination of numerous drinks and inflamed airborne spirit, gave me the following orders:

'Troopy! New orders. We're all going to rally on the bridge at sunrise! Spread the word, re-org on the bridge at zero six hundred hours.'

Needless to say, despite all our collective best efforts, we all became far too hampered by the countless glasses of fine Dutch beer to carry out, or indeed remember, these orders;

Greece, sadly, was not to be rated too highly by my soldiers whom I sent there as part of a number of Battlefield Studies, for although its regions and peoples are infamous for titanic struggles, especially against tyranny, and for their love of life and liberty, its modern day facades did not seem to impress themselves too much upon the visiting representatives from HM forces. For although they delighted in meeting and working with people, and the military, from across Greece, it was perhaps on their R&R visits in the cities and towns that their opinions varied. As I was eventually to find out when the first group of my Sprs returned from their Hellenic trip and reported their findings and experiences to me one morning in my office:

'Yep, it were pretty crap sir, we thought. We visited Athens and the only good bit were the ruins, and they built them a couple of a thousand years ago. Everything since has appeared to have gone to the dogs, they pay everything in cash so they don't have to pay tax, no wonder they ain't got no bloody money!'

One wonders what it'd be like if some British broadsheet paper was to publish a British soldier's or officer's travelling critiques of countries and cultures around the world. I for one would read it.

My thanks go to Major Sticky and his department for all the instruction and guidance they gave. Allowing soldiers and officers alike to visit foreign fields and aside from learning important lessons from the past, also giving them the opportunity to see more of the world and the various nations, cultures and people that inhabit it.

From witnessing a heartrending spectacle of a nation solemnly keeping with its promise to its soldiers and allies of past years and paying tribute to them every evening at the Menin Gate, surrounded by a countless multitude of onlookers, young and old, to standing in a sunny field in Southern England and watching a man dressed as a Soviet soldier driving a hovercraft at full speed around a racecourse whilst soldiers in the near background clambered joyfully over a fully functioning US Sherman tank, the Battlefield Studies I was fortunate enough to be sent on, as well as the activities I took part in or witnessed, were worth every single penny spent by HMG.

***

Throughout my time as a troop commander in 21 Engineer Regiment with the rascals of 7 Support Troop, my general approach was us to deploy away onto some real military escapades and exercises, far away from the clutches of

RHQ, from sports qualifications programmes to career courses that they actually wanted and were applicable to their particular trade.

I discovered that this approach was perhaps the best method available to me in order to enable a soldier to not only progress and increase their professional skill sets, but actually enjoy their time in the military. These various opportunities to get away from regiment also meant that there was less chance for me to get myself into trouble if I was deployed out of the gates, doing some actual soldiering instead of being sat behind my desk.

My approach to normal regimental life, and trying to get away from it as much as I could, be it on my own or more preferably with some of my soldiers, was epitomised by my OC in his speech during my farewell lunch at 21 Engineer Regiment Officers' Mess at the end of my two years as a Troopy:

'Everyone is aware of Troopy Beeching's appetite for getting out of regiment. I think that over the two years he was stationed here, he never spent more than two weeks in a row in his office.'

I could not have wished for a more fitting final statement on the time I spent whilst employed on 21 Engineer Regiment's nominal role.

I always strongly recommended this approach, for the benefit of the soldiers and also for the beleaguered officer in charge of them, to all those I came across during my time in the military, regardless of the screams and indignant emails that spewed forth from RHQ. The fact of the matter was that they were my soldiers, my military family, and thus they were always my priority, no one else.

Ultimately I loved my soldiers, the good and the bad, a strange sort of feeling that I suppose only someone who has been in the military would really understand, and it was with an extremely heavy heart when I eventually said goodbye to them at a farewell BBQ kindly arranged by SSgt Dixon at his family home.

The two years of good fortune and heaven sent luck, as well as a boatload of misfortune, errors and self-made mistakes, taught me a range of experiences that were although sometimes painful to learn, others were an absolute joy and I wouldn't have traded for all the tea in China. The lessons I learnt, I feel, were not particularly new or ground breaking, but ones perhaps that I believe have been cited by leaders throughout the centuries and are as applicable to Alexander's or Hannibal's time as they are now.

Listen to your NCOs, take on advice, soundboard your ideas off them and form your own command style, but remember that you are in charge and despite all the highs at times, in the end, it is very lonely at the top and this is the burden all commanders must bear. The buck stops with you, your soldiers don't want a friend, they want a leader. They want to have the absolute confidence that you will make the right decision, even in the most challenging and difficult of circumstances. This is where, if possible, checking your ideas or proposed plans with your NCOs previously come to the fore; from how to give an effective briefing, deal with a tricky discipline issue or doing what is best for one of your soldiers in terms of their career or family life.

There will be times when as a leader, within the first week or perhaps in their twentieth year of command, where they'll be forced to make decisions that will make them unpopular. Decisions that might mean, for a while, that they are not offered a brew or casual conversation in the office as regularly as before.

But it is those moments where true leaders shine through, the ones who do or say the right thing, even when they don't necessarily want to do. Or, to put it in the words of a Sergeant Major I knew:

'Troopy, you can be an officer they would follow into battle, one they would follow onto the dance floor, or just one they would follow just out of plain curiosity. Maybe you'll be lucky enough to be a combination of all three.'

Paperwork. It will rule your life; accept it, study MS writing and get good at it, for your soldiers' careers and lives depend on it, however farcical that may sound. Get on best terms with your unit chief clerk, civilian or military, for they will have the relevant know how and will be able to provide guidance to you that will be worth its weight in gold. Such as how to handle soldiers' annual reports, financial claims or career course applications.

The tiniest alteration made on a form, correct or incorrect, can make or break a soldier's career.

Adventure Training expeditions, both in the UK and abroad, will be thrown at you quick and fast, thus you must prepare for them as best as possible. Forewarned is forearmed. Key to this struggle is communication; it is vital. Find out who in the regiment, squadron or company has done a similar trip or venture before and then get the necessary guidance from them.

If in doubt, speak directly to the event organisers, no matter how intimidating it may feel for a Second Lieutenant to ring up an unknown Major or Brigadier.

Fools learn from their mistakes, whereas I think it's best to learn from theirs.

There are numerous websites available, some accessible from the military intranet, others on civilian computers, as well as groups on social media, that list persons who can not only be informally contacted to find out the necessary do's and don'ts, but also for little insider tips that will make all the difference between enjoying the trip or just seeing it as another trawl or assignment arriving in the inbox from the 2iC.

'Lead by Example', the mantra and all prevailing single most important lesson that is taught at RMAS and it must never be forgotten, regardless of how long a leader may have served in the forces. In my view it focuses particularly on, bearing in mind the line of work the British military involves itself it, to fitness, both the physical and mental aspects.

A leader, be they a soldier or officer, experienced or novice, must endeavour at all times to be as physically fit as possible, as well as concurrently developing their mental agility and command ability. It is not easy and the work never stops, as one can always do better, but commanders must remember that in order to be worthy of the rank that they wear and the obedience that they demand, they must be the leader of their particular pack, the strongest, the fastest and the most understanding of not only the situation, but also of their subordinates.

Besides, one of the best things about effective teamwork is that it gives the enemy other people to shoot at than just you.

On that note, there are very few things worse than a commander, especially an officer, who cannot make a decision. Whether you are sat in the office, or stood in the field watching the battle unfold, make a decision! Make a good one, a bad one, or even an excellent one, just for heaven's sake work up your courage and take the leap. For that's your job, it is the reason for you being there and, more importantly, it is what your soldiers are looking to you for.

Lastly, but most importantly, practise in making the correct decisions, for you never know when the day will arrive where your life and your soldier's lives will solely depend on what choice you make.

A good leader can make their followers do things, a great leader can make them do things they don't initially want to do.

When the work is mounting up, and your desk is positively groaning under the weight of piled up paper, remember that time is a commander's most precious resource, aside from your soldiers, and should be preserved as such. When walking around the barracks, say between offices, in order to avoid being waylaid by people coming to you with meaningless trivia, try walking at a slightly above average pace, with a sheaf of papers in your arms, muttering quietly to yourself; no one will bother you. If in the field, use an open training manual or TAM.

I was once told that in regards to my own career development and direction 'leave it to your chain of command, they will steer you in the right direction', and it took me a while to realise that although this is correct in theory, in reality it is often very wrong. The reason being that often, due to the tempo of life within the British military nowadays, individuals of all ranks are typically rushed off their feet and it is often very difficult for them to find time to sit down and accurately develop their subordinates. Inexcusable yes, but a fact of life none the less. As a result, bearing in mind my appetite for languages, overseas work and non-conventional jobs, I soon came to the following conclusion.

Find out what you want to do. It could be anything you like, from an arduous course to a basic university programme, sports qualifications, Special Forces selection, overseas travel or learning a new language. Find out what you want to do, what direction you want your career to take and then fight tooth and nail for it every step of the way. Accept the fact that there is never a good time to go away, but go away you must in order to develop.

For me personally, it would have been a crying shame to look back on a two year career as a YO, or as a section commander or SNCO, for instance, and realise that all that you achieved was to dance to RHQ's tune, with no personal development having been achieved at all.

You must develop yourself, your soldiers even more so; as often your chain of command will be too busy to do it themselves.

A soldier once turned to me in the field and said jokingly:

'When I die, I want my chain of command to lower my casket into the ground so that they can let me down one more time.'

Get your soldiers away on activities as much as possible; they all, hopefully, joined up to serve their country, they didn't sign up to sit in the squadron smoking area or doing shifts in the guardroom.

Key to this is asking them what they're interested in doing, as often you'll be surprised at the answers you get in reply.

In regards to sports, utilise the numerous websites, such as the 'Adventurous Training Group Army' website, and publications advertised in most regimental gyms and HQs to find out what courses are available, what dates they are running and how to best apply to get soldiers onto them.

On the subject of trade qualifications and career enhancement, such as short and long language programmes or arduous courses, such as the AACC or SRR PTA, find out what your soldiers want to do, tell them to go away and find the courses details and dates. When they then return to you with the information in their hands, use every brain cell and stretch of moral fibre in your possession to get them onto said courses.

In my view, a soldier's or officer's resettlement training starts the day they sign up to the military and it is every commander's responsibility to ensure that their subordinates use their available time as productively as possible.

You will find that amongst your unit you will have some very good soldiers indeed, such as the ones I knew who volunteered to step in and help the newest Spr in my troop manage his personal finances and debt so that he didn't starve or end up in prison, succeeding far quicker and more effectively than any official regimental department could have done.

There will be some excellent soldiers, like the ones I knew who always pushed themselves onto the most arduous of courses and overseas deployments they could find so that they could best support their families back home and provide them with the best life possible.

There will also the bad ones, the bastards, such as the one who, when he deployed to Germany, kept his additional overseas pay a secret from his family so that whilst they had to tighten their belts, he could secretly hit the bars and clubs in town.

But all of them, the good, the bad and the ugly, are your responsibility and it is up to you to develop and lead them, your loyalty is to them.

Work for them, care for them and lead them. If this is done correctly, they will follow you to hell and back.

As Field Marshal Viscount Slim once said:

'No man can be given a more honourable task than to lead his fellow countrymen.'

HENRY B BEECHING

7

Joke & Dagger Work

Defence engagement is in our blood. A globally minded nation requires, and is well served by, globally minded Armed Forces. We do much of this well, and by instinct. But we could do it better; and both the Armed Forces and the nation would be the richer and more fulfilled by our doing so.

Lt Gen Simon Mayall CB

Throughout my weeks and months of training, and then the two year stint as a troop commander at 21 Engineer Regiment, I tried my absolute hardest not only to maintain my knowledge of Arabic and French, not easy even in the most accommodating of situations, but also get involved as much as I could in Translator and Cultural Advisory (CULAD) work, in partnership with overseas Defence Engagements.

I also was to undergo and pass a number of selections for a range of Joke and Dagger units that exist throughout the Tri

Services of the British Armed Forces which specialised in languages, working closely with MENA nations and dealing in irregular warfare.

But over time I was to discover that although the British Army loves 'upstream capacity building' and working closely with allies to solve problems overseas before they begin, in reality anyone trying to get involved in this line of work, typically by trying to learn a language and get an overseas posting, will find themselves struggling severely, especially within the Royal Engineers.

This is typically because of a general lack of understanding and interest by the chain of command, as well as a subsequent severe difficulty in securing a non-conventional post due to dire regimental manpower shortages across the whole Army and British military.

The reality of an officer, especially one within the Corps of Royal Engineers, trying to secure a line of work either overseas or as part of a UK based Defence Engagement unit, or even short term loan service work from a conventional Field Army regiment (known as an E2 Post), is that they will find that it is less akin to 'upstream capacity building' and more like a salmon trying constantly to swim upstream against the prevailing current. More's the pity.

But still, despite the resistance, usually by senior officers thinking that I was off on a 'jolly' and the blank incomprehensible stares from across the desk I often faced, due to an apparent widespread severe lack of interest or knowledge by senior officers of the importance of sufficient engagement with our allies, bearing in mind how small our armed forces are nowadays, I became determined not to become deterred and to get involved in an unconventional line of work that I was extremely passionate about.

To follow in the footsteps and try, even in a small way, to emulate, in my view, some of the greatest military minds and careers in British military history:

Lassen. Brooke. Lawrence. Churchill. Maclean. De La Billiere. Gordon. De Wiart.

From studying in my spare time and eventually qualifying as a military translator in Arabic and French, to managing meetings and translating between the various heads of Arab military units and their British counterparts, or frantically casting around Portsmouth one rainy afternoon in the search of four Arab Colonels who had failed to return to their designated pick up point on time, eventually compelling me to start searching the locals brothels and telephoning everyone shy of the Egyptian Ambassador to the UK before I eventually managed to find them.

The CULAD assignments I managed to get onto were always trying, but also always immensely rewarding. In the words of one of my idols, 'Harry Flashman', an accomplished (albeit a fictional one) linguist and a political agent himself:

'It's hell in the diplomatic.'

Straight from the early days of my youth to the stress filled but immensely rewarding days as an officer in the Royal Engineers, my heart was set upon exploring the vast, and largely secret, world that existed out there in the form of overseas postings, working with foreign militaries and operating in places where it would not be strongly recommended to be wearing a British Army uniform.

I knew that in order to qualify for such lines of work, I'd have to establish my pedigree to my various chains of command first, and aside from getting a university degree in Arabic and Middle Eastern Studies, I'd also have to prove my worth in military circles before I could be vouched for any overseas 'secret squirrel' posting.

'Beeching, you speak Arabic right?'

I sigh inwardly. This senior officer not only had access to my personal military files, but also had turned down a number of previous requests from me in the past for Arabic CULAD jobs. Bring a horse to water and all that....

'Yes, I can string one or two words together if needed.'

'I've just been contacted by some Defence Attaché who is taking some Egyptian Colonels over the UK for a number of days and he needs a translator. You'll be put up in the same accommodation as them and will go wherever they go, helping translate during meetings, answering their questions and all that. Fancy getting away from regiment for a few days?'

'I think you know the answer to that.'

My first steps towards sipping fine Bordeaux at multinational powwows in refined chateaus whilst reclining in chesterfields by the fire or sporting a fine rugged beard whilst working in the mountains with some pro-government tribal militia had begun!

Although it was clear right from the start that for the foreseeable future, before I could be packed off to some North African desert or desolate mountain village, I'd have to pay my dues and put up with sipping cups of tepid tea in mundane conference rooms and working with portly Middle Eastern officers in quiet of barracks in Southern England first.

Over my career as an Arabist there were a number of lessons that I learnt, initially whilst cutting my teeth as both a penniless student studying Arabic and then afterwards as an eager but nervous CULAD. A number of the lessons came about through trial and error, some through pure chances of luck and some, thankfully not too many, were learnt through making mistakes and determining never to repeat them.

For instance, when it comes to hosting individuals from overseas, civilian or military, one simply cannot overestimate the importance and significance of providing gifts (aka gifting), official photos and certificates. This is not meant to be patronising but instead aimed at putting across the absolute importance of such things. All countries and cultures around the world regard different social aspects as important and it would be foolish to think otherwise. This must be borne in mind by any aspiring young officer or NCO who is taking their first tentative steps towards becoming a CULAD.

The importance of when an overseas delegation comes to visit, setting aside an afternoon, or longer, for the individuals to go shopping and buy presents for their families back home, as well as their senior officers, is often simply vital and key to any successful visit. The significance of government figures, as well as military, bringing back gifts for their family and friends, as well as the senior officers that gave them permission to travel overseas in the first place, is such that many airlines, especially in MENA countries, often allow persons to bring two suitcases on board as hand luggage, so often overburdened are they with gifts.

For the duration of any visit, be it five days or five months, it is important for the visiting delegation to feel assured that their assigned CULAD, for instance a young cheerful Royal Engineer Second Lieutenant, is firmly on their side and will do their utmost to be as helpful as possible. This should not done in a smarmy, lizard like manner, as that would repel anyone, but in a manner that you deem appropriate to the time, people and place. In short, assume the rank and concerns of the person you are speaking to.

There is no correct or set way to put this across to the visiting persons but as soon as they feel comforted by the fact that their host, their CULAD, will do everything in their power to help them achieve what they came over to the UK to achieve, the sooner they will open up and become easier to host, thus making life easier for all concerned. Also hopefully explaining what, for the duration of their visit, their military and social obligations and aims are, so that the hosting chain of command can then obligingly react to them and thus make the whole event more of a success.

After a number of times spent in the company of military officials from Islamic countries, many of whom spoke a number of languages themselves, it was interesting to see how when during an exchange between two groups of people, both desperately wanting to get along and achieve a common goal, how the translator can unwittingly become the power broker. The amount of times I was enabling conversations between groups of senior officers and politicians and I realised that if I so wished, through a greedy or selfish manner, to influence a conversation so that I personally benefited, say financially, no one would have been the wiser.

Militaries around the world have always suffered from this, such as the British Army in Iraq and Afghanistan, where the interpreters have often taken a dislike to the locals due to religious or social differences. And as a result they have influenced the incumbent military representative to the detriment of the military and the locals. Be it either out of petty spite or local rivalry.

This was an important lesson to me and should be borne in mind whenever a translator is required, as if their total honesty and integrity cannot be vouched for, there is no telling what damage they might cause. It also brought across the absolute importance of me brushing up on my linguistic skills beforehand and ensuring that I had a full working grasp of the vocabulary I would most likely be using, as well as always having my trusty and almost battered to pieces dictionary to hand.

Now when it comes to the Army's collective amount of serving linguists, one imagines that there must be a vast database where one can specially search for, say a Spanish speaker. Once found, they can be contacted, using the information provided on their file, and then seek permission from their chain of command to release them for the upcoming task.

Annoyingly, there is such a database, but no one seems to use it.

Instead what happens is that a junior NCO or officer will suddenly be informed that a deputation from, say Turkey, is coming out to visit their unit and its capabilities and would they mind being an awfully good chap and organise the whole thing?

At which point the unfortunate individual panics and immediately soars to twenty thousand feet and starts to hyperventilate. Once they've calmed down, usually after a hot brew provided by a sympathetic colleague, they then immediately go social media or bring out their mobile phone and send out a raft of messages to all and sundry, asking if anyone knows of someone who can speak the lingua franca and thus help host the visit. After an exhausting number of hours and days, unanswered emails and frantic phone calls, at the eleventh hour, a linguist is usually found and the day is saved.

It used to drive me mad when I found out how difficult it had been for the hosting officer to find me. If only they had accessed the online military database, they would have found me, as well as half a dozen others, in a matter of minutes.

Work smart, not hard.

Through this tenuous and temperamental network, I was to receive no end of last minute CULAD tasks, all of which I gladly accepted, mind you, and as each visit was concluded successfully and the delegation boarded the plane all smiles and handshakes, I was to find that my name as a CULAD was becoming bandied around more and more in the relevant Defence Engagement circles.

But sadly, despite my successes, all hard won, I must say, and reports from those I'd worked with, my chain of command at 21 still proved remarkably reluctant to release me. Often citing, for instance, that although helping our military teach the Egyptian, Jordanian or Omani militaries about counter IED procedures was indeed important, being in barracks for the mandatory officer development lectures run by the Adjutant was another thing entirely!

The Army is slowly starting to relearn the lesson of the past, one of our favourite hobbies it seems, in that in order to effectively work with, and fight next to, overseas militaries, it's probably a good idea if our soldiers and officers can actually talk with them in the first place. As such, before an officer can become an OC, he or she now must be able to talk competently in a second language; although due to manpower shortages and the stubborn refusals to actually release people for language training, a curse I know only too well, the various HQs within the British Army haven't actually stipulated how its personnel are to find the time to learn such a skill.

But, having always been one keen to turn lemons into lemonade, or preferably some form of liquor, I realised early on that the work I was trying to do was not only worth doing and immensely good training, but also bloody good fun, and I'd be damned if I was going to let any stuffed shirt of a Royal Engineer senior officer get in my way.

Although knowing the language of the people whom you will be talking with, a CULAD must also have a thorough understanding of the history and culture of the people whom they are talking with. For without a thorough historical knowledge of the country they are from, how they perceive their own role within the national stage or how they view common topics, (such as the current situation with the State of Israel, women at home and in the workplace or which candidate they'd like to see become US President), you simply cannot succeed.

If it were between a choice of having a thorough understanding of someone's language or their culture, I would choose the culture every single time. For I've known people who are expert linguists but cannot function in social interactions due to a lack of understanding, whilst persons of limited linguistically ability but who know their subject, have positively soared time and time again.

To give an example, twice I was called on to host delegations from the Egyptian military and both times they were an absolute success. Not just because I could converse with them in Egyptian Arabic, but because I'd spent a considerable amount of time in their country and thus knew what would interest them, how to best interact with them both socially and in the workplace and I knew a number of topics they'd be eager to talk about during any lulls throughout the day.

I knew that they'd probably wish to go pray at certain times of the day and I adapted each day around these pious obligations. I knew that everywhere we would stop there would have to be some tea and biscuits, just like a visiting British unit. I knew that they'd want, and need, to dedicate at least an afternoon to go shopping for their family and military superiors back home and that at the end of their stay, they'd most likely provide us with a small token or gift to which we would have to give something in return.

All simple stuff, agreed, but if I had just studied their language but not their country, culture and habits, our time spent with them would have not been as nearly as successful. And it was simply remarkable at how often I found UK military personnel unaware of this requirements or insider facts about overseas visitors.

Towards the end of my time at 21 Engineer Regiment, when I was again tasked at the last minute to be the CULAD for a visit from a military unit from the Middle East, I'd learned a few tricks on hosting and how to best put my guests at ease. The phrase that always springs to mind, which sums up the working relationship a CULAD must have with their guests, was what I thought to myself whilst I was waiting for my group in the arrivals area of Gatwick:

'If I was going to be a guest in their country, how would I like to be treated?'

Whenever I have ventured abroad to visit MENA militaries and their establishments, the absolute generosity and heartfelt desire of my hosts for me and my companions to enjoy ourselves, as well as find out whatever we intended, is often almost overwhelming. I was once sat in the office of the Omani Tank Brigade Commander and upon finding out that the next day, our day off, my group and I were planning to go hiking up the 'Jebel Akhdar', arguably the most famous mountain in Oman, it was all we could do to stop him loaning us his official private military car, fluttering pennants included, for the day.

The reason being that he simply couldn't get the idea of going hill walking on one's day off and thought that we were shorthanded for transport.

At times, especially early on in my fledgling career as a CULAD, I found myself wishing that there was an official handbook where naïve translators or cultural advisors could turn to and flick through the various pages, each chapter detailing dos and don'ts for hosting and working with persons from many different countries.

Food and drink are always an interesting issue, especially when the visiting persons are from a country or region that does not allow the serving of certain items; such as pork, alcohol or beef. I believe that if the situation does not allow for the guests to be asked directly what they prefer to eat or drink, which can indeed be very awkward, an excellent option that is available is instead, when arriving somewhere for drinks or a meal, have a range of foods and beverages laid out before you get there and just let the guests decide what they prefer.

Sometimes individuals will prove themselves to be extremely devout in their religious or cultural beliefs and will adhere to them rigidly, thus stressing the importance of having alternative foodstuffs, others will happily display a complete laissez fait attitude towards these issues, seemingly leaving their obligations behind them back in their own country and tuck into the booze and bacon sandwiches with wild abandonment. Some others, for instance from a predominantly Islamic country, will clearly wish to loosen their obligations somewhat but will be afraid of what their colleagues might think, suffering a form of Islamic 'Catholic Guilt', and consequently will ask for an orange juice whilst hungrily eyeing the bottles of single malt whisky behind the bar.

These situations must indeed be handled carefully.

It must be borne in mind, especially by those taking part in discussions between two groups of different nationalities and language, of exactly mentally exhausting being a translator can be. Any language, especially one as difficult as Arabic, which is as different to English as right is to left, is a significant drain on the mental ability and fortitude of any linguist, regardless of how accomplished they are.

Translators, even if they might be working in a language similar to their own, must be given regular breaks in order to rest their weary brains, recuperate and then return to the field of battle, fully refreshed. Else their capabilities will start to wane and a breakdown in communications will occur. In my experience, two straight hours of dialogue is about the maximum any normal translator can take before their brain starts to drift.

Since my time spent in the University of Leeds, Egypt and afterwards in the British Army, I've spoken and worked with people, both civilians and serving officers and soldiers, from across the length and breadth of the Islamic world. From Algeria to Qatar, Iraq to Afghanistan, and what has always struck me are the different subjects and phrases I've had to learn in order to be able to converse with and adapt to each and every one of them.

For instance, in the past, when I found myself conversing with someone from one of the monarchic nations in the Middle East or North Africa, I would typically cover topics such as elections, holidays, films, trade and much more.

Whereas when chatting with a soldier or civilian from one of the Islamic Republics, I quickly learnt that I'd have to know the words for civilian deaths, weapons of mass destruction, terrorists, civil war, refugees, corruption and suchlike.

A wiser person might be able to draw an observation on how the words and topics used by people of a region, or country, in everyday conversation might perhaps be one of the best ways of figuring out the lie of land and current state of affairs, despite what their politicians or national newspapers might say. But that would be way above my pay grade and for someone who has a lot more letters in front of their name than I do.

Through a combination of blind luck and bloody hard work, as the weeks sped by, I was also fortunate enough to get on a range of interesting, and at times very challenging, specialist courses and unit selections which were aimed at preparing individuals in the finer and lesser known methods of intelligence gathering and influencing operations. These various courses and selections were hosted and taught by a number of both civilian and military organisations, the instructors often being from a plethora of different backgrounds and specialities.

They ranged from university professors, undercover police officers to quiet, but clearly determined and deadly, army officers and soldiers of all ranks.

Over a number of days, weeks and months, I was to learn such skills, to name but a few, as to how to get certain information out of perfect strangers without them even suspecting that the conversation was anything but casual, how to influence entire populations, from a single street of houses to a whole region, in a number of ways so that they'd assist with achieving a specific goal, or how to create propaganda in various forms, depending on the area and cultures within it that would stir, invoke feelings in even the most timid, or even resistant, of souls.

Information warfare, intelligence gathering and cultural influencing; three skills that the wider British military would do well in remembering the utility of, and sequentially allowing its personnel to learn and train how to deploy such battle winning tactics.

The number of miniscule non-conventional units that exist through the Army, as well as the courses they, and their civilian counterparts, teach, hidden in variety of semi forgotten barracks and secluded non-descript buildings around the UK, do wonders in promoting excellent skills and techniques vital to the success of the military, at home and abroad.

Their problems, however, lie in the fact that no one in the Regular Army seems to know much about these various selections and brush up courses, such as the excellent language brush up programmes run by a number of UK academic institutions.

The number of times I returned from, say an intensive French course or E2 unit selection, and my chain of command viewed my time away and what I had achieved almost absolute with disdain, was truly disheartening and bloody annoying.

But I kept at it, and looking back on what I've seen, been taught and subsequently done over my past career, I'm so damned glad that I stuck to my guns and did the career that I enjoyed.

From sitting Ministry of Defence Language Examination Boards (MODLEBs) where I was put through numerous university grade military languages assessments, and as a result getting nice pay bonuses through qualifying to certain grades, munching croissants and sipping delicious coffee whilst attending week long brush up language courses in central London, to being able to travel the length and breadth of a number of countries in the Middle East and work with their inhabitants, the career of a linguist and CULAD was certainly a rewarding one and I do not regret a second of it.

To be honest, when I think back to it, I count my lucky stars for that day, all those years ago, when I was sat in my sixth form college and I made up my mind to follow in the footsteps of my heroes and to see something of the world through the guise of an officer in the British Army.

Captain Sir Alexander Burnes FRS (aka Sekunder Burnes), a British officer in the time of the Raj and a true adventurer, perhaps one of the greatest CULADS, or 'Politicals', as they were once known, ever to have picked up a dictionary or trod a desert path, is the alleged creator of my most favoured phrase on the importance of having translators and cultural advisors in the British, and wider, military:

'Soldiering is all very well, but the men who make or break the army in a foreign country are we Politicals. We meet the men who count, and get to know em' and sniff the wind; we're the eyes and ears, aye, and the tongues. Without us the military are blind, deaf and dumb.'

8

End Game

Over my time in the military, it was incredulous, as well as intensely angering and frustrating, as to how indignant and annoyed RE senior officers would suddenly become when they realised my desire to serve within an overseas defence engagement post after finishing my time as a troop commander. Despite the fact that I'd stated my career aspirations to them from day one.

Perversely, I often narrowly missed out on actually being punished by them for my desire for non-conventional postings, even when I was once the only person to pass a certain unit selection. I found their attitudes simply ridiculous, bearing in mind the British Army's proud lineage for 'Ungentlemanly Warfare'.

From the WW2 Special Operations Executive (SOE) who under orders from Churchill leapt from planes and ships into the dark of night to fight the Nazis and set Europe ablaze, to those crazy individuals from the history of the British Empire who spent years living amongst the tribes and clans in the far off soaring mountains, scorching deserts and thick jungles that lie dotted across the globe. Utilising their understanding of languages and cultures, as well as their own self-reliance and determination, to achieve goals that would have been impossible for conventional soldiers and officers to even think of, let alone accomplish.

I initially took this reaction of various higher officers rather badly and I quickly grew to resent the lack of support, and amount of opposition, I faced. Thinking that as the units I was applying to join were not particularly well known by the conventional military, it was the general ignorance of their abilities that led to the stubborn refusal of many to let me join them. But after speaking to a number of fellow officers, I soon learned that the lack of understanding was not the biggest contributor to the opposition I was facing.

The fact of the matter is that, in Army 2020, there are so many officers, and soldiers, leaving the service that even those who wish to join infamous units, such as the SBS or SAS, also run a severe risk of having their efforts hobbled by senior officers.

The reason being that even if an officer is willing to put themselves through the toughest military training in the world, it is still likely that when their Adjutant or CO realises that they will have to then report to their higher chain that they'll be losing an officer for a couple of years, they get cold feet and stop the officer from going.

Inexcusable and craven, in my view.

Even if that means that the challenge and adventure seeking officer will come back happier and significantly more experienced and capable, with a strong desire to serve for longer once they return to their regiment.

Numerous HQs have a depressing tendency to show a worrying degree of career cowardice and inevitably clip the aspiring individual's wings to suit their own needs.

Cutting off one's nose to spite one's face.

The British Army, and wider military, does offer so many fantastic and simply unbelievably good things for its personnel to do but sadly these are now, more so than ever, over shadowed by the mistakes it continually makes. It is a shame that so many of the errors it commits, such overburdening its personnel and abusing their dedication to their jobs, can be easily addressed. As such, these unintentional self-harming policies are driving personnel away in droves whom otherwise would have willingly stayed within the then British military, if only their grievances had been listened to and addressed.

In the words of Richard Branson:

'Train people well enough so that they can leave, treat them well enough so that they don't want to.'

Despite the numerous conflicts existing around the world, many of which have arisen due to previous and unsolved British military interventions, and often very few (if any) junior military personnel seem able to deploy to them. Our people signed up to be soldiers and officers and serve their nation proudly abroad, to help people or help put people in the ground. They didn't sign up to sit behind desks and deal with peacetime army madness, especially when the army isn't at peace; bearing in mind the current domestic and overseas threats we and our allies face.

I believe that the capability of the military has been seriously degraded over recent years due to cutbacks in finances, personnel and training opportunities and unless the abilities of the Army are substantially increased, we will undoubtedly face a scenario where we do not succeed or win; we've reached our culmination point.

Bust.

To look at the situation in broad speaking, the British Army, and wider military is, in my view, too small for the objectives now set to it by its politicians and senior officers. We have fallen into the trap of sticking to our proud and time honoured mantra of 'can do!' but sadly there is a limit to how much soldiers and officers can manage with severe shortages of manpower, resources and time.

The spirit that kept men going through the dark days of Dunkirk, Kohima Ridge, The Chosin Reservoir, Basra and Sangin, can only go so far before it snaps under the strain of lack of men, experience and material.

The maxim by Napoleon that 'the Morale to the Physical is as three to one' is very true, but there is a limit and in order to continue to succeed, soldiers must be reinforced with recruits, finances and sufficient war materials.

The retreat by the German Army after the Normandy landings in WW2 sums up the situation perfectly. For the German soldiers were retreating torturous mile after torturous mile, through country after country, suffering huge losses at the hands of the Allies but their morale and motivation was still high and despite everything they kept on fighting, even attacking through the Ardennes, for the second time. But morale and motivation can only count for so much when facing an enemy who has vast resources and capabilities and knows how to use them.

In the words of the German Army, what they eventually lost and thus helped increase the speed of their retreat, was the war of materials; 'Die Krieg von Materialien'. Or, as the Soviets aptly described it:

'Quality over quantity, but quantity has a quality all of its own.'

Speaking as an engineer, compared to what the Royal Engineers used to do, such as building of the Chatham Docks, the Royal Albert Hall or bridging various expansive and dangerous rivers whilst under heavy enemy fire (the longest bridge built by the Engineers in WW2 was 343m long) our capability now is very limited indeed. Whilst using issued equipment, the largest gap that Royal Engineers can now bridge, utilising extremely rare and frail assets, is only 60.96m wide.

Even the non-equipment bridging that gets taught to all RE recruits is taught with standardised equipment, with no cutting down of trees or improvisation of any form taking place whatsoever.

Heaven forbid the British military ever has to deploy en masse to a large country that has arduous terrain and weather, with numerous large and difficult rivers and countless local factions siding with enemy forces for their own gain. Such as North Korea, the Congo, Iraq, Syria or the Ukraine.

A lot of this has stemmed from not only financial cutbacks and time restrictions, but also due to the loss of 'Crown Immunity'. Meaning that as soon as the British military lost the ability to conduct its own standards of training in sometimes, but necessary, hazardous environments, it began to lose its ability to best prepare for conflict and sudden large scale adaptation. As every exercise planning officer and NCO becomes hogtied and weighed under by reams of needless paperwork, legal restrictions and the fear of being brought to court by advantageous and unscrupulous lawyers. The focus now is very much on risk aversion, than training our soldiers for war.

Commanders must bear in mind the importance of watching over the protection and maintenance of their forces during peace time, as it is typically during these times that they degrade the most.

But despite all the harm done to them by their chains of command and political masters, the loyalty and ethos of the British Army personnel is as still as strong as ever, and the soldiers and officers of British Armed Forces would make their forefathers proud.

There is still complete loyalty going upwards from the junior ranks to their HQs, but sadly not a lot of loyalty coming back downwards from the HQs members themselves.

One of the best things the Army ever did for me was not just help me realise my strengths and build new ones, but, arguably even more important, it made me realise my weaknesses and address them. For through the military, and the instruction and lessons it gave me, I developed more, for the better, I would like to think, than I possibly could have ever could have done elsewhere.

As a point to any future commanders, large and small, I would say that military personnel, soldiers and officers alike, will always surprise you. Meaning that sometimes they will let you down, as either a one off error through simple human error or through a bold faced lie and sheer bad discipline, and it is down to the commander to find out as to how it happened and what disciplinary action should be taken. But also they will leave you astounded to how intelligent, capable, brave and quick thinking they, come the moment, can be.

These sorts of things should be borne in mind when meeting and working with military personnel, as I have seen, more times than I would have liked to, a commander to initially take the wrong idea of an individual and they then suffered as a result.

By either the commander being let down by a scoundrel posing as a saint and letting them off practically scot free, or by them crushing a subordinate who otherwise should have been allowed to a bit of grace, then the opportunity to prosper and be a future credit their unit.

But to be honest; for better or for worse, good or bad, officer or soldier, young and old, I am as proud as punch to have served with them all.

But, over a number of years, after passing a number of linguistic examinations, writing two separate papers on the evolution of radical Islam and the importance of comprehensive cultural, linguistically and historical understanding in the British military, as well as taking on a number of cultural and translator assignments and passing three separate Joke & Dagger unit selections, all of which specialised in a mixture of overseas defence engagements, mitigating religious extremism at home and abroad, and utilising military personnel who have significant experience in the MENA nations, I still wasn't permitted an E2 post and so with a heavy heart, I resigned my commission.

I became sick of talks given to me by senior, often very tough and experienced ones at that, but sadly woefully out of touch with their troops, that I must desist from my attempts to get onto a tour or get involved with overseas defence engagements or loan services, but instead:

'Listen, cut your teeth on a few more regimental posts, such as Regimental Signals officer or a 2IC of a squadron. Maybe afterwards you could be sent somewhere, but not before another four years I'd say. The Engineers may have sent people off to E2 posts in the past, and it's known that a few other cap badges do allow their personnel non-conventional posts at your current rank, but the Engineers just don't do that anymore and that's just the way it is. Now buck up and make sure that your manpower plotter and weekly reports are up to date, there's a good chap.'

If I was going to be miserable behind a desk, my job role restricting me to merely shifting paper around, I might as well get paid a lot more for it in Civilian Street. Being no less patriotic or keen to help my country and people around the world, I was also tired, as were many of soldiers and officers I knew, of being severely disillusioned and disappointed with not being permitted to do a job where I could make an impact for the better, at home or aboard, despite the incessant demands by the British military for the skills I acquired over years of training. Thus, I left.

It was interesting to think back over my career in the British Army, and the Corps of Royal Engineers, and realise that the reasons I had decided to leave were as simple as they were compelling.

Firstly, I'd achieved everything I had set out to do as an aspiring junior officer. I was damned if I was going to spend years frustrated in the Regulars sitting behind a desk, hoping against hope of utilising what I had learnt and experienced over the past years and deploying somewhere fun.

Secondly, but even more importantly, I was tired of seeing not just myself, but more importantly my men, let down by senior officers and the career management system, and yet the offending officers or management programmes were never brought to account. I forget the amount of times I saw men whom I would have gladly followed into hell armed with a snowball, true war fighters and with a range of operational tours under their belts, have their careers and aspirations mismanaged and destroyed by senior officers who seemed to have no desire to promote the interests and desires of their soldiers, only their own.

It got to a point I couldn't support, or agree with, the decisions of my chain of command anymore, as I saw the damage they were doing to my men, and I had to leave, for my own integrity and sanity.

Lastly, I had met the woman of my dreams. My life had found another direction in life and although I have no doubt that I will, somehow or someway, maintain my link with the military, she had become my priority, not the Army.

This was combined with the fact that postings have become even more irregular, sudden and irrational than ever in Army 2020, and that I didn't want my job to risk my marriage, as I forgot how many divorces occur due to rapid and long lasting overseas deployments. The choice was clear.

In the end, I would never command a group of men like those in my first troop ever again, and as time goes by and my memory begins to fade, despite what I may start to lose memory of, I will never forget the boys of Support Troop, 7 HQ & Support Squadron, 21 Engineer Regiment.

Out of everything that I left behind when I left the British Army, it is the brotherhood that I miss the most.

Recommended Reading

Ask Forgiveness Not Permission by Howard Leedham

Band of Brothers by Stephen E. Ambrose

In the Service of the Sultan by Ian Gardiner

Eastern Approaches by Fitzroy Maclean

Quartered Safe Out of Here by George Macdonald Fraser

Panzer Commander by Col. Hans von Luck

Shooting Leave by Sir John Ure

Homage to Catalonia by George Orwell

The Forgotten Soldier by Guy Sajer

Loan Soldier by Bruce Duncan

Callsign Hades by Patrick Bury

The Flashman Papers by George Macdonald Fraser

Fight, Dig and Live by General Sir George Cooper

Notes on the Handling of a Field Company R.E. by Major Denis Eadie

Scorched Earth, Black Snow by Andrew Salmon

Pegasus Bridge by Stephen E. Ambrose

Looking for Trouble General Sir Peter Billiere

Congo Mercenary by Mike Hoare

Acknowledgments

My utmost and sincere thanks to all those who were there for me during my career; to those officers and soldiers who inspired me to try and emulate their efforts, dedication and selflessness.

The boys of 21 Engineer Regiment.

And finally, and most importantly, to my wife, Katie.

About the Author

Henry Beeching was born in 1989 in Hastings and was educated in Luxembourg and Brussels, before finally settling in Sussex. Whilst studying Arabic and Middle Eastern Studies at the University of Leeds, he joined the UOTC and then completed Reserve P Company and obtained a Reserve Officer Commission.

Afterwards, he attended Regular Sandhurst and then joined 21 Engineer Regiment for two years as Troop Commander of Support Troop, 7 Squadron, 21 Engineer Regiment.

He then served throughout the UK and across Europe, in both capacity of Troop Commander for almost 50 Sappers, and on lone assignments.

During that time he also led teams from 21 Engineer Regiment in boxing, alpine skiing, shooting and sailing, as well as qualifying as an Arabic Cultural and Linguistic Advisor.

Thereafter he served within both 1 Royal School of Military Engineering Regiment and 36 Engineer Regiment, which culminated in him deploying to Somalia in support of the African Union and United Nations.

Ubique.

Printed in Great Britain
by Amazon

12691177R00198